Business Process Mapping

Business Process Mapping

IMPROVING CUSTOMER SATISFACTION

Second Edition

J. Mike Jacka

Paulette J. Keller

To Theresa —
Hope you find it
Helpful!

WILEY

John Wiley & Sons, Inc.

Published by John Wiley & Sons, Inc., Hoboken, New Jersey.
Published simultaneously in Canada.

For general information on our other products and services, or technical support,
please contact our Customer Care Department within the United States at 800-762-
2974, outside the United States at 317-572-3993 or fax 317-572-4002.

Wiley also publishes its books in a variety of electronic formats. Some content that
appears in print may not be available in electronic books.

For more information about Wiley products, visit our Web site at
www.wiley.com.

Library of Congress Cataloging-in-Publication Data:
Jacka, J. Mike.
    Business process mapping : improving customer satisfacion / J. Mike Jacka,
    Paulette J. Keller—2nd ed.
        p.   cm
    Includes index.
    ISBN 978-0-470-44458-0 (cloth)
        1. Consumer satisfaction.   2. Customer relations.   3. Reengineering
    (Management)   I. Keller, Paulette J.   II. Title.
    HF5415.335.J33   2009
    658.8'12—dc22

                                                                2009005647

Printed in the United States of America

10 9 8 7 6 5 4 3 2 1

For Kathy and Ralph

Contents

Preface

You are looking for a way to create efficiencies. You are looking for a way to analyze the work that is being done. You are looking for a way to provide better customer service. You are looking for a way to provide innovation. In any of these situations, you are ultimately looking for a way to better understand processes.

In business, just as in life, processes underlie everything we do. It is processes that allow us to come to work, it is processes that allow us to complete our work, and it is processes that bring people together to accomplish objectives. The intertwining of these processes ultimately leads to the success or failure of any enterprise. So, we are all looking for a tool that can help us untangle those processes, understand how they work, and how they can work together toward successful achievement of objectives.

Process Mapping is that tool. It allows reviewers the opportunity to get a better understanding of the process, effectively find ways for that process to be more successful, and ensure that true value is being provided to the customers.

Throughout the years, a number of approaches and techniques have used the name *Process Mapping*. Technically, there is no clearly defined Process Mapping approach, nor is there a wrong or right approach to Process Mapping. Each approach has its merits and may be applicable in various situations.

However, we have found that our approach to Process Mapping has resulted in numerous successful process analysis engagements. These have ranged from quick one-week reviews of small units to multimonth projects analyzing entire operations. We have used this approach in the past and continue to do so. Our success is measured by the continued requests for this type of review.

Not to put too fine a point on it—our approach works.

It may be misleading to call the overall approach we describe as Process Mapping, because the final product—the *Process Map*—can sometimes be nothing more than a glorified flowchart. (In fact, our working title for the book was *Process Mapping: Flowcharting with an Attitude.*) But it is the work around those maps that provides the real insight. What we will do is show an entire approach that leads to a holistic understanding of the process under review.

We begin by taking a closer look at processes and what they are. Starting with a concept that is the cornerstone of moviemaking—storyboarding—we show how Process Mapping can drill down into the area under review. While describing the steps used in Process Mapping, insights into how an operation functions will be discovered. This approach includes working with the client to ensure that everyone has a full understanding of the processes involved; learning the underlying concepts behind the process, such as objectives, risks, and key controls; building the actual maps that are the cornerstone of this approach; and using various approaches to help determine how to make the process better. A number of tools are also provided to more effectively complete the various analyses. Finally, we discuss different applications for Process Mapping, the things that can go wrong while Process Mapping, and additional process analysis approaches that work nicely in conjunction with Process Mapping. We also introduce an application of Process Mapping called *Customer Mapping*, whereby the principles of Process Mapping are more closely tied to the customer.

For some projects, every step in the book is the right answer. In others, just a few sections are necessary. But it cannot be emphasized enough that the approaches, concepts, and practices outlined in this book can be successful. Ultimately, that is what we want to share with you. Through the explanations and examples that follow, we will show you how to use Process Mapping as an effective analysis tool. The approach is simple yet powerful and can be used by anyone who needs to analyze a process—whether you are working within the department, within the company, or externally.

No doubt, when you are finished with this book, you will have a good understanding of the Process Mapping approach, along with a set of tools to help facilitate the project. But you should also better understand how the work that is done helps achieve company objectives and leads to better customer satisfaction. Finally, when you apply these techniques, we are firmly convinced you will find the same successes we have found.

Let us just end by noting that, while we are Internal Audit professionals, the concepts of Process Mapping go beyond the discipline of Internal Audit. Yes, it is a tool for that profession, but anyone who wants to effectively analyze processes will benefit from this approach.

INTRODUCTION

Pinocchio and the World of Business

A film is a petrified fountain of thought.

—Jean Cocteau

In 1938, Walt Disney held a meeting with his animators to discuss an idea he had for the follow-up to his blockbuster *Snow White*. He brought the entire group into one room, sat them down, and proceeded to tell a story. He began by describing a lonely woodcarver. He told of how the man carved a wooden boy and wished that boy was real. He told of the Blue Fairy who heard the old man and brought the little wooden boy to life, but left him made of wood. He then told of the boy's heroic struggles—being captured by the evil Stromboli, going to Pleasure Island where he began to be turned into a donkey, and eventually saving his father from the whale Monstro. At the end, he told of the boy's transformation to a real boy.

The story he told was *Pinocchio*, based on the book by Carlo Collodi, and Walt Disney intended it to be his next movie. As he told the story, Disney took on the parts of all the characters. He spoke the words. He acted out the scenes. He led the group on the roller coaster ride that would become his next triumph. When

1

the entire story had been spread before them, he told the animators, "Make that movie."

The animators were thrown the challenge of taking that series of events—Disney's re-enacted story of the transformation of Pinocchio into a real boy—and making it into a movie. This was a daunting task. Disney had an exact image—from start to finish—of the animated movie he wanted to make. By talking and gesturing and becoming that movie, he spelled out its story. The animators had the challenge of taking that story and making it a finished product. However, a tool already existed that had proven invaluable in the development of cartoons—storyboarding.

Storyboards are large areas (at that time, four-by-eight-foot boards) on which sketches can be pinned. Key steps of the story are drawn and placed in order. As the story is fleshed out, additional drawings are included. If something is wrong, it is discarded. If the sequence is particularly complicated, more drawings are put in for detail. What results is a pictorial flow of the movie's transformation from beginning to end.

Using Disney's vision and the existing tools of the trade, the animators succeeded, and *Pinocchio* became Disney's second animated feature movie—another smash. The world fell in love with the puppet boy who wanted to become real. They watched as the Blue Fairy brought him to life, as his naiveté caused him to succumb to Foulfellow and Gideon, and as he saved Geppetto from Monstro—a series of actions that led to his final transformation into a real boy.

At its very core, the story of Pinocchio is a process. As all good processes do, it has an input (Geppetto carving a puppet and wishing it were a real boy), it has an output (Pinocchio becoming a real boy), and between those a series of events—the actions—that achieve that transformation. Disney's animators documented the process of that transformation through storyboarding.

Every individual has many stories to tell. Each of these stories is a process, a series of actions that takes input, transforms it, and produces an output. Some are dramatic transformations, life-altering events that shake and move them. For example, a person may tell a story about surviving an earthquake. The story begins with the earth shaking around the person (the input). A number of actions are taken—grabbing the children, running out of the house, or just falling to the ground. And the final outcome is safe survival. Other stories are less thrilling, but a process nonetheless. Take, for example, waking up in the morning. The alarm goes off (the input), the body goes through a series of movements (the process), and the body eventually is in an upright and (hopefully) alert position (the output). Each story is a process.

In the business world, every company has a story to tell as well. At its most basic level, that story is the transformation of investments into profits. But for that story to reach a positive conclusion, there are a series of more fundamental stories to tell. One story may be the transformation of steel into an automobile, another may be the transformation of a phone call into customer service, and another may be the transformation of computer data into information. But no matter what the process, it is a story told by a group of individuals. Just as each story is a process, each process is a story.

The tool that brings this all together is Process Mapping—storyboarding for the business world. The development of Process Maps comes from the reviewer sitting with an employee who tells the story. As that story unfolds, the reviewer documents the process in a way that will help the employee visualize the transformation that occurs. At the end, the employee can see the finished product and ensure that the story has been told accurately. Each scene can be put together to provide the reviewer with the final movie that is the entire process. Then, much like a director, the reviewer can analyze the finished product to show how to build a better movie, one that does just what Disney hoped *Pinocchio* would do—result in a profitable enterprise.

Process Mapping is a way to graphically represent the transactions and stories that make up a business. However, just as storyboarding in and of itself is not a movie (rather, it is a tool used to make that final movie), Process Mapping by itself is not a complete analysis. Instead, it is a tool that helps complete the final analysis of the process under review.

What follows is more than just a description of how the tool called Process Mapping works; it is a description of how it works as part of an overall approach to process analysis. We discuss processes and how to drill down into them. We talk about how processes interrelate with other processes and the information that must be obtained to understand them. Then we discuss the actual mapping of a process—how the Process Mapping tool works and how it can be used to analyze the process.

Before us we have a challenge much like that faced by Disney's animators. Every company is telling a story, and every employee within that company has his or her own story to tell—a scene to share. We, as reviewers, want to learn those stories and understand those scenes in order to find out what is going on. Our task is to take those scenes and come up with the final movie—the overall epic of how initial input leads through a transformation to final output.

Our review has to determine whether the movie is the right length. It may take three hours to tell the story, but if no one wants to sit through a three-hour movie, you will sell no tickets. Likewise, if it takes four months for you to deliver your product, there may be no one waiting at the end to buy it. Does the story require a miniseries, or is a one-reeler enough? Is the process taking three hours to tell a ten-minute story?

Our review also has to determine whether each scene benefits the whole. Anton Chekhov was once famously quoted as saying, "If in the first act you have hung a pistol on the wall, then in the following act it should be fired." What part of the story is truly needed, and what parts are missing? Does every pistol go off? Is every process necessary to build the final output?

Finally, our movie (as they used to say in vaudeville) has to "play in Peoria." Even if we have developed the world's greatest widget in the shortest amount of time, it is useless if the world has moved on to sprockets. Do the customers need the product? Do they need part of it, but not all? If it is unnecessary, what should we be doing instead?

Process Mapping helps us achieve that task, just as storyboarding helped Disney's animators. And when we are done, we will have a blockbuster, too—an analysis that gives us a holistic view of the process, as well as the cooperation and buy-in of all levels in the company.

We're ready for our close-up, Mr. DeMille. Lights, camera, action—let the Process Mapping begin.

CHAPTER 1

What Is This Thing Called Process Mapping?

I may not have gone where I intended to go, but I think I have ended up where I intended to be.

—Douglas Adams

Who Cares about Processes, Anyway?

Most companies spend a great deal of time each year developing strategic objectives and goals. High-level objectives are developed that reflect the overall strategy of the company. Business objectives are then developed at the department level to support overall company objectives. Goals are developed to measure the progress toward achieving particular business objectives. And every employee has individual objectives that support overall strategies.

In a perfect world, there would not be any conflicting goals. All department objectives would actually support the company objectives. Every employee would understand these goals and objectives and understand how the work he or she performs contributes to the achievement of those goals and objectives. The company's plans would be executed flawlessly and the story would always have a happy ending—the wooden company would become real.

5

However, such happy endings seem far too rare. Strategic objectives may be developed in isolation—from the top and communicated down. Department objectives may be self-serving and may not support strategic objectives. Department objectives may be in conflict with one another. Employees below the management level may not have any idea what the company's goals and objectives are or how the work they do contributes to the achievement of those objectives. People only see their own story—follow their plot—and have no idea what is going on around them. They do not always understand the company's or department's story, and certainly have no idea how they can help achieve that happy ending.

The accumulation of activities that takes place in each business process is what ultimately determines a company's success. So processes must be analyzed to ensure that they support key business objectives. Process analysis is particularly useful in ensuring the accomplishment of business objectives relating to customer service, efficiency, effectiveness, and profitability.

"Tell Me a Story": Analyzing the Process

A vital key to transforming a business is the complete understanding of the processes involved in it. This understanding is necessary for any change management approach to be of value, and it can be included in total quality management, Sarbanes-Oxley analysis, process re-engineering, International Organization for Standardization (ISO) certification, and even in developing a Baldrige Award–winning approach. But getting a handle on the processes is one of the more daunting tasks reviewers must face.

However, this task is not unlike the one Disney's animators faced. The animators had to find a way to transform the narrative Walt Disney had told them into a movie. Likewise, reviewers must find a way to transform the company's story into a concrete, tangible product that can be viewed, verified, and manipulated. To help understand that story, the reviewer needs a storyteller to bring the stories to life. The animators had Walt Disney; reviewers have the company's employees. Walt Disney knew Pinocchio's story inside and out. He would tell it to anyone who would listen. The company's employees know their stories just as well, and they are willing to tell the details of those stories to anyone who will listen—where things are going right and where the plot is not quite so good. Each employee knows the job and knows the processes that are completed. These are movies that go on constantly in their minds. Although they often have not thought about it, they know the beginning, the transformation, and the end.

The challenge for any reviewer is to get that information and develop a finished product that anyone can look at and understand, not unlike a finished movie. This requires the reviewer to talk with that employee and learn each of the steps—each of the "scenes"—that make up that process. Process Mapping is the technique that helps the reviewer transform that employee's movie into a finished product that anyone can view and understand.

Benefits

We've already enumerated some of the more obvious benefits of Process Mapping, including better documentation of the review process, the ability to visually represent the process, and an overall view of the various aspects of the process. However, that only scratches the surface.

As previously noted, if the only step taken when developing Process Maps is to graphically document a process, then Process Mapping can become nothing more than glorified flowcharting. Instead, the Process Maps are part of a larger system. When all the steps of this system are used, there are additional benefits that may not be as readily apparent.

Holistic

In daily life, processes constantly come in conflict as the objectives of one process directly oppose the objectives of another. For example, every workday, millions of individuals climb into their cars to start the process known as going to work. For many, the primary objective of this process is to arrive at work at the proper time. If the individual feels that this primary objective may not be achieved, then speed is at a premium and other objectives fall by the wayside. This individual then runs into a significant conflict with another objective. Municipalities have developed a series of processes intended to ensure achievement of their primary objective related to safe travel. Speed limits, stop signs, and traffic lanes all work together to thwart the time-conscious traveler. The driver's objective (the need for speed) comes in direct conflict with the municipality's objective (the need for safety).

In every aspect of our lives, every process is forced to interrelate with other, coexisting processes. The same is true in business. To meet the objectives of keeping shareholders, customers, and employees happy, executives and managers must juggle conflicting priorities—the objective of paying expenses comes in conflict with the objective of making a profit; the objective of keeping employees satisfied comes in conflict with reducing expenses; and the objective of making a top-quality product comes in conflict with the customer's objective of paying a low price.

Far too often, analysis is done "in a vacuum" without considering how these processes interrelate. Reviewers will talk to one person or one function and find what works best for that single perspective. As a result, the reviewers may focus on one set of objectives at the expense of another. This analysis in a vacuum far too easily provides benefits to one while taking from another.

Process Mapping provides a method for taking a holistic approach to this analysis. Before sitting and talking with people, the reviewer gains a full understanding of the process's objectives and how they interrelate with the company's overall objectives. The objective of each part of the process is also reviewed to ensure that it benefits some greater objective. And, when identifying and recommending changes, the reviewer will keep all these objectives in mind to ensure that the effect of this change is fully understood.

By looking at the whole picture and integrating the various parts, the reviewer sees not only what needs to be changed, but also how the proposed change will affect everyone. With an overall view, the benefits for one can be weighed against the detriments to another, and the ultimate good can be appropriately considered.

Employees' Buy-In

Too many reviewers come in with the mind-set that management must be pleased. Often, reviewers have preconceived notions of what they will find. And even if the reviewer is open-minded, the review is often done in isolation from the employees. Discussions may be held with management. There may be reviews of procedure. Files may even be reviewed. But the people actually doing the work are never brought into the picture.

Even if discussions are held with line personnel, the ultimate product may still be geared toward management or executives. Many reviewers obtain information on how things are supposed to be done, but they do not use the employee as a resource for understanding how things are *really* done or how they can be improved. And employees are not so slow-witted as to misunderstand what is happening. They recognize that reviewers are often in the room, but not listening.

Process Mapping allows a true buy-in to the completed product. Maps are developed in real time, and the employee can see exactly what is being recorded. They are developed in an interactive atmosphere that allows the employee to physically change what is occurring. Plus, it allows them to provide input on where the system can be improved. In our experience, we have gone back to offices where employees were excited about the process. They told new employees about the review that was going to be completed and looked forward to their turn to talk to us.

Despite the fears previously addressed, employees are still happy to have someone actually listen to them. They have a story to tell. That story can take up to eight or more hours of their life each day. And when someone actually listens, they are more than willing to share. We have had employees share ideas that changed the way processes worked throughout the company. They were willing to tell anyone who would listen—it is just that no one was listening.

One of the biggest mistakes we made when first implementing Process Mapping was something as simple as not sharing the finished product with all employees. We discussed the results with the manager and supervisors, giving them the completed maps. We left assuming that they would share the information. In short order, we heard from the employees that they were very upset. They wanted copies of the completed maps. Even those who had only a small part in the process were interested. It was a product they helped develop. They had ownership, and the owners wanted their product. Ever since, we always make a point of ensuring that all employees are provided with the final product.

Sense of Pride

The previous two benefits lead to the third benefit of Process Mapping. Many employees come to work and understand what they do (their story). They take something, transform it, and make it something else. Some are lucky enough to actually interact with customers and see the effect of what they do. But many see only that input and output.

Process Mapping not only provides management with an overall view of operations, but also provides employees with a view of how their work adds value and how they are part of a team. The holistic approach allows them to see where their work comes from. They can see the steps that lead to the product they receive and understand the work that has gone before. They can also see why they are doing what they do. Each step in the process should lead to further steps in the map. Eventually, this should lead to a final benefit to the customer. Process Mapping is often the first time employees understand why they are doing the work they do. It helps them understand why a bothersome statistic they are required to generate is important to a report that drives future customer transactions. Or it may show why they should not use a certain code they thought would make things run smoother.

In the book *Gung Ho!*, Ken Blanchard and Sheldon Bowles talk about the "spirit of the squirrel"—the need for people to believe their work is worthwhile. They go on to state that *worthwhile* means that people must understand their work; it must lead to a well-understood and shared goal; and values must guide everything they do in their work. Basic to all of this is that people must understand how their work makes the world a better place.

For some jobs, this is easy. Doctors see their patients become healthier, pilots know they take people safely from one place to another, and politicians . . . well, let's not press it. Other jobs seem so menial or useless that people only think they are part of a cog that makes larger cogs. But looked at as part of a greater process, any job takes on meaning. On one level, the file clerk may only be pushing paper, but on another level, he is ensuring that paperwork is available when decisions must be made. On one level, the janitor handles trash and dirt, but on another level, he is ensuring that the people in the building can achieve their work at its highest level. On one level, the factory worker just puts rivets in metal, but on another level he ensures that the product meets customer specifications in order to achieve customer satisfaction. Process Mapping, done correctly, helps provide the information that will show employees the true value of their jobs.

During one review, we asked employees what their work accomplished. They were not able to tell us. In fact, they told us that when they asked their supervisor why they did the things they did, they were told, "You don't need to know." We showed them how their work fit in with the overall process. Not only did it provide them with a sense that their work accomplished something, but also it led them to suggest changes and elimination of paperwork that cut days off the processing time. Not bad for a bunch of clerks.

Customer-Driven

If a process leads to completion of an output that nobody wants, it is a waste of time—there is no customer. The successful analysis of processes must take customers into account, and that can be any level of customer. Maybe it is the primary customer—the one who buys the product; the one who purchases the car or insurance or legal advice. Or it may be an internal customer—the one who uses that output as their input to their process; the accounting department or the chief executive officer (CEO); or the next step in the production. Bottom line, any analysis must take the customer into account; it must be driven from the customer's perspective.

Possibly the most important benefit of Process Mapping is that it is customer-driven. To complete a Process Map, everyone must understand what is being delivered to the customer and why. Initial reviews with employees are established in a way that begins this process—the idea of identifying outputs and how they benefit a customer. Likewise, analysis of the inputs helps the reviewer understand whether the customer is getting a useful product.

In addition, evaluation of the process is meant to help ensure that the operation is as transparent to the customer as possible. And transparency is an important component of internal processes. Timely response is the hallmark of perfect customer service, and looking for efficiencies in a process directly affecting customers is a good start. But it is just as important to identify process-caused delays that should not be affecting the customer. For example, if administrative duties such as timekeeping cut into an individual's ability to provide customer service, a nonsupporting process is affecting the customers. And customers are much less willing to accept the excuse that there was a delay because of administrative issues. These are the processes that must become transparent to the customer, and finding ways to create transparency (what they cannot see, they do not object to) should be the objective of any review. Process Mapping helps make that step.

What Can Go Wrong

As previously indicated, we will be including a number of the mistakes and pitfalls we have encountered as we have implemented Process Mapping projects. However, there are two overall issues to keep in mind—two basic mistakes that can undermine the entire project.

The first is the nightmare of a hidden agenda. Inherent within the benefits listed earlier is the need for trust—trust among all participants: management, employees, and the reviewers. Destruction of that trust will result in a failed project. The movie *Office Space* has almost reached cult status, primarily because people see their everyday lives in the problems and miscues shown in that particular office. Central to the problem are the Bobs—two external consultants ostensibly brought in to determine how things can run better, but with the real agenda of driving layoffs. (As one character notes, "Good luck with your layoffs, all right?") In the movie, every employee lives in fear of meeting with the Bobs, because they all know what is really going on. If you go into a Process Mapping project to carry out management's agenda, if you go in with preconceived notions, if the review is a foregone conclusion, then it will never succeed. You will only prove what you think you know, and there will be no trust (meaning no truth) in any of the work accomplished.

Closely paralleling the hidden agenda issue is the second issue—losing sight of the customer. Customers are central to the methods used in Process Mapping, and customers are where it all starts. If the outcome is more concerned about management, if it is more concerned about the shareholders, if it is more concerned about the consultants, then it will eventually fail. Each of these groups is important. But more important is to remember that long-term success is tied to the customers' satisfaction. As long as everyone has their eye on that prize, then the Process Mapping analysis has that much better chance of succeeding.

The Process of Process Mapping

Somewhere out there, someone has an idea for a great movie. It may be the next *Ben-Hur*, or it may be the next *Plan Nine from Outer Space*. But in that person's mind, it is a great movie. Everybody thinks they have an idea for a great movie. Of all those great ideas, a small percentage is actually put on paper. Of all the ideas that are put on paper, a small percentage are picked up and read by someone who can do something. Of all those that are read, a small percentage are purchased. And, surprisingly, for all the ones that are purchased, only a small percentage is actually produced. And by the time the idea goes from one person's idea to being captured on film, the person with the original idea may not recognize the finished product.

Once a script is accepted, it gets changed. It gets researched and changed. It gets storyboarded and changed. It goes into rewrite and gets changed. It goes into filming and gets changed. It gets edited and gets changed. Sometimes it gets tested by focus groups and gets re-edited—and changed. The story that is "the movie" evolves as the many people working on it come to a better understanding of what the story is.

A company's processes go through numerous changes, too. As a result, the understanding of those processes is changed. The CEO and executives have one idea of the processes, the managers and supervisors have another, the line personnel have a third, and the person who first imagined the processes that would be "the company" probably would not recognize the finished product.

Just as the storyboard is used to anchor a visual understanding of a movie's changes, the Process Map is a visualization of the changing understanding of the process. When all is said and done, the Process Map should bring together everyone's understanding of the story to show the "real" process.

The steps that go into changing the map to reflect reality are what make the map effective. These steps are process identification, information gathering, interviewing and map generation, map analysis, and presentation.

Process Identification

We know intuitively what a process is. We think we know what the start and end points are. We think we know where the process resides and who the owners are. And we think we know what is important and what is not. However, until we really dig in and find these answers, we are only fooling ourselves.

A scriptwriter sits down thinking the plot will fall into place. However, the characters have their own ideas. Many writers talk about how they knew exactly where the story was going to go, but the characters had a different idea. As the story develops, the good writer allows the characters to determine an outcome that is true to their spirit. That final script looks nothing like the original idea, but it is a better script because it is true to the characters.

Presupposing what makes up the process leads to the same false results that occur from forcing characters to act—well, out of character. The reviewer must sit down with the people who know how the processes work and learn the story. But the reviewer needs to do more than just get their story. The reviewer helps them begin to understand that their story is only part of the overall movie. Just as a good writer must think about the audience, a good reviewer must think about the customer. This means taking a trip through the customer's eyes and seeing the triggers that interact with the customer.

Data Gathering

Digging deeper into the process, we must understand the information that is available. This information may be in statistical reports, it may require talking to specific people, and it may simply mean spelling out what the process does. But if we jump into Process Mapping without all information necessary, we can easily miss what is important.

A scriptwriter must have a basic understanding of the subject before writing. The more the writer "guesses" at what the real facts are, the more the viewer's suspension of disbelief is tested. Think about *2001: A Space Odyssey*. In the entire movie, based on what was known at the time, there was only one scientific error (and it is not the zero-G toilet—that was based on evidence available at the time). As the scientist experiences free fall shuttling from the Earth to the space station for his briefing, he sips on liquid food through a straw. After the liquid is sipped, it falls back into the container. Weightlessness would not allow this to happen.

Now think about *Plan 9 from Outer Space*. People who are killed in one scene show up in later scenes (and they are not the zombies), scenes that have nothing to do with the movie are included, and headstones in the obviously fake graveyard are knocked over by people brushing into them. Ignoring facts shatters what little credibility the movie might have had.

Okay, it may be unfair to compare a megabudget movie to one shot on a shoestring, but you can think of examples of your own—a soda bottle visible in a scene from *Cleopatra,* a watch on a gladiator's wrist in *Ben-Hur,* and the fact that Krakatoa is west of Java (not east, as the movie title says). Factual data are the key to suspension of disbelief.

For Process Mapping, factual information is the key to sustaining belief. The reviewer must have the facts at hand and be able to use them. This will keep the reviewer from going down roads that are unimportant. It also helps the reviewer understand the information being received through the mapping. Finally, and maybe most importantly, it provides credibility to the reviewer.

Interviewing and Map Generation

Once the basic information is in hand, the reviewer actually starts making the map, but this process is not done in isolation. It is a give-and-take interaction that makes the maps living, breathing items. Every interviewee has input and, if desired, a hands-on opportunity to make the map. And every interviewer is one of the artists building the final product.

After a script is done, it is time for the rest of the players to become involved. As we have already discussed, the storyboard provides the medium to begin translating that story. But the director has ideas, the producer has ideas, and the actors and actresses have ideas. The filming of the movie is the time when the words on paper transfer from the storyboard to the film. As each person provides input and change, the storyboard changes. When the film is "in the can," the storyboard may not look at all like the original script.

Each person has an idea of what the process looks like. They know their stories and expect them to match everyone else's stories. The map and interviews help build on those stories until there is a final product that, although it might not match the original map or the original stories, does represent the final, real process.

Analyzing the Data

This has been happening since the project was first undertaken. Even the first discussions should provide the opportunity for analysis. During one recent review, we began by talking to the head of the department. He told us that, although the processes were the same, the two sections were doing them differently because the heads of those sections each thought that was the better way to do it. Later, while talking to the head of a third department, she stated that she bypassed the mechanical system and used her own spreadsheets. The initial analysis is accomplished. A major problem has been identified. The only question left is why.

Editing the movie starts when the script is being written. No scriptwriter submits a first draft. If so, it will be rejected every time. Changes are made during the writing process, during the negotiation process, during the filming process, and, most important, during the editing process. In fact, the editing process is what really brings it all together; this is where the final storyboard is brought to film, where the final product is really completed, ready for the world to see.

Analysis has been going on throughout development of the maps, but only at the end can the full effect be seen. The reviewer can look at the entire picture, seeing the full interactions, identifying the most significant delays, and determining the effectiveness and efficiency of the entire process. This is where the final product and final report come together for all the world to see.

Presentation

Putting all the process definition, data gathering, interviews, map generation, and analysis together should result in a final report. This is the product the reviewer has been working to build, and it is the product that management wants to see.

Eventually, a movie is shown to an audience. That proves its ultimate value. All the writing and research and storyboarding and filming and editing have led to this product. If it is successful, it is used and used again. And the results of that work are successfully apparent to the audience.

Eventually, a report of the process under review is provided. This can be written, oral, or anything that grabs the audience's attention. But all the process identification, data gathering, interviewing, mapping, and analysis have led to this product. A successful map is used many times. And a successful mapping project will lead to more. And the results of that work are successfully apparent to the audience.

Process Defined

Before getting into the details of a Process Mapping project, we want to examine how processes can be subdivided to better understand how they are constructed. And to do that, we need to ensure that we all have a similar understanding of what we mean by *process*.

Life is a complex intertwining of processes. Every action we take is a mixture of inputs, actions, and outputs—the classic definition of "process." Some of these processes are simple: The input is an old piece of paper, the action is wadding and dropping, and the output is trash disposal. Other processes are infinitely complex. The input is raw materials, the action is the combination of those materials into a product, and the output is the space shuttle. Others seem simple, but are infinitely complex. The input is sound, the action is hearing, and the output is enjoyment of a fine piece of music.

It is important to understand that more than an action occurs, however. A better term for what happens is a *transformation*. If the process does not transform the input, nothing has happened. The output is the same as the input, and there is no real need for the process. Sometimes, this discovery is the most surprising part of evaluating a process—and the most valuable.

To fully analyze and understand processes, there must be a system for classifying and understanding the actions within the overall process. This requires breaking a single process into the various elements that make up that process. The reviewer can then drill down as needed, getting into the details that make up a process. Even a simple process like throwing out the trash can be broken down into simpler elements.

Each section of a process is really a smaller process. And when that section is broken down, it too is a process. And, possibly, the sections of that process are another process, as are the sections of that process, and the sections of that process, and so on. As this drill down takes place, a reassessment of the inputs and outputs should also occur to ensure that true value is being added. In this way, the particular parts of the process can be evaluated, just as the overall process can be.

Drilling Down the Movie

To understand how these processes can be subdivided, let's return to the movies. To better understand the story that is being told within a movie, there already exists a systematic way of drilling down the parts of the movie so the individuals involved in its creation can understand how it is put together.

Movies are broken down into acts. Each act has an overriding theme or point to it that helps support the overall movie. Each act is then broken into scenes. Again, individual sections that help support the individual acts. Each scene has individual shots, which help support the tone of the scene. Finally, there is the actual script, the specific words and directions that make up the movie.

Exhibit 1.1 shows how this drill-down might look.

The Movie

Think about the classic movie *Psycho*. (Warning—minor spoilers alert. No, we won't give away the ending. But some of the movie's details are about to be included.) There is the overall movie about Marion's misappropriation of funds and the events that transpire when she meets Norman Bates. This is actually a process. There is an input—a sum of money and a young girl (Marion) who acts on an opportunity for theft. There is a transformation—people's lives are changed after Marion meets Norman Bates, especially Norman's

Exhibit 1.1 Drilling Down the Movie

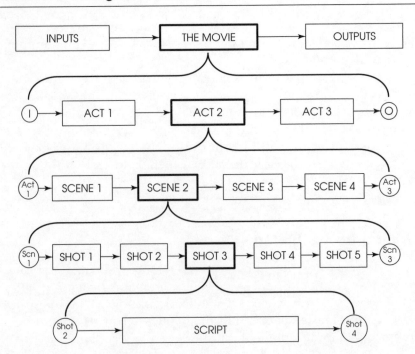

and Marion's lives. And there is an output—Norman's final run-in with the police and the shocking surprise. The movie is the process.

Acts

Each movie or play is broken into various levels to better facilitate an understanding of the action that is to occur. Movies are composed of a number of acts—usually two to four. These are the major subsections of the movie that represent overall structure. *Psycho* might be broken down into the following acts:

Act I: The opening theft and flight from Phoenix.

Act II: Marion's meeting and interaction with Norman.

Act III: The search for Marion by her sister and the detective.

Act IV: The final confrontation with Norman.

Each of these acts can further be viewed as an individual process (or movie) with an input, a transformation, and an output. The input comes from the prior act and the output goes to the next act. Using Marion's initial meeting with Norman as an example, the input is a young girl and her arrival at a strangely empty hotel, the transformation is the subsequent discussions with Norman that begin to reveal his character, and the output is a body left in the trunk of a car that is dumped in a swamp. You can also see that the output of the first act (Marion's flight) leads to this act, as the output from this act (a dead girl) leads to the third act.

Any process must add value, and any section of a movie must add to the final conclusion. In this case, Norman and Marion's meeting brings to conclusion the events in Marion's life and sets the foundation for her sister's search. Accordingly, a true transformation has occurred.

Scenes

The next level is the scene. Each act is composed of a number of scenes. Just as the acts are subsections of the movie, the scenes are subsections of the act and represent the overall flow of that act. Act II of *Psycho* (Marion's meeting and interacting with Norman) might be broken into the following scenes:

Scene 1: Marion checks into the hotel.

Scene 2: Marion comes over for a snack.

Scene 3: Norman watches her in her room.

Scene 4: The infamous shower scene.

Scene 5: Norman cleans up.

These can be seen as little movies that come together to build the final movie. And, just as with each act, these can be seen as little processes. The input for the shower scene is running water and an unsuspecting girl. The transformation is from life to death. And the output is a body. Again, the input comes from the previous scene (Norman's and his mother's reaction after Norman talks with the girl), and the output leads to the next scene (a body can raise questions and must be disposed of). The scene adds value by providing the impetus for the search that occurs in the next act, and it begins to show the characters' twisted minds. The obvious transformation of Marion's death is accompanied by the transformation of the movie into a deeper mystery.

Shots

Each scene is composed of a number of shots. These are the actual images that make up the movie. As with the previous levels, they are the subsections of each scene, representing the flow of that scene. In the shower scene, for example, Alfred Hitchcock used almost 50 shots from as many as 20 different camera angles. These included shots of Marion's feet, shots of her turning on the shower, shots of a mad person with a knife, and a final shot that pans back from Marion's lifeless eye.

Again, each of these is a small process. While not profound, a well-crafted movie needs every one of them to establish its purpose and mood. At first blush, the number of shots Hitchcock used might seem excessive. But people who watch the film do not notice the number of shots. Instead, they are wrapped up in the action captured in those shots. And each shot has its own input and output. The input for the final shot is the eye of a dead girl. The transformation actually occurs inside the viewer—the realization that we have seen Marion's last breaths. And the output is the dead body. Again, the previous shot's output provides the input for this shot. And the output provides the input for the next shot and, in this case, the next scene.

This shot adds a finality to the scene that would not have existed otherwise. It provides the transformation described and, as with the items described previously, propels the movie to the next level. The shot adds many levels of value.

The Script

Finally, there are the actual words that make up the shots, the scenes, the acts, and the movie. These are a written representation of what is supposed to occur. In some scenes, those words are the dialogue. In other scenes, the words are the camera instructions, such phrases as "hard cut to face" or "dissolve to shower" or "fade to black." For the final shot in the shower scene, the script might read:

> FADE TO:
>
> MARION'S eye. Camera slowly pulls back as image turns
>
> showing face. As full face begins to come into view, stop turn.
>
> Continue pull back until full face in view.
>
> HARD CUT TO NEXT SCENE.

Ultimately, words and direction cues build to make the final movie we watch. However, the organization of these words is built around the various subsections of the movie—the acts, scenes, and shots. Likewise, it is these sections that are storyboarded to help the producers, directors, editors, and everyone else involved understand the direction of the movie. The storyboard helps synthesize the script into graphic images.

Business Processes as Movies

To fully understand processes, they must also be broken down into manageable segments. This approach allows a more detailed analysis of the parts that make up that process. The subsections used to organize and understand movies work well in a business environment. And, just as with movies, this substructure makes Process Mapping (storyboarding) that much easier.

To help understand these subsections, we will take a look at the process of making breakfast (see Exhibit 1.2). At first blush, this might seem to be a trivial process, but even the analysis of something this mundane could be an evaluation if it were completed at a hotel or restaurant to identify an existing snafu in the food production unit.

Exhibit 1.2   Making Breakfast

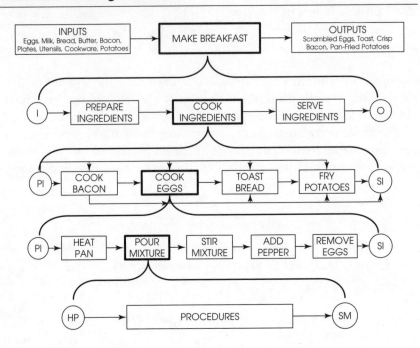

The Process

First, we need to understand making breakfast as a process. The input is the ingredients that go into making a breakfast (e.g., eggs, milk, bread, butter, bacon, plates, utensils, and pans). These ingredients go through a transition we call making breakfast. The output is the finished breakfast (e.g., scrambled eggs, toast, crisp bacon, and pan-fried potatoes). (This is not a particularly healthy breakfast.)

Units

The first subsection (equivalent to a movie's acts) is the unit. These are the major subsections that make up the overall process. This breakdown can be made based on location (home office, field office, branch office), type of work (building, testing, installation), stages of work (preparing, cooking, serving), or any other logical subset. The intent is to provide the best understanding of what makes up the process.

The process of making breakfast is probably best understood based on the stages of the process. These stages might be Prepare Ingredients, Cook Ingredients, and Serve Ingredients. Just as we saw each act of the movie as a smaller movie, each unit can be seen as a smaller process. For example, the input for Cook Ingredients is the prepared ingredients (the output from the prior unit), the transformation is the application of heat and other stimuli to the prepared ingredients, and the output—edible food—becomes the input for the last unit, Serve Ingredients. Any process must add value to be a true transformation. In this instance, value is added by taking raw food and making it into an edible—and hopefully tasty—dish.

Tasks

Just as each act of a movie is broken down into scenes, each unit can then be broken down into tasks. Determining the tasks that make up a unit is done in much the same way as described for units. However, it is less likely to be dependent on location and more likely to begin focusing on the actual work.

The unit Cook Ingredients might be broken down into the tasks of *cook eggs, cook bacon, toast bread, and fry potatoes*. Again, each is a small process that uses output from a prior task or unit and produces output to the next task or unit. It is interesting to note that these tasks are not dependent on any of the other tasks in this unit. *Cook eggs* does not require input from *cook bacon* and does not provide an output to *toast bread*. While a very simplistic example, this is the type of analysis that can take place during Process Mapping.

The input for *cook eggs* would be the mixed eggs. This would come from the first unit, Prepare Ingredients. The transformation would be the cooking process. The output would be scrambled eggs and would provide the input for the last unit, Serve Ingredients. This process adds value by taking raw eggs and transforming them into edible eggs. Therefore, there is a true transformation occurring.

Actions

Each task can then be broken down into various actions. These are the equivalent of the shots that make up each scene in a movie. Moving from units to tasks, the description becomes more focused on actual work done by the individuals. Actions reinforce this focus with descriptions that are more closely related to individual work.

The actions for *cook eggs* might include heat pan, pour mixture, stir mixture, add pepper, and remove eggs. (Note that we have tried to use two-word descriptions for these actions. This is a fundamental approach when developing Process Maps, so it is a good idea to practice doing so now.)

Once again, each of these actions can be considered a very minor process with its own inputs, transformations, and outputs. The input for pour mixture would be a container holding mixed eggs and other ingredients already added. The transformation is the act of transferring the contents from the container to the pan. The output is the mixture sitting in the pan. Customer value has been added during the process, because cooking the eggs cannot be accomplished without this transference. Therefore, there is a true transformation and a true process.

Procedures

The final stage is the actual words. With a movie, this is the script. With a process, it is the procedures. These are written descriptions of how each action is completed. Often, it is the way things are supposed to be done. Pouring the mixture might be composed of the following procedures: "Take the container in your right hand, grasping it between the thumb and fingers. Hold the container above the pan. Slowly tilt the container until the mixture begins pouring into the pan. Continue tilting until all contents are in the pan. Place the container on the counter."

But just as with a movie script, there is room for interpretation or improvisation. Looking at the directions, the following questions might arise. If I am left-handed, do I have to use my right hand? How high above the pan should the container be held? How fast should I pour the contents? Good employees know there is room for interpretation. They may even find better ways to do something than the basic description. Less able employees might see instructions and assume that, despite being left-handed, they must pour with the right hand.

It is also impossible to write down everything that must be done. Accordingly, much procedure is passed down from worker to worker over the years through oral tradition. This lends itself to misunderstanding and the use of procedures that have no basis in need.

During a review, we tried to understand how a certain document was used in the process. We continued to ask for the form by name—the "Journal for Unearned Premiums." Employee after employee gave a dumbfounded stare. Finally, while describing how we thought the form was used, a light went on for the employee who gladly stated, "Oh, you mean the greenies!" Oral tradition, describing the green form as "greenies," had long taken over the official procedures, which called them the "Journal for Unearned Premiums."

Employees' interpretations and misapplication of these instructions speak to the root of what is occurring in a process. The good employees are adjusting these procedures to the needs of the situation. The employees ingrained with the "it's a rule, so I'll follow it" mentality are busily using their right hand when they are left-handed or, even worse, sitting waiting for someone to tell them how fast to pour the mixture. And, to make things easier, we will not discuss the companies who insist that better ideas should not be accepted because they are not in procedure or, even worse, think these should go through a committee before being accepted.

That is one of the purposes of the hierarchy of processes. To fully analyze the overall process, the reviewer and the employees must understand the interrelationships of the sections within the process.

As you will see when Process Maps are developed, they allow you to identify the processes that exist on their own and those that rely on other processes. You can see how one unit leads to another, how one task leads to an action, and how they all work together to the final product.

A Real Business Example

Making breakfast is an interesting example, but it does not lend itself to deep analysis. To get a better feel for the hierarchy of processes and its uses, we will use a more realistic business example— Payment by Check Request. This scenario is used throughout the remainder of the book, so this is a good time to get acquainted with it (see Exhibit 1.3).

The first thing to notice based on this description is that the process we are examining is really a unit of another process. Payment by Check Request is a unit of *Expense Payment*, the basic units of which are Payment by Check Request, Travel Expense Report Payment, and Purchase Order Payment. Likewise, Expense Payment is a unit of *General Disbursements*, which might include Payroll, Expense Payment, and Refunds. Ultimately, every process is a subset of the overall process that is the company.

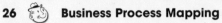

Exhibit 1.3   Expense Payment Process

Travel expenses are reimbursed through *expense reports*. These reports are prepared by the traveler, approved by the traveler's supervisor, and processed through the payables departments—field office and home office.

Purchase order expenses are all those that require preparation of a *purchase order*. These are required for all purchases over $5,000 and all repairs over $2,500. They are prepared by the purchaser, require two to five approvals, and are processed through the purchasing department.

This scenario focuses on *all other* expenses. These are paid through use of a Check Request. Portions of this part of the expense payment process have been centralized in the home office disbursements department to increase efficiency and to reduce costs. Other functions are handled by the local payables departments (one in the home office and one in each of the 11 field offices). The company has committed to having all requests completed within 48 hours.

The requester completes a Check Request (form #1292) online. The form requires the payee's name and address; amount; budget codes; and (if applicable) tax ID information. In addition, if the check is to be returned to the requester, manual form #1293 (*Return to Requester*) must also be completed and included with the supporting documentation. Once completed, the requester submits the request electronically. Upon submission, a check request reference number is immediately e-mailed to the requestor. This is used to reference all further transactions relating to this request. Once the reference number is received, the requester faxes all supporting documentation to the Documentation Center, where the documents are scanned into the system. The reference number must be on each document. The requester then notifies his or her immediate supervisor that a request has been submitted and provides the reference number.

Upon notification that a request has been completed, the immediate supervisor will check the system to determine whether supporting documentation has been posted. Once the documentation is online, the supervisor will indicate approval. This review is intended to ensure that the request is completed correctly and to verify that supporting documentation matches the request. In addition, if the check is to be returned to the requester, the supervisor must approve an additional section of the check request. If the request is for more than $1,000, a second-level approval (the supervisor's supervisor) is required. The immediate supervisor will advise of the need for a second approval by e-mail. In the event either approver feels there is a problem with the request, they will notify the requester that additional information is required.

Once all approvals are complete, the last person providing approval will notify the local payables department via e-mail.

Twice daily (at 9:00 A.M. and 2:00 P.M.) the local payables clerk processes all requests. The clerk verifies that all required sections are completed, that they are completed correctly, and that all required approvals are present. The verification process includes comparing support to the request, verifying proper coding, and ensuring proper authority. In the event that there is an error, the requester is notified via e-mail. The clerk then approves the form to show the review has been completed. At that point, copies of all requests and supporting documentation are printed out and filed, by date reviewed, with a five-day hold-file. When the batch is complete, an e-mail is sent to the home office check issuers listing all requests.

There are three home office disbursement check issuers. One of these handles home office requests and those from one of the field offices. The other two check issuers handle five field offices each.

At 1:00 P.M., the issuers each print out the e-mails listing the requests, sign on to the check issuance system, and access the check request system. Each request is reviewed to ensure that the approvals clerk has approved the request. Two of the check issuers maintain a log listing those requests that do not have the clerks' approval. The third check issuer (the one handling home office expenses) prints out copies of the requests which have not been approved by the local approvals clerk and maintains them in a file. The required information is then entered in the check issuance system. A copy of each check request is printed out upon completion. Once all checks are completed, the issuer enters the print command and then signs off the system. The physical checks are printed at this time.

The check printer is maintained in a locking cabinet in a centralized location within view of most employees. The home office disbursement supervisor keeps the key for the cabinet and the key used to enable the printer. At 1:00 P.M., one of the issuers notifies the supervisor that the check issuance is about to start. The supervisor will enable the printer, then relock the cabinet. The treasurer maintains backup copies of the keys.

Once the checks are printed, each issuer gives the copies of the check requests to the check retriever. When all three issuers have turned over the copies, the retriever notifies the supervisor, who unlocks the cabinet. After the retriever gets the checks from the check printer, the supervisor disables the printer and relocks the cabinet.

The retriever processes checks in field office code number order. The home office is code 01, the southwest office is 02, the northwest office is 03, and so on. She matches each check to a request. The retriever enters the check number on the request and then initials it. The initialed copies of check requests are filed by date, in check number order. All exceptions (a check with no request or a request with no check) are set aside to be researched later. As each office is completed, the non-exception checks are bundled for overnight delivery. Those offices not completed are given priority handling the following morning. Overnight deliveries are required in the mailroom by 3:00 P.M.

Research of missing items is usually completed first thing the following morning. For requests with no checks, the retriever verifies in the system that no payment was made. The request is then returned to the issuer, who processes it in that day's batch. If the review in the system shows that a check was ordered, the request is marked "Stop Pay/ Reissue" and returned to the issuer. These are also processed with that day's requests.

For checks with no request, the retriever verifies with the issuer that there is no request. If the request cannot be found, the check is voided in the system, "Void" is written across the physical check, and it is stored in a separate file with other voids.

Checks are received in the field office at approximately 10:00 A.M. the day after shipping. Home office checks are hand delivered to the payables clerk

(Continued)

Exhibit 1.3   (Continued)

at approximately 8:00 A.M. The payables clerks open the package and pull the appropriate day's folder from the hold file. Each check is matched to a request. The clerk verifies that the amount and payee are correct; enters the check number on the original request; and initials the request to show that the check was received.

If the check is to be mailed directly to the payee, the clerk prepares an envelope and routes the payment to the mailroom for delivery. If the check is to be returned to the payee, the clerk completes the delivery log. This log includes the check number, the check amount, the requester's name, and the requester's department.

Once all checks have been recorded, the clerk hand delivers those checks that are to be returned to the requester. The clerk takes the check to the requester or an authorized individual in the department. The check is delivered, the clerk signs the log, and the requester (or authorized individual) signs for receipt.

If the clerk has a request for that day but no check, the request is returned to the folder. At the hold-file date, the clerk prepares the Check Locator Form (#1922) and e-mails it to home office disbursements. This includes all information necessary for home office disbursements to locate the check. A copy of the form is printed out and put in the hold-file established for that day.

When a check locator form is received in home office disbursements, it is set aside for the following day. The next morning the issuer reviews the system to see if the check was issued. If it has not been issued, a new check is issued using the check locator as support. If it has been issued, the check locator form is e-mailed to the field office with any necessary information.

When the check locator is received by the field office with an indication that the check was already issued, the clerk will verify that the check was not received. If not received, the clerk will complete a stop pay form and prepare a new request. When the new request and stop pay are received in home office disbursements, the check issuer will verify that the check has not cleared, process a stop payment in the system, and issue a new check using the stop-pay form and the new check request as support. If the review shows the check has now cleared, the check issuer will obtain documentation from the bank to determine if an Affidavit of Forgery will be required and a potential fraud should be reported (using the Potential Fraud Form-#1099).

If the local payables clerk receives a check for which there is no request on record, the check is marked "Void," and a Void Check Form (#0086) is completed. The check and the form are returned to the home office in the next overnight shipment. When received in the home office, the check issuer voids the check in the system and stores it in the void check file.

In the event that the check retriever is unavailable after 1:00 P.M. (absent or detained with other business), the backup is another clerk within the department who is not a check issuer. In the event that a check issuer is out for one day, the work is held until the following day. If the issuer is out for more than one day, the other issuers pick up the additional work. Backup for the payables clerk in the field offices depends on the office. Some use the supervisor, some use another clerk in the department, and some do not designate a backup.

This is a good reminder that the process, units, and associated levels are really defined by the reviewer. The primary process under review provides the base point for further defining the units and lower levels. Keep in mind that the reviewer may have decided to do this review of Expense Payments after identifying it as a unit (or possibly even a task) associated with a broader process within the company. But now it is time to evaluate Payment by Check Request by itself, so it becomes the primary process.

The Payment by Check Request process begins with a bill. This is the most usual form of input. The transformation that occurs is the completion of a request leading to a payment. The final output is the check delivered to the payee.

The process might be broken down into the three units based on location: Field Office Prepares Request, Home Office Prepares Check, and Field Office Delivers Check. Each unit is a process in which the output from the prior item provides the input for the next item. Since the first unit is Field Office Prepares Request, the input for this unit is the same as the overall process—the bill. The transformation is the completion of a request that meets home office requirements. The output is the original and photocopy of a properly approved check request.

The Field Office Prepares Request unit might be broken down into four tasks: *complete request, approve request, verify request,* and *mail request.* These subsections are starting to be based more on people than on location. However, the location issue is still important in that there is a task for the employee, one for the supervisor, and two for the disbursements section. The input for the *approve request* task is the check request. However, depending on the disposition of the final check, the input could include a *return to requester* form. The transformation is the bestowing of authority on the request form. The output is an approved form.

The *approve request* task has a number of actions associated with it, including some decision items. It starts with a decision— "Is check request correct?" If not, return request. If so, approve request. Then another decision—"greater than $1,000?" If not, mail request. If so, send to superior and the superior will approve request, then mail request. You can see from the description that the breakdown now is totally function-specific, and each continues to have a basic input and output. The input for the *approve request* task is the completed request. The transformation is the review and approval of the request. The output is the approved request.

Take note of the use of a verb-noun approach in the task and action descriptions. As mentioned before, this is the way maps are eventually generated. Sometimes it can be tough, but it is good to get into the habit as soon as possible.

Finally, there is procedure that underlies every action. In some cases, this may be straightforward, as in "The individual giving final approval to the expense will submit the form to the disbursements clerk." Other procedures may not be as explicit. For example, "All amounts over $1,000 must be approved by a second level" does explicitly indicate the approval, but it implicitly indicates that a decision must be made (is the amount greater than $1,000?).

This is the act of drilling down, finding the processes within the processes. The degree of drill down is at the discretion of the reviewer. Likewise, the reviewer determines how broadly the overall process should be defined. But, whatever that level, an understanding of the layers of the process is a prerequisite of understanding the full process.

Recap

The first step in understanding the value of Process Mapping is understanding the reasons for process evaluation in the first place. Ultimately, quality process evaluation is intended to ensure that all processes are in alignment with key business objectives. In particular, these should focus on customer service, efficiency, effectiveness, and profitability objectives.

The ultimate value of Process Mapping is in getting employees to tell their story—the stories that make up the movie that is the company. Process Mapping is a way of recording these stories in a way that documents the movie.

Four major benefits can be obtained from using the entire system of Process Mapping. First, it is a holistic approach that helps explore the interrelationships of processes. Second, it is accomplished in a way that gives all employees—from executives to line personnel—buy-in to the finished product. Third, it helps employees understand how their work adds value and instills additional pride in their work. Fourth, it focuses on the customer and how that person sees the company.

As mentioned before, Process Mapping is more than making a map; it is the whole system that results in a successful project. The steps in that system are process identification (learning what makes up the process under review); data gathering (learning what exists within the process and with whom we will be involved); interviewing and map generation (learning and recording the actions within a process); analyzing the data (learning what can be done to make the process better); and presentation (showing others what we have learned).

To understand process analysis, processes themselves must be understood. A process is an input, a transformation, and an output. The transformation is the important part. Just as a movie can be broken down into acts, a process can be divided into units. Acts can be broken down into scenes, and units can be broken into tasks. Scenes can be broken down into shots, and tasks can be broken down into actions. Finally, the script of a movie provides the actual words that are the movie. Likewise, the procedures of a process are the words that make up that process.

Key Analysis Points

Analysis is the key to success for Process Mapping, so it cannot be isolated to any one stage. Later, there is a discussion of analysis as a final step of the Process Mapping system. However, since analysis is ongoing, each chapter identifies some key analysis points that were brought forward during the chapter.

No Transformation: No Need

For a process to be truly effective, some transformation must occur. Transformation implies a change to an input. If there is no change, why does the process exist? Look for processes in which no real transformation occurs and eliminate them.

Analyze the Written Descriptions

Policies and procedures hold the basic information on how a process should go. Some are too detailed. Others are too vague. Take a close look at these documents, and determine whether enough latitude is available to allow people to get their jobs done. Also ask for those handwritten instructions—the ones that the employees really used to learn their jobs.

(Continued)

Keep Alert for Oral Traditions

Listen closely to the stories that are told about how people learned their jobs. There may be an excellent procedure manual, but it is too detailed and boring. Instead, the employees learned their jobs by swapping stories. This oral tradition (sometimes written down in the handwritten instructions described previously) is the actual way the world works. Until you know about the "greenies" (the common reference name of a form or report), you will be the one talking a foreign language.

You Define the Process That Defines the Project

The ultimate process is the company. Within it are numerous processes that support the main process. Defining the level of process helps define the overall review project. By defining that process, the limits of the project are also defined.

CHAPTER 2

Process Identification

As for the outside world, you will be confronted by what you see.
And what you see is primarily what you look at.

—Zen saying

What Do You See?

When we operate within the business structure, the movie we see focuses on the work we do. We see our individual jobs, the tasks within those jobs, and not much else. We often see the purpose of our work as just getting the tasks done. We do not think about the impact of our work on our customers or on the company as a whole. We do not take the time to look at what we do in a different way, to see it as a novice, the way our customers may see it when they first come into contact with the business. We see the organization as it has been defined from within.

The movie our customers see, however, is defined by the experience they have when they touch the organization. They do not know about our internal structure, and, frankly, they do not care. It is, or should be, transparent to them. So we must start looking beyond what we normally see and look at what our customer is seeing. What are our visible processes?

Put yourself in the shoes of an insurance company's customer.

Day 1: You are in a car accident. This is a traumatic event and may be the first time you have any experience dealing with the insurance company. It all begins when trying to report the claim. Who do you call? Trying the claims office would seem reasonable. After searching to find a valid phone number, you call the claims office. The receptionist tells you no one in the office can take the report of your claim and you will have to call your agent. You call the agent's office, but he and his secretary are out for the day. You leave a message on voice mail and spend a worrisome night wondering what to do with your car, how you will get to work the next day, and what to do about the pain you are starting to get in your neck.

Day 2: You reach your agent. He takes down the information about your claim and tells you that someone from the claims office will be contacting you soon. You wait for the phone call all day. Nothing.

Day 3: You phone the claims office. The receptionist tells you that your claim must be assigned to a claims representative. However, assignments for claims reported yesterday have not yet been made. You should be hearing from a claims representative soon. You ask what to do about getting transportation and about the pain in your neck. She says you will have to talk to your claims representative. You remind her that you have not yet been assigned one. She repeats that yesterday's assignments have not yet been made. You hang up and wait by the phone all day again. Nothing.

Day 4: A friend gives you a ride to the store to pick up aspirin for the pain in your neck. You return home and the claims representative has left a message. You call back and get his voice mail saying he will be out of the office for the rest of the day.

Day 5: You finally speak to the claims representative. He explains what you need to do to get your car repaired and arranges for a rental vehicle. You tell him you are experiencing some headaches and pain. He explains that he only handles the auto damage portion of your claim. He will report that you are injured and another claims representative will be assigned to handle the medical portion of your claim.

Day 6: You take your car to the mechanic (thank goodness he is open on Saturdays) and get your rental car. Back at home, there is no message from the second claims representative. Your neck continues to ache.

Day 7: It is Sunday and, while you had a slim hope that you might receive a call from the claims representative, it appears they do not work on weekends.

Day 8: At last! A call from the second claims representative.

It has now taken just over one week for you to complete the process of reporting your entire claim to the company. At this point, you probably are not very impressed with the service delivered by the insurance company. And you would probably be very surprised to find that the insurance company's measurements indicate this claim was handled successfully.

How does that happen? Here are the measures of success established by the company. To ensure agents are aware of the activity on their insured's policies, all claims must be reported through the agent—Success #1. To ensure prompt assignment of the claim, assignment must occur within one business day of being reported by the agent—Success #2. To facilitate timely contact with the claimant, the claims representatives must make the first attempt to contact the customer one business day of receiving the assignment—Success #3. To ensure the claim is handled by an individual with sufficient expertise, claims must be assigned to claims representatives based on specialty—Success #4. The customer may not have been happy, but the company is celebrating its resounding success.

You see what you look at.

Now imagine a different scenario. When you purchased your insurance, you were given a sticker for your glove compartment and an ID card with a number for reporting a claim. You are in the same accident. This time, while still at the scene of the accident you call that number. The person on the phone says the company will have a claims representative to you in 10 minutes. He will have a rental vehicle delivered, find a repair facility for your vehicle, have your vehicle transported, and assist you in obtaining prompt and immediate treatment if you are injured. The claims representative arrives in five minutes and first asks about your injuries. He gives you a list of physicians you can see at no cost to you. He arranges to have a rental car delivered to the scene in the next 15 minutes and a tow truck within 30—again at no cost to you. It is one hour after the accident, all your questions have been answered, your vehicle has been delivered to a repair facility, you have arranged to see a doctor tomorrow morning, and you are driving away in a rental vehicle.

Would you rather be a customer of the first company or the second?

The first company defined the claims reporting process from the company's point of view, setting measurements of success from an internal rather than an external perspective. While they attempted to consider the customer's experience, they still thought only in terms of the internal processes when developing measures of success. The second company structured the reporting process around the customer's experience. The measure of success is significantly different. This company built processes to support a rapid resolution of the problems facing customers when they are involved in an accident. Success to this company was having a person on-site to deal with the customer within 30 minutes of the time the company is notified of the claim. The company representative was empowered to resolve all immediate customer problems such as removal of the vehicle, obtaining a replacement vehicle, and even authorizing medical treatment for injured parties. The actual reporting, processing, and authorization for both companies may take a week. But while the first company is a slave to the processes at the expense of the customer, the second company has allowed these processes to take a backseat to customer service.

When a company makes the decision to examine business processes, it has the opportunity to look at its business differently, outside its normal organizational structure.

Finding the Story

The reviewer's first job is to identify the processes within the area being reviewed—and this will be one of the first challenges. The organizational structures within companies are seldom process-oriented. Some businesses are organized geographically, some functionally, and some as a mixture of both. One department may be responsible for a certain piece of a process and another department for another piece. The reviewer must find the relevant parts that make up the entire process.

A company that is not organized around processes may never have identified the broad processes that help it achieve its objectives. If this is the first attempt by the company to classify operations as processes, the exercise will take some time and discussion. It is not always easy, and the classification process can be somewhat arbitrary.

For example, if the business is organized around functional areas, such as accounting, marketing, and support services, it will be necessary to define the particular processes taking place in each of these functions. Job titles, rather than actual processes, are often used to classify the work being done by an employee. Titles such as Accountant I or Accountant II do not offer much information about the actual processes involved in these particular jobs. The reviewer must look beyond the department name—beyond the traditional job titles—and systematically determine what work is being accomplished. The goal is to make sure that all critical processes have been identified and defined.

We once reviewed a new department responsible for the accounting activities related to sales. As such, it was under the finance department, and our initial understanding was that we would be reviewing accounting processes. However, as we began analyzing the work that was actually done, we found that over half of the operations had more to do with marketing administration than pure accounting. Accordingly, there were two sets of processes at work in that department—those related to accounting and those related to marketing. This discovery led to two completely separate analyses.

Trigger Events

There must be an input at the beginning of every process. But input does not, in and of itself, get that process going. Something must occur to trigger the start of the process. This may often be the same as the input, but it is important to ensure that the trigger has been identified.

In the movie *Psycho*, the trigger that starts the movie rolling is the money. The existence of this money tempts Marion to leave her current life and sets the events in motion for her meeting with Norman. In the breakfast process, the trigger may be one of the two things. The most obvious trigger would be hunger. The less obvious trigger might be the act of waking up in the morning. Sometimes we are not hungry, but it is morning and we know we should eat or we will not make through the day.

The trigger is also important because it is often the point at which the customer is first involved. Some action by a customer (internal or external) will be a trigger. If the trigger comes from a different source, it may be an indicator that the process is not customer-driven, meaning radical change may be needed, including elimination of the process.

Looking at the business through the eyes of the customer will help identify the most important triggers, the ones that indicate contact with the customer. Customer trigger events can be defined as those started by the customer or initiated to react with the customer.

Identifying the customer triggers requires putting yourself in the customer's shoes (just as we did in the claims example). You are look-ing for the interaction points your company has with its customers. In *At America's Service,* Karl Albrecht calls each of these interaction points a "moment of truth" for the company. He gives credit to Jan Carlzon, president of Scandinavian Airlines System, for adapting this metaphor from bullfighting. He defines a moment of truth as:

> . . . any episode in which the customer comes into contact with any aspect of the organization and gets an impression of the quality of its service.

Albrecht goes on to state that these moments of truth are the "basic building blocks of the service product . . . the basic atom of service, the smallest indivisible unit of value delivered to the cus-tomer." The moments of truth are the real products the company delivers to its customers. These are used by customers to judge the company, so it makes sense to focus on moments of truth when analyzing business processes.

> The moment of truth is typically neither positive nor negative in and of itself. It is the outcome of the moment of truth that counts. The sum total of all the possible moments of truth your customers experience, both human and nonhuman, becomes your service image.

We want to make sure we look at all the critical trigger events. We want to see the complete movie, not just clips from the movie. Just as the audience in the theater is in the best position to under-stand the final movie, the customer is often the only one who sees the big picture. The complete movie will cross many organizational and departmental lines, but the customer perceives it as a single experience with the company. Failure at any point along the way can mean failure for the entire company. Every business is the sum of its processes. We must identify just what the processes are so we can step back and take a look at how they affect business outcomes.

To ensure a customer-focused approach to analysis, begin by telling the story of the business from the customer's perspective. What is the first scene in which the customer is involved? What is the next scene, and the next, and the next . . . all the way to the final scene. What triggers the movement from one scene to the next? And, eventually, what is that process called?

Consider the scenes involved in a customer's interaction with a cell phone company. Start the camera rolling and record all the actions and trigger events chronologically as they occur.

Scene 1: Customer sees a commercial on television regarding "free non-roaming delegable minutes" and is able to remember which wireless company is holding the promotion. A potential customer is born when there is a need or desire. This need or desire is one of the two triggers for the first scene. A potential customer's first interaction with the company is usually a response to these needs. A second trigger for this scene is the commercial that catches the customer's attention. For this potential customer, the commercial has focused on his need for free non-roaming delegable minutes. The company's commercial specifically addresses the potential customer's need or desire, setting off the trigger. This first scene is really the initiation of the overall cell phone customer interaction.

Scene 2: Customer responds to commercial by visiting the company's retail outlet. The next interaction with the company comes when the potential customer pursues his need and makes contact to obtain further information about the product. The contact is the trigger that starts this process. The first moment of truth has gone well, and the customer responds by visiting the company's retail outlet. (Note that there could quite easily have been another scene in this movie—the customer visiting the Web site to gain additional information or even purchase the phone online.)

Scene 3: Customer asks about costs, coverage, and features. This is the first voice-to-voice interaction with a company representative. It is the first moment of truth that depends on instantaneous interaction with the company. The potential customer solicits information about the particular product or service needed. The customer's questions are the trigger for the scene. The success or failure of this customer's translation from potential to actual will depend on how the customer's expectation matches what the company delivers—both in terms of customer service and quality of the product.

Scene 4: Customer purchases phone and service plan. While it is true that each scene relies on the success of the prior scene, this seems no more evident than now. Unless the potential customer's needs have been met in the prior three scenes, the potential customer will not become an actual customer. The acceptance of the terms and conditions by the potential customer is the trigger that elevates him or her to an actual customer. Upon purchase of the phone and service plan, the importance of the process under review increases. Studies show that the cost of getting new customers can be anywhere from three to ten times more expensive than the cost of keeping them. Therefore, the efforts spent on enhancing the processes existing from this point forward are far more effective than those spent on getting to this point.

Scene 5: Customer's phone is connected. At this point, there is a lot going on behind the scenes. But none of these processes affect the customer. At least, they should not affect the customer. These processes are an excellent example of transparent processes. Notification may need to go to billing and connection. The customer database probably needs to be updated. And while the customer may never recognize that these are occurring, errors in the processes will become quickly evident. Connection may need to wait until billing verifies credit card authorization. All computerized systems may go down. However, if any of these causes a delay, the moment of truth is not faring well. It is also important to point out that scenes four and five may not seem like separate series of events to the customer. The individual expects to walk into the retail outlet, purchase a phone, and have connection. However, separating these scenes (and even the following one) provides a better understanding of the processes involved, and that is the true purpose of this exercise.

Scene 6: Customer uses phone. There are actually two triggers to this scene. The first is the customer receiving the phone. The second is the customer desiring to make or answer a call. This all leads to the ultimate moment of truth. Once all is said and done, if the phone does not work, the customer has not received what was promised. Keep in mind, it is not only a matter of the phone working, but also whether the reception is good, whether the caller gets cut off, and whether the customer experiences any of the various service issues that arise with cell phones.

Scene 7: Customer receives bill. This event is triggered by a date—the date the billing period ends. The resulting process is another test of the customer's satisfaction. This is the moment the customer decides whether the service received warrants the associated expenses. Once again, there are a number of processes behind receiving the bill, processes that should be transparent to the customer. And these processes should ensure that the bill arrives on time, includes only the services requested, and is billed at the agreed-upon rate.

Scene 8: Customer pays bill. This is the final scene in our movie. The happy ending in which the company receives compensation toward making a profit and the customer rides into the sunset, receiving excellent service for as long as the two do business. The trigger is the payment actually arriving (by check, credit card, Internet, etc.) at the billing center. Once received, the cycle starts over with the customer using the phone again.

Experiencing the business from the customer's prospective can help identify obvious processes. Each of the scenes represents processes necessary for the successful completion of the overall process, but it has also helped us identify processes that should be transparent to the customer. Even if the customer does not know these processes exist, they will directly or indirectly affect the customer's experience with the company.

In the preceding example, we identified billing, connection, and database management as transparent processes, but there are many more support processes. The first direct contact with the company is the sales representative, so the recruiting and training of sales representatives is an extremely important process for this company, but one that should be transparent to the customer. Another example might be supply management. Without a solid process here, phones might not be available to potential customers. Again, although we have identified eight "moments of truth," there are a number of transparent processes that must exist to make the moments of truth go right.

Naming the Major Processes

After listing the key trigger events from the customer's perspective, take a look at these events from the company's perspective. A process name may already exist and be obvious for the event. If so, you are in luck. If not, you must put on your creativity hat and come up with a descriptive name for the overall process. Keep in mind that there may be several units making up the process, but you are trying to first identify the overall major business processes.

A Process Identification Worksheet can be used to facilitate documentation (see Exhibit 2.1). The title of the form should be the area of the business being reviewed. The first column is a list of all the trigger events corresponding to the scenes encountered by the customer. The second column lists the process name. The example shows this completed using the cell phone purchase and subsequent billing as an example. It is a good idea to start with the overall process and the broad trigger that begins the process. This approach will help you focus on the work to be completed.

In listing the process names, use a name that has been agreed upon by you and the client to describe those overall processes. Again, the names are somewhat arbitrary. Two people may look at the same triggers and see different groupings or come up with different names, but there should be agreement from everyone working on the project about what processes they represent.

Exhibit 2.1   Process Identification Worksheet

Cell Phone Customer Interactions	
Trigger Events	**Process Name**
Potential customer has need or desire for cell phone. Potential customer sees commercial.	Marketing
Potential customer contacts company.	Customer Inquiries
Customer gets details.	Sales
Customer accepts offer.	Order Completion
Company initializes service.	Service Initiation
Customer begins using service.	Phone Support Services
Billing period ends.	Customer Billing
Customers make payment to the company.	Customer Payment
Customer does not make payment by specified date; or customer cancels service.	Termination of Service

In the example shown in Exhibit 2.1, an additional pair of triggers has been added. These represent the customer not making a payment or canceling the service. This is the unhappy ending to the story. For whatever reason, the processes have failed to fill the customer's needs, and the Termination of Service process must begin. Notice that, while these two triggers are different, either can set the process in motion.

Look at the example and see how the triggers described in the previous scenes lead to the associated processes. The overall business under review—Cell Phone Customer Interaction—is initiated by the needs and desires of the potential customer for a cell phone. When the customer sees a commercial that resonates with his needs and desires in such a way that he takes action, the overall process has begun. The process of *Customer Inquiries* starts with the potential customer making initial contact with the wireless provider. The *Sales* process begins with the customer making inquiries and the sales representative providing information in a way that responds to the customer's perceived needs. (Note that, rather than describing this process in terms the customer would use—for example, information gathering—it is named after an existing process within the company.) The *Order Completion* process begins when a customer places an order and ends when information is forwarded to the service department so that service can be initiated. *Service Initiation* begins when the request to set up a phone is received and ends when the service is established.

The *Phone Support Services* process involves the ongoing use of an existing phone, and while in most instances there is only one type of trigger (the customer uses the phone), the various circumstances that result may be reflected in many different units within the process. The *Customer Billing* process begins at the end of the billing period and involves the actual generation and circulation of the bill to the customer. The *Customer Payment* process begins after the bill is received and involves the method of payment and determination of whether a payment has been received. (Depending on the circumstances, this process can trigger the next process.) *Termination of Service* begins when one of two triggers exists—a payment is not received or the customer requests cancellation. The process ends when the service is actually disconnected.

Process Timelines

Development of the initial storyboard for the business can now begin as the major processes or acts have been identified. This is completed at a relatively high level processes and can be done through a traditional Process Map (you can see an example in Chapter 6). However, the use of a Business Process Timeline Worksheet (see Exhibit 2.2) can help identify missing processes and the way certain processes interrelate. This worksheet is designed to show how the customer experience processes lead from the first trigger event to the last. It also is used to show how transparent processes support the customer experience.

Identify the first and the last events in which the customer is involved. These visible events make excellent bookends for the timeline. In our example, *Marketing* is the starting point and *Termination of Service* is the ending point. Between these you can list the processes included in the Process Identification Worksheet (see Exhibit 2.3).

Next, determine whether there are other transparent processes that do not specifically involve the customer but are necessary to ensure success at the process's beginning. One example might be the hiring of employees. If we do not have employees, the *Marketing* process cannot begin. So, before that process can begin, the company must hire employees. This business also uses commercial

Exhibit 2.2 Business Process Timeline Worksheet

Process Name					
Process 1 (first trigger event)	Process 2	Process 3	Process 4	Process 5	Process 6 (last trigger event)

Exhibit 2.3 Visible Process Timeline (Customer Perspective)

Cell Phone Customer Interaction								
Customer Process								
Marketing	Customer Inquiry	Sales	Order Completion		Customer Billing	Customer Payment	Terminate Service
Support Process								
			Service Initiation				
			Support Services				

retail outlets to handle sales. Therefore, there must be a process for purchasing or renting commercial property and for maintaining those offices. Before there can be a response to a commercial, that commercial must be designed and distributed. There must be a *Sales and Marketing* process in place to accomplish these objectives. Finally, some processes may be administrative and have their own unique timelines. For example, financial reporting may be done on a fiscal-year basis. *Gathering of and Reporting on Financial Data* is another process.

Another good way to identify transparent processes is to look for gaps in the customer experience processes. From the company's standpoint, there may be a gap in the process between the initial use of the phone and the end of the billing period. There are transparent processes occurring in this period. These may be shown on the timeline by leaving gaps in the initial customer experience timeline. Below that timeline, the transparent processes that fill the void can be shown.

Processes that are not specifically part of the overall customer experience should begin on separate lines. If possible, they should be placed to show how they relate to the customer experience. For example, *Advertising* and *Marketing* actually occur before the customer makes first contact and should be placed accordingly. Employee hiring occurs throughout the experience, providing support at every stage. This should also be shown graphically. Within these supporting processes, identify those that are dependent on the completion of another process for a beginning and show these linked together next to each other in the timeline.

An attempt should be made to capture all the major processes relating to the particular business or segment of the business being reviewed. This should include visible processes and transparent processes. Exhibit 2.4 shows an example of a Business Process Timeline Worksheet that includes processes required to support potential customer solicitation, to obtain and support actual customers, and to terminate the customer relationship.

By defining the beginning and ending events and identifying the interrelationship of processes, we have set the overall boundary or frame for each process. You can see at a glance how one process may depend on another.

Exhibit 2.4 Comprehensive Business Process Timeline Worksheet

Cell Phone Customer Interaction							
Customer Process							
Marketing	Customer Inquiry	Sales	Order Completion		Customer Billing	Customer Payment	Terminate Service
Support Process							
			Service Initiation				
			Support Services				
Human Resource Management							
Employee Recruiting	Employee Training				Employee Compensation		
Employee Evaluation							
Call Center Development							
Call Center Selection	Call Center Purchase	Facilities Management					
		Call Center Evaluation					
Marketing							
Advertising Design	Campaign Proposal	Advertising Distribution					
		Campaign Training					
		Advertising Evaluation					
Financial Reporting							
		Capture Payment/Expense Data	Prepare Financial Statements	Distribute Financial Statements			
		Evaluate Company Financial Performance					

Customer Experience Analysis

A customer-focused business wants to ensure the customer has a starring role in each and every part of the story. For processes such as *Marketing, Sales, Customer Service Inquiries,* or *Customer Billing,* it is easy to understand that relationship.

Other processes may have no direct interaction with the customer, but have a profound impact on areas such as quality of products or services delivered. These critical supporting roles can determine whether your customer is really a star or a mere extra on the set. Areas such as asset management, distribution, facilities, supplier management, human resources, and training all indirectly affect the relationship with the customer.

Let us take a look at how understanding the overall customer experience processes, along with supporting processes, can give us a better understanding of the customer's role in our movie. Billing is always a critical interaction point with customers. As mentioned before, it is the point at which the customer makes a real decision about the value of services versus the expense. If the billing process itself goes wrong, businesses run the risk of losing customers immediately. Consider our cell phone customer:

Scene 1: The sale. A customer visits the company's retail outlet to purchase a cell phone. After discussions with the sales representative, she decides to purchase a phone with free long distance for $19.95 a month. The sales representative activates the phone and inputs the details of the sales transaction into the computer.

Scene 2: Preparation of the customer bill. A computer-generated bill is prepared once a month. The date is based on the original sales transaction. The amount is based on the initial agreement plus the actual minutes used.

Scene 3: Delivery of the customer bill. Bills are mailed 20 days before the due date to the address on the original sales transaction.

Scene 4: Accepting customer payments. Customers can make payments at the retail outlet, by mail, by phone, or by Internet.

Scene 5: Recording customer payments. Payments received at the retail outlet are posted at the close of the business day. Payments received by mail are posted the day after they are received. Payments accepted over the phone are posted two days after they are received. Internet payments are posted two days after they are verified.

Now we will look at a comedy of errors that we want to edit from our movie:

Outtake 1: The customer traveled frequently and relied heavily on the cell phone for contact with the office. At a critical time, she went to make a call and could not get service. When she was finally able to contact customer service, she was told that the phone was disconnected because of nonpayment of her bill. She stated that she had not yet received her initial bill. On further review, it was discovered that her billing address had been incorrectly input and the bill had never been received.

Outtake 2: When the customer received the bill, it was for $250 for two months. She again phoned the customer service department for an explanation. They informed her that the "free long distance" was not available from her calling area. While her base fee was still $19.95 a month, she would be charged additional fees unless she was calling from a specified city. She also learned that she was being charged for call waiting, which she had not ordered. Customer service informed her that she must pay the full amount by the 15th or they would be unable to reinstate her service.

Outtake 3: The customer decided to use the Internet to pay her bill. She logged onto the site on the 15th, made her payment by credit card, and logged off. She went to use her cell phone the next day and it still did not work. The customer service representative informed her that her payment would not be posted until the next day.

Exit—stage right!

While the customer was ultimately lost as the result of problems with the billing process, the real problems initiated with what should be a transparent process—order completion. The company's failure to ensure the accuracy of transaction inputs caused two potentially lethal problems: (1) failure to receive an initial bill and (2) inaccuracies in the bill. From the customer's standpoint, she only knows that she provided someone in the company with all the information necessary. This included the required service, her personal information, and where she wanted the bill sent. The incorrect input from the order fed directly to the preparation of the customer bill and directly impacted its delivery. These processes should have been transparent to the customer. However, the process became visible to the customer because of a failure in performance.

In analyzing this situation, it may be that sales representatives are measured by the number of customers handled and not on the accuracy of information recorded. The company could have determined that the prompt handling of customer transactions is a good measure of customer satisfaction. If so, the company has not considered the entire customer service picture. In this case, the company-defined measure of success contributes to the flow of inaccurate information. If the sales representatives were measured on the number of correct transactions or percentage of errors made in the original order entry process, a different outcome might have been realized.

Let us consider the *Claims Reporting* process from the beginning of the chapter in the same way. The customer will be lost because of this process, but it is really the supporting processes that cause the problem. For example, in an effort to ensure that claims representatives are fully trained, the company has made the decision to have them specialize. However, the result is that customers may have to work with a number of different people to solve what they perceive as a single problem—bringing order back to their lives.

This focus on the supporting process of training has caused the company to lose sight of what the training is meant to achieve—better claims service. In the example, additional support processes also need improvement—the customer service training of the receptionist, the availability of employees empowered to handle the steps of the process (the agent and the claims representative), and the use of the dreaded voice message. In such situations, it is not uncommon to see a company blame the customer for not understanding its procedures. But customers do not pay for procedures, they pay for results. Transparent processes that become visible only inhibit customer satisfaction.

In the expense payment scenario introduced in Chapter 1 (see Exhibit 1.3), we see some of the same things. To the customer (in this case, the company's employees), there are only two visible processes—submitting the request and receiving the check. In an effort to make a better controlled or more streamlined operation, the company has lost sight of this internal customer and built significant delay and bureaucracy between those two steps. Companies often give their internal customers less attention. While there is much debate about whether the internal or external customer is the most important, a company still has to recognize the importance of all internal customers. In this instance, the customer is not likely to take his business elsewhere. It is likely, though, that a more expensive option may occur—employees may go to a company where they can get their expenses reimbursed more easily.

Recap

The first step in identifying processes involves identification of trigger events. However, identifying these critical triggers and their associated processes requires viewing them from an external, not an internal, perspective. This approach means walking in the shoes of your customers and understanding your business processes from their perspectives. Look for the events that lead to interaction with the process.

Trigger events may be thought of as "moments of truth." These are the episodes in which the customer comes into contact with an aspect of the company and forms impressions of the company's quality of service. While these moments of truth are not in and of themselves positive or negative, the customer's experience with the company—the sum of all customer interactions—makes the experience positive or negative. One negative event can outweigh all other positive moments. Identifying these trigger events will lead to the most critical processes. The Process Identification Worksheet can be used to capture this information.

The next step is to identify the supporting processes. When customers perceive the company, they do not see all the processes. In fact, they do not see most of them. Underlying the customer experience processes are a multitude of transparent processes. These transparent processes are necessary to support the customer processes, but must not interfere with those processes. When a transparent process is exposed, it may result in a negative event—the type of negative event that makes the overall experience negative.

Once all processes are identified, they must be named. While this may seem a trivial task, it is often the first time anyone in a company has been required to consider what the actual processes are. Some names will be obvious, whereas others will take creativity and a lot of negotiation.

The next step is to prepare a Business Process Timeline Worksheet. This is a graphic representation of the major processes, including how they interrelate and support each other. It can be thought of as a broad overview process map. It should include the starting and ending events for the process, visible and invisible processes, and dependent and independent processes. These will help focus the review on the areas most sensitive to customer needs.

The five basic steps in process identification are:

1. Identify the trigger events.
2. Identify the customer critical processes.
3. Identify the supporting processes.
4. Name the processes.
5. Prepare the broad overview process map.

Once processes have been identified, it is time to start summarizing the information that has been gathered about the overall process and start developing plans for gathering additional detailed information about each process.

Key Analysis Points

Keep an External Perspective

Throughout the analysis process, from the moment you take on the engagement to the moment you leave, you must think like the customer, not like the company. The failure of many reviews occurs because the reviewer approaches the problem just as the company did, and that usually means ignoring the customer's perspective. "If you are not serving the customer, you had better be serving someone who is" is as true for the reviewer as it is for the employees.

"Moments of Truth"

Identify each and every time the customer comes into contact with the company. Every one of these is a moment of truth, the chance for the company to make a lifelong ally or enemy. If these are not adequately identified, the real value of underlying processes may never be known.

Measure the Right Things

Make sure that measurements are focused on the customer, not on the company. For a company to be successful, its measures of success must relate to customer satisfaction. Do not be fooled by measurements that claim to support customers but still look only at internal processes. You get what you measure. If that measure is focused internally rather than externally, you measure only internal success. Ultimately, the measures of success must be geared to reach the overall objectives.

Supporting Processes Must Be Transparent

Look for supporting processes that are inhibiting the success of critical customer processes. A large number of internal processes are necessary for a company's success, but they can never be more important than the key customer processes. As soon as these internal processes begin to intrude on the customer's experience, they become visible. If it is not important to the customer, it need not (and should not) be seen. When you find a transparent process that has become visible, you have found one of the focal points of your review.

CHAPTER 3

Information Gathering

The fog of information can drive out knowledge.
—Daniel J. Boorstine, Librarian of Congress

What You Need to Know and Where You Go to Learn It

Before performing any detailed review of a process, the reviewer must gather as much background information as possible. If we were Walt Disney's animators, trying to put together that first storyboard, we would need to reaffirm and establish our understanding of each scene. Disney knew what actions should take place in every section of the movie. He knew which characters were playing in each scene, what each character should do, and what he wanted to accomplish with each action. Those attributes are what he showed his animators while acting out the movie. But one exhibition was not enough (just as one discussion will not tell you everything that is happening in a process). Before the animators could start the storyboard, they talked with each other and went back to Disney to better understand what made up the movie.

Process reviewers, too, must have a complete understanding of the business movie they are reviewing before they try to put together a process map. Just like Disney's animators, they have heard the story, but now they must go back and piece together information to capture the essence of the process.

Information gathering occurs from the first moment you consider analyzing any process and continues throughout the completion of Process Mapping. A thorough understanding of the process under review is critical to the success of any Process Mapping project. However, it is almost like coming in as the movie is being filmed—without the benefit of understanding how it was developed. And to make things worse, there usually is no single "director" in charge of the process, someone you can approach to understand the master plan. The result is that people involved in one action may not have any idea what is going on in the entire scene. The answers lie in bits and pieces of each act and scene and in the actions taken in those scenes. The reviewer must start assembling the story with information that is coming in one piece at a time, much like putting together a jigsaw puzzle.

The challenge for the reviewer is to identify the resources that will provide the entire picture. To do this, someone with a good overview of the entire process must be found. It may be difficult, especially if functional or departmental lines are crossed as the process occurs, but it is integral to an effective start on Process Mapping. Therefore, managing the information gathering process begins by identifying the individuals who own the whole process. These process owners have both the responsibility and the authority to affect the processes under review. They will be your key resource and are most likely your key customers in the Process Mapping engagement.

If the company is not organized around processes, you may find it a bit difficult to determine who actually owns an individual process. There may be a multitude of owners and little or no accountability for the entire operation. Process owners may be somewhat elusive. A collaborative effort on the part of the reviewer and company management personnel is necessary to develop an accurate picture of the processes under review.

Preliminary Information

The analysis of processes requires a systematic methodology for gathering and documenting information. Following is the approach that has worked best for us:

- Identify the process (described in Chapter 2)
- Describe the process
- Identify the process owners or unit owners
- Interview the process owners or unit owners:
  - Verify your understanding of the process
  - Determine the business objectives
  - Determine the business risks
  - Determine the key controls
  - Determine the measures of success

While there is a logical flow of information implied in this list, it is not always possible or practical to gather information in such a linear fashion. For example, information about measures of success may become available before process owners are identified. The reviewer must understand what information is needed in each step and be alert for information sources early in the review.

The goal is to use your information sources in the most efficient manner. As you gather information, you will need to sort it and store it in the appropriate buckets. The worksheets described in this chapter are your buckets for sorting the different bits of information you will be getting.

You will be putting together this puzzle one piece at a time, finding straight-edged pieces to get some framework around your story; arranging certain colors to identify the pieces of each part of each scene; and identifying shapes to find the pieces that interlock. Unfortunately, you do not have the top of the box that shows the puzzle picture. Instead, the picture is emerging before your eyes as the pieces come together.

Process Identification

The first pieces of information gathered are at the macro level. As described in Chapter 2, the reviewer is trying to identify the processes involved in a given business or function. Individuals with a good understanding of the overall business operation—executives and managers—are the best sources for this type of information. It may be beneficial to have joint meetings with people who represent a good cross-section of the business when attempting to identify key processes. Face-to-face meetings are preferable. Maybe most important, sufficient time should be set aside. This meeting can easily take half a day.

The reviewer should facilitate this session, helping to identify triggers and categorize processes as discussed in Chapter 2. While the owners of the process have the best understanding of what is occurring, they probably do not have an understanding of the framework the reviewer is trying to establish. By facilitating the session, the reviewer can ensure that the outcome matches the needs of the review without forcing a particular result.

Process Description Overview

After major processes are identified, a complete description of each process should be prepared. The Process Description Overview summarizes all business processes by name and basic definition. The simple two-column form consists of the Process Name and the Process Definition. (This form can be built from the Process Identification Worksheet.)

These processes are the major acts in the business movie. Optimally, the process names will have been determined during the Process Identification phase, and now you will be developing descriptions for each process. Each description should include enough information to determine where the process begins, where the process ends, and what major actions occur in the process. A partially completed worksheet based on the cell phone example from Chapter 2 is shown as Exhibit 3.1.

There are some interesting things to note from this example. In general, the beginning and end points of the processes are evident from the descriptions. In addition, the *Phone Support Services* process is unique in that it is really an amalgam of many processes. Rather than try to identify all the processes that might be included in *Phone Support Services*, the reviewer has chosen a broad definition. This approach could imply that the various services will not be reviewed in depth, or it may be intended to allow additional flexibility in the review of the area. This process is also unique in that its start and end points are defined with the phrase "monthly usage." The same type of situation is reinforced by the use of the phrase "appropriate day of the month" in *Customer Billing*. Finally, the *Customer Payment* process uses a definition that helps point out the various modes of payment available—mail, phone, or Internet.

All these nuances are intended to enhance the reviewer's understanding of the process and help others who may look at the

Exhibit 3.1   Process Description Overview

Cell Phone Sales and Service	
Process Name	**Description**
Customer Inquiries	Sales representatives receive inquiries from potential customers, providing requested information.
Order Completion	Upon the customer's acceptance of the company's terms, sales representatives record sales transactions in the company order receipt system.
Service Initiation	The service department receives the customer order from the sales center to initialize service based on product and features ordered by the customer.
Phone Support Services	The unique usage of the product and services by the customer on a monthly basis.
Customer Billing	On the appropriate day of the month, the system mechanically issues a bill to the customer.
Customer Payment	The customer makes payment to the company by mail, phone, or Internet.
Termination of Services	If payment is not received by a predetermined date, or at the customer's request, service is terminated.

supporting work to better understand what has been accomplished. These descriptions may be revised as additional information on each process is gathered.

Identifying the Process Owners

During the initial meetings, you should have been able to identify the major processes. At the same time, you also should have obtained a good understanding of who the process owners are. In fact, you probably have been speaking with some of them. Creating a visual image of the key processes and associated owners helps the reviewer better understand how the people who own those processes relate to overall operations. A Process Owner Chart (Exhibit 3.2) is the perfect vehicle to accomplish this.

The Process Owner Chart may pertain to the entire business or to only a specific area of operation. The reviewer should begin only with process owners and then create additional charts that drill down to the unit owners. If the operation is relatively simple, the reviewer may develop one chart that includes both process owners and unit owners.

You probably will be unable to name all the processes when you begin the project, and, accordingly, you will not know all the owners. But as you gather information, the picture will become clearer, and more and more owners will become apparent. The people identified in the Process Owner Chart should be process owners—the individuals ultimately responsible for the overall process. Depending on the circumstances, these can be one-to-one, one-to-many, or many-to-one relationships.

In Exhibit 3.2, the first node identifies the operation under review. Separate nodes are then created for each process (Processes A through D). Again, at the beginning you may not have these all identified, but start with what you know and add information as you gain it. The major process owners are listed next (Person 1

Exhibit 3.2   Process Owner Chart

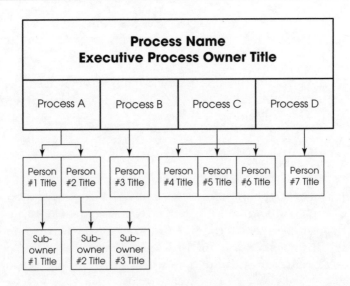

in the examples). If appropriate, you also may need to identify subordinate owners. These should not be unit owners (these will be identified later) but should be individuals involved in complicated processes who work as deputies to the process owners.

The exhibit shows the situation that might occur when processes cross functional lines. Processes B and D are all contained within one function and have only one owner (a one-to-one relationship). These also could be within the same function, and the owner could be the same person (a many-to-one relationship). Process A covers two areas and Process C covers three areas, resulting in two and three separate owners, respectively (a one-to-many relationship).

The Process Owner Chart can be completed using any basic flowcharting or drawing software. A traditional organization chart structured by process can also be used as a Process Owner Chart, but it is important to remember that the identity of true process owners may not be obvious. The goal of the chart is to be able to see at a glance what processes are involved and who owns them.

To make best use of an individual's time, as thorough an identification as possible should be completed before any detailed data gathering. This way, if an individual is responsible for more than one process, questions regarding all appropriate processes can be addressed during one interview.

Meeting with the Process Owners

Meetings should now be held with the highest-level individual involved in the processes under review. It may be a good idea (depending on the politics of the situation) to have all the reviewers who will be involved included in the initial meeting. In fact, it is important to have all reviewers involved in all aspects of the project. This helps ensure a team approach, makes sure all clients know everyone involved, and helps build trust with all participants. Most important, however, it allows the reviewers to better understand the broad perspective, resulting in a better evaluation.

These initial discussions should include the objectives of the mapping project, the approximate time frame in which the project will be completed, and the names of individuals who will be included in the project. This also is the point at which the reviewer can begin to obtain information on the process owners, subordinate process owners, business objectives, business risks, measures of success, and key controls. (These last concepts are discussed in more depth later.) The reviewer also should request that process owners be notified about the details of the project, including when they should expect to be contacted by the reviewer.

Interviews should now be conducted with process owners, subordinates, and eventually unit owners. Discussions should again include the objectives of the mapping project, the approximate time frame in which the project will be completed, and the names of individuals who will be included in the project. In addition, the process owner should be informed which units will be the focus of the review and approximately how much time the reviewer will be spending in each unit. An indication of the amount of time expected to be spent with each employee should also be given.

The reviewer now starts obtaining contact information and specific information about the process from the process owner and subordinate process owners, including business objectives, business risks, measures of success, and key controls. At this point, the reviewer also starts obtaining information about specific steps in the processes. While it is not time to start the actual map, the reviewer should be aware of this and record the information to be used in the map generation phase.

Some of these meetings may be held with groups of clients. For example, the highest-level owner may be included with the process owners. This will make for a longer single meeting, but can be more efficient than a group of individual meetings. It is also a good time to hammer out differences the owners may have in their own understanding of what makes up the process.

During one initial meeting, we began discussing our understanding of the primary processes in an operation. The department head was new and wanted us to help him gain an understanding of the entire operation. We met with the department head and his four managers. We explained what we saw as the first major process, and everyone agreed. We explained what we saw as the second major process, and there was general agreement, although one manager looked uncomfortable. We explained what we saw as the third major process, and a riot ensued. What we had found was that, although three of the managers had identical operations, the processes were being done three different ways. When we left that meeting, we had identified the differences and reached an agreement on how each was running. We also received the thanks of the department head, who was finally beginning to understand why there was no consistency in his department.

Ultimately, the information obtained from process owners may or may not agree with the information provided by the high-level process owner, but it is important to resolve these differences immediately. If conflicting information is obtained, identify the sources and document all the issues. All individuals involved in the review (the client and the reviewer) must approach the project using the same metrics. If there is already disagreement on something as basic as objectives, the project may be doomed to failure. The discrepancy probably will be a significant portion of a final report, but the reviewer cannot wait for that report before discussing the information. Only with agreement by all major parties can the reviewer have a basis for the review that will be accomplished.

If process definitions have been developed, review these with the process owners and the subordinate process owners. If they have not yet been developed, a portion of these meetings should be used to identify and define the processes.

Units and unit owners will generally be identified during your discussions with the process owners. Once their identities have been revealed, the Process Owner Chart can be revised to include the individual unit owners. If there are too many owners to make this practical, a separate chart for each individual unit may be necessary. As stated before, the goal of the Process Owner Chart is to visually depict each process owner, the units in each process, and the unit owners of each unit. Including all unit owners will only make this understanding more complete. When completing the chart, remember that one process owner may head a few units or all of them.

By now, you should have created a visual diagram of the ownership relationships. This will help you determine who you need to talk to about different issues. Exhibit 3.3 shows a combined Process Owner/Unit Owner Chart for the Expense Payment process introduced in Chapter 1.

In this exhibit, the Treasurer is the owner of the *Expense Payment* process. Within that process are two subordinate process owners, the Home Office Accounting Manager and the Field Accounting Manager. In this instance, the subordinate owners reflect different aspects of the *Expense Payment* process—home office and field. Within this process are the units that make up payment of all other

Exhibit 3.3   Combined Process Owner/Unit Owner Chart

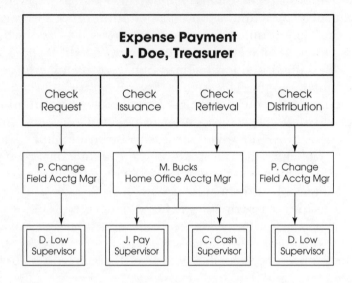

expenses. For the home office, there is one unit owner—the Home Office Disbursement Supervisor. For the field office there are 11 unit owners—one Field Disbursement Supervisor for each office.

What to Discuss

Some of the points to be covered in the owner interviews have been mentioned and discussed in depth already. These include the process name, process description, triggers, and process or unit owners. However, some additional areas must be included in the interview because they are core considerations when analyzing the process. These are the areas that everyone must understand and on which they must have a basic agreement.

Business Objectives

In talking with owners, one of the primary questions the reviewer should ask is, "What is the process trying to accomplish, and how does that tie to the theme of the business?" As discussed earlier, every movie has an underlying plot or theme. Each act within the movie and every scene within the act should have a purpose or objective that supports the overall theme. In the same way, every business has key strategic objectives it is trying to accomplish. Every business process should support one or more of those key strategic objectives. If any process does not support the objectives, it may not be warranted and may need to be eliminated. Even if it does support a strategic objective, a complicated process may be supporting one of the less important objectives and may represent a waste of resources. The true success or failure of a process can be determined only if specific, measurable objectives are identified that tie in with the company's strategic objectives.

If management does not specifically identify objectives, processes may be completed based on employees' perceptions of the right thing to do. The reviewer must understand what the process owners expect from that process and what they expect the process to achieve. Then the reviewer must determine whether the process owner's goals and objectives conflict with the company's strategic goals and objectives. More often than not, the goals for a process (or unit) were developed at a high level. However, when these high-level goals were passed down to the employees, the intent of those goals (how they tied in with the company's strategic objectives) was not included.

Without a firm understanding of the true objectives, differing perceptions result in inconsistent low-level objectives. The high-level owner may have an objective of making a certain profit while delivering a certain level of customer service (a very common objective). However, if the subordinate owner has heard only the need for profit and interpreted this to mean that costs should be cut, there is a miscommunication. Thinking that the primary objective is reduced costs, the subordinate owner may be eliminating costs that turn out to be essential to the performance of the process. By putting policies in place that fly in the face of a true profit objective (it takes money to make money), the subordinate owner has undercut the success of the process.

In one of our first attempts to apply objectives to processes, we learned how seldom numerical objectives are actually given in strategic terms. Before reviewing a claims office, we spoke with senior executives about the claims department's objectives. They were very simple and straightforward—objectives such as "ensuring that our claimants' lives were restored to order" and "maintaining the highest quality staff." We had no problem assigning these objectives to the major processes we had identified. We then began working with the manager. Again, we started with a discussion of his objectives.

He gave us copies of his objectives for the year and we went on our merry way. Once we actually looked at the information that was provided, we were very disappointed. What we received were numerical requirements. Examples included "return all phone calls within 4 hours," "set up all files within 24 hours," and "use computer-generated letters for all correspondence." There were also some very esoteric goals, such as "placing an emphasis on outside education," "increasing teamwork between claims offices," and "improving communication with the sales force." Immediately, you can see that there are either no measures of success for these goals or that the measurements may not be available. We discuss measures of success later in this chapter, but it was painfully apparent as we reviewed these measures that there was no context for the goals. Each had the same weight and each stood alone. When we talked with the manager, even he had no understanding of how these objectives supported the strategic objectives of the company. He only saw that he had to meet all these goals.

This example demonstrates that it can sometimes be a bit difficult to match goals and objectives at the process level to the overall objectives. For advertising, a business strategic goal may be to maximize sales. It is very easy to see how a process-specific objective of increasing sales in a certain target market by 20 percent in 6 months helps support this goal. However, the process of *Customer Inquiries* would have the identical business strategic goal of maximizing sales—in this case through superior customer service. The process objective could be answering 45 calls per hour; answering calls in two rings; or another goal established based on the number of sales per hour or day. The tie-in to the strategic goal is less obvious, which shows how important it is to make sure that the people responsible for the goals understand why that goal exists. In particular, the first two measures can be reached without affecting sales at all. Only when customer service understands how those goals impact the overall strategic goal will their efforts be effective.

We are discussing measures of success a little prematurely, but to determine whether people understand the reasons for objectives, it is important to see how measurements affect their perception. Different service results will be received depending on the actual or perceived objective of the process. If customer service employees are measured on sales alone, simple customer inquiries may not receive the appropriate attention. If customer service employees are measured on number of calls per hour, each customer may not receive the attention he or she deserves. If customer service employees are measured on the quality of results, including required rework or complaints, representatives will take more care with each call. Unless given evidence to the contrary, people determine important objectives by how they are measured. The old saying "you get what you measure" (or what people perceive you are measuring) is very true. Conflicting goals and objectives can often be the root cause of a service breakdown.

Looking at the cell phone example, if maximizing sales is the main objective, sales representatives may have an incentive to add additional features that the customer did not order to boost the employee's sales numbers. They may also have an incentive to hurry through the process to get to the next order if accuracy is not part of the measurement. In the customer billing process, a business strategic goal may be to maximize revenue with a billing objective of providing accurate bills to all customers by the 10th of each month. In this situation, a conflicting objective may occur in the *Prospect Inquiry* or *Recording Sales Transaction* process. If sales representatives are paid by the numbers, not by accuracy or quality, billing errors may occur and go undetected. The billing process in isolation may be working perfectly; however, inputs to the process may be corrupted.

Taking business objectives down to the process level is not intuitive. We normally write business objectives and set budgets on a departmental basis, not at the process level. One department may be involved in phases of many different processes. Process objectives may be dictated by procedure or policy, or they may be set by management as a performance standard. Many people involved in part of the process do not have the slightest idea what the process is trying to accomplish or how their particular piece contributes to the overall picture.

Actors in the movie that is the business have been exposed only to their individual frames. They may play bit parts, walk-ons, one frame out of hundreds or thousands. They have never seen the entire scene or act, let alone the whole movie. They may have an idea what the movie is about, but they cannot provide you with many details. If these actors at least know about the scene, its purpose, and their motivation, they can help make sure that their performance is consistent with the whole movie. By providing clear process objectives, employees can know their motivation and provide performances consistent with the strategic needs of the company.

Likewise, the reviewer must understand these objectives and motivations to determine how each part of the process fits the big picture. Process Mapping facilitates the accomplishment of goals and objectives by providing a holistic, visual representation of how the business processes individually and collectively fit together to achieve the desired results. By defining the business processes and associated objectives, the reviewer increases awareness of the different points of impact with the customer. The reviewer can more clearly see how action taken in one area may influence another—the plot of the movie is known, the scenes that are a part of the movie have been defined, and it is now easier to determine how those scenes support the plot. Even if you as a reviewer go no farther than this point—never creating a single process map—you would be ready to help your clients handle their business in the future because you had identified clearly each process and associated objective.

Business Risk

Once an understanding of the objectives has been accomplished, the next question to be asked is "What would prevent the accomplishment of the key business objectives?" Many processes are developed with the purpose of achieving some objective—making things go right. Often, however, very little thought is put into determining how the process should be developed to ensure that the objective is completed—making sure things do not go wrong. Process owners should be aware of key business risks and have plans in place to address them. One value of working with the client to identify the key business risks is to ensure that they have thought about these risk issues.

The other purpose of the risk discussion is to help the reviewer spot issues related to key business risks as maps are created. The goal is to have a process that eliminates or at least mitigates the business risks. In many Process Mapping projects, the reviewer will focus on efficiencies. Usually there is an implied understanding that the key objective is reducing costs, and the risk is that processes will not run efficiently. Therefore, the reviewer is trying to address those aspects of the business. While it is true that efficiency detection is a large benefit of Process Mapping, focusing on one risk hobbles the reviewer. Looking only at efficiency is much like trying to watch a movie without sound and color—you get only part of the story, and the part you get is out of context.

Getting the full range of objectives is the first step, but getting the broad view of risks is the next step. Basic risks could include poor detection of fraud, customer dissatisfaction, low morale, and increased fines and penalties. These seem obvious, and most reviewers keep them in mind, but it is easy to get caught up in the "efficiency" paradigm.

One of the most obvious objectives is fraud prevention. Every company has a number of processes in place to prevent or reduce fraud. Two-party controls are one of the most common. By the same token, any review will show that having two people involved in a process is less efficient than having one person involved. A pure efficiency review would suggest reducing the workforce. A review that encompasses all risks will recognize that the need to reduce fraud in this situation far outweighs the need for efficiency.

A mapping project's effectiveness is increased by including as many of the key objectives and associated business risks as possible, and the company's exposure to risks is decreased if the mapping project has a broader focus than just efficiency. Working with the client to determine these risks helps everyone understand the exposures.

Key Controls

For each objective, we have found the associated business risk. The next question is "What controls have been established within the process to ensure that these risks are eliminated or mitigated?" Process owners often understand their objectives and may even have an understanding of the risks inherent in those objectives. They probably also have a thorough understanding of procedures in place within the process, but they have seldom made the connection between risks and the procedures put in place to control those risks.

Unit owners are more likely to know what controls are in place because they will have a much more detailed knowledge about the process, but they may still not have made a connection between the controls and the risks they are addressing. And individuals actually performing the process often do not have a clue about controls—they are just doing their jobs. As a result, the reviewer is often the one who has to identify the existence or lack of key controls. This represents a good opportunity to educate process owners about controls and how they help achieve objectives.

During discussions about key controls, reviewers may find that people misunderstand which controls are important. During a review of an accounting process, every person we spoke with could outline the office's procedures to make sure the check printer key was secure. There were procedures for when the manager was there, there were procedures for when the manager was not there, there were procedures for when the manager should use the key, and there were procedures for what type of lock should be used on the desk where the key was kept. This one aspect of the risk of loss from fraudulently issued checks was mitigated—and then some.

There also was a procedure requiring each supervisor to review a certain number of files for every employee on a monthly basis. Because these employees were given a great deal of autonomy, it was the only real review of supporting documentation. Much like the prior control, this review helped prevent fraudulently issued checks. However, it was also a key control to ensure that files contained all regulatory-required documentation. Furthermore, since this provided the supervisors with an opportunity to review the employee's work, it was an important control to ensure that all employees were receiving proper training. However, every single supervisor told us the same thing—there was not enough time to do the reviews.

The good news was that the check printer key was secure; the bad news was that it was being used to turn on a check printer that could be printing improper or unsupported payments. Because of the emphasis on the key as an important control, everyone in the office had lost sight of the importance of the file review as a control. This "key" control for three different areas had lost out to a control over a physical key.

Process owners or unit owners may not have a good understanding of their key controls. The initial discussions should try to identify them, but the interviewees may not have the detailed knowledge necessary. The question of what key controls are in existence may go unanswered until mapping of the process begins. Once these key controls are determined, the reviewer can also use the mapping to determine if the key controls in place really are the important ones and to help determine whether control breakdowns are occurring.

Measure of Success

Once we know the objectives, there is another important question to be asked: "How does the process owner measure the success of this process?" As mentioned when discussing objectives, it's probable that the process owner is measuring a number of areas, but he or she may not always make a direct connection to strategic or even process objectives.

First, come to agreement on the existence of specific measures. If there are none, you will need to work with the client to determine what they think those measures should be. It is better to develop them with the client early in the project than work without any measures. This approach provides clients with a new way to measure their own success and provides a benchmark to eventually show the Process Mapping project's success.

At this point, you should start taking a hard look at these measurements. Misplaced measurements can be as detrimental as a lack of measurements. Make sure that the measurement in place matches the identified objectives, risks, and controls. As an example, we reviewed an area that wanted to increase the number of independent marketers selling a product. The overall objective was an increase in sales, and there was a determination that more salespeople meant more sales. One of the business risks identified by the client was that the objective could not be reached with a stable or declining sales force. In discussions, they were unable to identify a true key control, although they cited numerous criteria that had been established to ensure that only quality candidates were accepted.

The measure of success was an annual net increase in the number of marketers. The measurement had been met for the past two years. We discussed the key controls with them in more depth, and they began to recognize that the controls they brought up dealt more with a customer service objective—providing customer service by ensuring contact with skilled individuals. Discussing this more, everyone realized that there was no measure for the existing sales force. In addition, while gathering statistics before developing the maps, we noticed that the number of independents removed from the marketing plan over the last two months of the year was almost zero. The department was successful in getting what it measured—a net increase in the number of bodies. However, this measure did not address the real key controls or the full business.

The reviewer also should determine whether information on the measures of success for the process is readily available. If reports are not readily available, determine whether they can be extracted from other data. Remember that if you cannot readily obtain statistics that are required for measures of success, the process owner probably cannot determine whether success has been met. In one process, a measure of success was maintaining or reducing the balance for outstanding receivables. However, discussions showed that the report containing this information had not been received for more than six months. This raised two questions: (1) How was success actually being measured? (2) if the information was not received for six months and no one noticed, was this a truly important measure?

Obtain the measure of success information as early in the review as possible. It will be helpful in discussions with process owners and unit owners. Also, pay particular attention to cycle times that are measurements. As the map is developed, these cycle times will be identified and will become an integral part of the analysis.

Maybe most important, if measures of success have not been specifically defined, how do the process owners know when the process has failed? Sometimes success can be measured only by the absence of failure. Ultimately, it is imperative that the process owners and the reviewer know the measurements of success to know whether the process is working.

Which Came First, the Objective or the Risk?

It should be apparent from the previous discussions that these four areas do not exist in isolation. Discussion with the process owners, unit owners, and even line personnel will all touch on various aspects of objectives, risks, controls, and measures. And these discussions will not flow directly from one to the next. It is the reviewer's job to ensure that the discussions stay somewhat on track while still getting as much information as possible. It is also necessary to ensure that all four questions are answered in as much detail as possible.

After the discussions are complete, the participants may not realize how much information they have given. The reviewer may have a hodgepodge of information—a situation in which everything necessary was recorded; it is just a question of finding it. Therefore, it usually is a good idea to have another meeting with the entire group. The reviewer should sort through the information and provide a summary (as discussed in the next section) that shows everything that was agreed upon regarding these areas. It is one more chance to ensure that everyone is on the same page.

Process Profile Worksheet

One of the most important worksheets you will put together is the Process Profile Worksheet (See Exhibit 3.4). This form will be created for each process under review. The worksheet is intended to be a centralized repository for critical information obtained about the process. It will be completed in phases as information is gathered from various process owners. This same form can be used to develop a profile of individual units in the process (a Unit Profile Worksheet).

This worksheet will help anchor the mapping process. A well-developed profile can also help focus the review on the most critical areas. One of the most difficult aspects of Process Mapping is determining how the details fit within the whole picture. In Process

Exhibit 3.4   Process Profile Worksheet

Process Name—Number	Process Owner
Description	
Triggers	
Event beginning: Event ending process: Additional events:	
Input—Items and Sources	
Output—Items and Customers	
Process Units	Process Unit Owners
Business Objective(s)	Business Risks
Key Controls	Measure of Success

Mapping, it is easy for the reviewer to see only the individual shots in the movie, often out of context. The Process Profile helps the reviewer identify the context of that shot within the overall scene and act.

Process Name and Number

The form provides a space for process name and number. The process name developed in the process identification exercise should be used. It can also be useful to assign each process a number. This approach can facilitate the numbering of units, tasks, or actions in documents to ensure that the reviewer understands what portion of the process is under review. They can also enable easier cross-referencing of the charts and worksheets maintained in the work papers. For example, the main process of *Paying Other Expenses* may be process 1. Units of the process might include Field Office Prepares Request (1.1), Home Office Prepare Check (1.2), and Field Office Receives Check (1.3). The tasks for Unit 1.1 might be *complete request* (1.1a), *approve request* (1.1b), and so on. The numbering method should reflect the process–unit–task hierarchy.

Process Owner

The process owner field provides a space for listing the individual process owners by name and title. These should mirror the information recorded on the process owner chart. Reference information (e.g., phone numbers or an assistant's name) can also be included. If the worksheet is completed at the unit level, the unit owners should be listed.

Process Description

The process description should reflect the overview descriptions developed after the processes were named. These should be taken from the Process Description Overview, developed during the first phase of the review.

Triggers

Key triggers were noted in the Process Identification Worksheet (see Exhibit 3.1). A process may include a number of trigger events. All of these events help explain what goes on in the process, but the most critical triggers are the events that begin the process and the events that end the process. Clearly outlining these triggers helps ensure that processes do not overlap and that a clear beginning and ending have been identified for each one. Very often, the trigger for one process is the final task or action from the prior process. Any additional trigger events should also be included. Additional triggers are significant actions that are required to keep the process going. They may eventually be recognized as triggers for individual units and tasks.

As an example, the event beginning for *Service Initiation* (as defined in the Process Description Overview) would be the customer order being received by the service department. The end of the event would be the successful hook up of the cell phone.

Inputs and Outputs

At the very beginning, we discussed the importance of inputs and outputs to the definition of a process. Identification of the key inputs in the process at this point—including the item and source of the item—helps clarify exactly what piece of information starts the process rolling. Both the item and the source of the input should be identified. In the *Service Initiation* example, the item that starts the process is an electronically entered customer order form. The source of this form is the sales representative. Likewise, the key output from the process should also be identified, along with the main customer for the output. The customer for the output could be an external customer or an internal customer. This output identifies what the process is supposed to produce. For *Service Initiation*, the output item is a functioning cell phone and the customer is the service purchaser.

Looking at the definitions for the prior two sections, you can begin to see the difference between triggers and inputs. In general, triggers represent a process or event, whereas the input is an actual thing. For *Service Initiation*, the trigger for the beginning of the process is receiving the customer order. The input is the order itself. The trigger is an event that is the culmination of a prior process (as shown in the Process Description Overview). The input is an item that is the result (output) of the prior process. Understanding both is necessary to get the full effect of how a process begins and ends.

Process Units and Process Unit Owners

By this point, you should have a good idea of the units within the process. Record them here. Take a look at the critical trigger events included as "additional events" in the Triggers section. These triggers are causing transformations during the process and can represent units within the process. Make sure that each unit represents a trigger and every trigger represents another unit. Also include the process unit owners. If you are taking the Process Profile Worksheet to a unit level (the Unit Profile Worksheet), gather similar information from unit owners to determine the tasks within the unit. The task information can then be recorded in this section.

Business Objectives

The business objectives determined in the meetings with process owners should be included here. There should be no more than two or three major objectives for the process being reviewed, and they should be stated in a fairly concise manner.

Business Risks

The risks recorded here should also be fairly high level. These may not have a one-to-one relationship to the previously listed objectives. However, if this correlation can be made, the information should be entered to reflect this. Completing this section will help the reviewer focus on all risks involved.

Key Controls

This section should include the key controls agreed upon in meetings. There should be a much clearer correlation between objectives and controls or risks and controls, which should be made clear by the way the information is entered in the worksheet. Again, these should be fairly concise descriptions intended to give the reader a feel for the control, not the exact process steps.

Measure of Success

Finally, enter the agreed-upon measures of success. These should be concise, specific, and most important, *measurable*. Do not fall into the trap of repeating objectives here. This is where the exact numbers that represent success or failure should be recorded.

Process Profile Worksheet Summary

The Process Profile Worksheet should be used as a work in progress. The reviewer should start with any initial assumptions and modify the worksheet as discussions occur. As each discussion takes place, the reviewer can go over the worksheet with the interviewee and make any necessary changes or additions. Bear in mind that the farther you go in the project, the less likely you should be to make those changes. You do not want the worksheet to strictly reflect what the last person says; instead, it should reflect the consensus of discussions. Intermittently throughout the project, you should go over the process-level sheets with the process owner and the unit-level sheets with the unit owners. This will accomplish two things. First, getting their agreement will validate your understanding. Second, it will help the owners begin to understand where misunderstandings are occurring.

Exhibit 3.5 is an example of a completed Process Profile Worksheet for the *Expense Payment* process.

This process would have been identified in an overall process identification exercise with the Treasurer, J. Doe. At that meeting, basic units of the general disbursement process were identified; these included Payroll, Expense Payment, and Refunds. If we were examining all of these processes, a separate Process Profile Worksheet would be developed for each one. However, in our example the project is focusing on *Expense Payment*.

After identifying each of the disbursement units, the reviewer asks J. Doe to identify the owners of the various disbursement units. J. Doe identifies M. Bucks of Home Office Disbursements as the owner of the *Expense Payment* process. J. Doe has a general understanding of how the process works, but he defers the discussion regarding the description, triggers, and other process details to M. Bucks. J. Doe says his objectives for this process are to ensure that no one steals any money; that no inappropriate expenses are generated; and that all bills are paid promptly, accurately, and within the discount period. This information is entered in the Process Profile Worksheet. From this, the reviewer is able to determine both the objectives and the initial business risks.

The reviewer then meets with M. Bucks, who is able to provide descriptions of the units involved in the process. These are added to the worksheet. M. Bucks also points out that she is responsible

Exhibit 3.5   Process Profile Worksheet-Expense Payment Process

Process Name—Number	Process Owner
Expense Payment Process – EP	J. Doe, Treasurer M. Bucks, Mgr HO Disbursements P. Chang, Mgr Field Accounting

Description
The process of paying for incurred business expenses other than travel and purchase order.

Triggers
Event beginning: Receive bill
Event ending process: Distribute check to employee or mail to payee
Additional events: Complete check request, obtain approval, submit request, issue check

Input—Items and Sources
Bill/Invoice or other support—employee

Output—Items and Customers
Disbursement check—vendor

Process Units	Process Unit Owners
Check Request Check Issuance Check Retrieval Check Distribution	Field Disbursement Supervisor Home Office Disbursement Supervisor Home Office Disbursement Supervisor Field Disbursement Supervisor

Business Objective(s)	Business Risks
Prompt and accurate payment of valid, properly approved business expenses	Fraudulent payments Delayed payments—missed discounts Customer dissatisfaction

Key Controls	Measure of Success

Segregation of duties
    Requester and approver
    Requester and issuer
    Issuer and retriever
	All checks issued within 48 hours
	Utilization of early pay discounts
	Complaints about delays
	Absence of duplicate payments

only for check issuance and check retrieval. The check request and check distribution processes are the responsibility of P. Change, the Manager of Field Accounting. This owner is added to the process owner portion of the worksheet. At this point, M. Bucks and P. Change might be considered subordinate process owners or co-owners of the process.

M. Bucks was a field accounting manager and is very familiar with the field process. The reviewer obtains an overview of the process from M. Bucks and is able to complete the Description, Triggers,

Input, Output, and Process Units portions of the worksheet. Additional refinements to the worksheet are made after discussions with P. Change. This includes determining that one measure of success is that the home office will issue all checks within 48 hours.

Once these discussions are complete, a brief meeting is held with J. Doe, M. Bucks, and P. Change to discuss the worksheet and fill in additional details. In particular, the key control of segregation of duties is identified, along with the additional measures of success— use of early pay discounts, complaints, and identifying duplicate payments. There is some discussion about measurements to identify fraudulent payments (e.g., terminal digit analysis, data mining, or address analysis), but the owners think the controls are sufficient to limit the need for this measurement. With complete agreement on the worksheet at this stage, the reviewer can continue.

Meeting with the Unit Owners

Meetings should now be held with the individual unit owners. If a unit-level Process Profile Worksheet is being completed, the same information discussed previously should be obtained from the unit owner. Even if a worksheet is not being completed, much of the same information should be obtained. At the very least, discussions should again include the objectives of the mapping project, a review of the detailed information-gathering plan, the approximate time frame in which the project will be completed, the individuals who will be included in the project, and final arrangements for the actual mapping interviews. In addition, you will want to let the unit owner know which tasks will be the focus of the review and approximately how much time the reviewer will spend with each employee.

If Workflow Surveys are used (see following section), let the unit owner know when the surveys will be sent and what the expected turnaround time is for the surveys. Establish a plan for conducting the interviews (for example, one every two hours). Determine who will control the flow of interviewees.

Measures of success should be specifically discussed. The unit owner is more likely to have the actual data than the process owners, so determine whether information on the measures of success for the unit is readily available. If reports are not readily available, find out how the owner obtains data. Get the actual measurement data as early in the process as possible. It will be helpful in discussions with the owners and line personnel. If it is not readily available, determine whether there are tests that can be performed at the time of mapping to verify the success or failure of the process.

Workflow Surveys

The next step is to start determining the actual tasks and actions within the process. Unit owners and employees working for unit owners are the best source for this information, and that means the reviewer is beginning to enter the interviewing and mapping section of the project.

However, before actual interviews are started, the reviewer must get a feel for what each employee does. To facilitate this understanding, a Workflow Survey should be sent to all employees involved in the process under review (see Exhibit 3.6).

The form is relatively simple, but it can reveal a wealth of information. The top section asks for basic information—the employee's name, job title, length of time in present position, and a quick summary of job duties. Then it gets into a little more detail. Employees are asked for information regarding the individual tasks they perform. This includes a basic name for the task, how they receive the work (from whom), what they do with it when they get it, the approximate cycle time, and to whom it goes when they are done.

This is an incredibly useful tool in the interviewing process. From the reviewer's perspective, it helps identify individuals who are involved in the process being reviewed and gives the reviewer an overview of the actions being taken to perform the process. By including cycle times, the reviewer is already becoming aware of bottlenecks and other efficiency issues.

However, there also is great benefit to the employees. Initially, the Workflow Survey helps take some of the mystery out of the process for employees. The information is laid out in a way that encourages everyone to think of their individual duties as processes. Once employees begin thinking in terms of processes, subsequent discussions and mapping go easier. The survey also shows the employees that someone is actually interested in the work they do. This may be the first time anyone has asked them to outline exactly what they do for a living. Although the survey is meant to be an overview, some people react by becoming very detailed in the completion of

Exhibit 3.6 Workflow Survey

We need the following information in order to complete a workflow study of your office/department. We are asking you to provide us with a summary of your job duties, as well as specific information on how you complete the individual tasks involved in your job. Please be as specific as possible and feel free to use additional copies of this form if one page is not sufficient. Thank you for your assistance.

Name:	Summary of job duties (list general job duties below)
ID#:	
Title:	
Length of time in present position:	

Task	Work received from? (Co-worker, mail, phone, supervisor, etc.)	What specifically do you do? (How to you process your work?)	How long does the process take? (Estimate for the task.)	Where does your work go when you are finished? (To someone in your department, a customer, mail, etc.)

the form. We often find that people attach several extra pages to provide us with the best picture possible of their job.

Surveys should be sent out one to two weeks before they are needed. This will allow employees the time necessary to give the survey some thought and complete it fully. Also, allow enough time for the reviewer to go over the surveys before conducting interviews. When surveys are returned, the reviewer should use them to begin understanding the tasks and actions within the process, determining who actually performs those tasks (this could be different from the owners' understanding), and highlighting any issues that must be pursued during the actual interviews.

Surveys can be customized to better reflect actions in a particular job. One survey may work well for clerical employees and another survey may work better for supervisory employees. For clerical employees, the reviewer is probably interested in the actual flow of work and the individual tasks. For supervisors, the emphasis is generally on known job duties—for example, approvals, training, supervision, budgeting, span of control, and other management functions. Rather than cycle times, a reviewer may be interested in the percentage of time management employees are spending on certain duties.

If an area has been reviewed before, the survey may emphasize known duties. As an example, we have used these in our claims office reviews. A number of these reviews are conducted annually, so many of the basic processes are well known. In spite of what we think we know, a Workflow Survey is still important. In response to this, the survey sent to our claims representatives focuses on areas where we know we need specific information. In general, tailor the survey to the individual and to your specific information needs. Examples of two surveys specifically tailored to claims processes are provided in Exhibits 3.7 and 3.8. Exhibit 3.7 shows a sample claims representative survey, and Exhibit 3.8 shows a sample for management employees. You can see how the same types of information are solicited, just in different formats.

Data Gathering

You may have noticed an interesting thing about our discussion. The title of this chapter is Information Gathering, yet we have talked very little about getting any hard data. Obviously, the focus

Exhibit 3.7 Claims Workflow Survey—Claims Representative

We need the following information in order to complete a workflow study of your office/department. We are asking you to provide us with a summary of your job duties, as well as specific information on how you complete the individual tasks involved in your job. Please be as specific as possible and feel free to use additional copies of this form if one page is not sufficient. Thank you for your assistance.

Name:				
ID#:				
Title:				
Length of time in present position:				

Claims type		Authority Level by Type of Claim		
		Reserve	Settlement	Negotiation
APD				
Liability				
Property				

Task	Action Taken
	Please provide the following information concerning how claims are processed
Assignment	When received? (times per day, week) How received? (fax, jacket file, paper file)
"Investigation"	Where is your investigation work documented? (field file, master file) If you use a filed file, when is documentation transferred to the master file?
Reserving	When are reserves established? How do you document your reserve request? (by memo, in the log) Who is your file routed to when you request a reserve? (Supervisor, secretary, input clerk)
Additional Units	How do you request additional units on a claim? (by memo, in log, special form) Who approves the request? Who inputs the additional unit?
Subrogation	How is subrogation potential documented in your file? (special form, log notes, stamp) What information do you gather for subrogation input?
Claim Settlement	Who is involved in the negotiation process for claims within your authority? (Explain when your supervisor would be involved and how) How is the settlement amount approved? (on check request, in log, on settlement advise) Are checks returned to you for delivery? What happens after final payment is processed? (return the file to you, file to closed file area, file to supervisor)
File	How often are case reviews scheduled? What files are reviewed at case review? How often do you submit a status report on a file?

Exhibit 3.8 Claims Workflow Survey—Management Personnel

We need the following information to complete a workflow study of your office/department. We are asking you to provide us with a summary of your job duties, as well as specific information on how you complete the individual tasks involved in your job. Please be as specific as possible, and feel free to use additional copies of this form if one page is not sufficient. Thank you for your assistance.

Name:	Summary of job duties		
ID#:			
Title:			
Length of time in present position:			
Task	**Work received from?** (BCO personnel, mail, phone, etc.)	**What specifically do you do?** (How to you process your work?)	**How long does the process take?** (estimate)	**Where does your work go when you are finished?** (To someone in the office, to the customer)
Assignments				
Reserving				
Claim Settlement				
Subrogation				
File Review				
Closings				
Quality Assurance				
Other (explain)				

of information gathering is learning about the process. It is about sitting and talking with people. However, some basic data should be obtained before beginning the real interviewing process.

Some of the first data to accumulate should relate to the measures of success. These should include not only the final statistics, but also the data used to drive the results. Obtain historical information to get a sense for the trends. Also, look for data that might be useful for additional measures of success—areas that the reviewer thinks might be important but have not been identified as such by the client. In the *Expense Payment* example, the reviewer has some concerns about fraudulent checks that are not shared by the client. The reviewer may look for data that would be used as fraud identifiers (e.g., numerous checks to one address or a large number of checks in round dollar amounts).

It is always wise to obtain personnel statistics if they are available. Turnover ratios and employee tenure information can help show which processes may have the most problems, either because a large number of new employees work on the process or because problems in the process are resulting in job dissatisfaction. Newer employees can often be a great source of innovative ideas. They often are unafraid to ask the questions everyone else thinks have been answered. However, longtime employees have a broader view and may be able to help identify longtime systemic problems.

Also gather any information about accounts involved in the process. Take a look at current information as well as trends over time. Wildly fluctuating balances or accounts that suddenly grow may be representative of a process problem. Additionally, aging account balances will help show where processes may have gone wrong.

In general, any data should be gathered that would help provide a snapshot of the current processes. Gathering the information will also help the reviewer obtain a fuller understanding of the process.

Recap

Information about a process will unfold a piece at a time. It is important to know what information you are going to need and identify who can provide you with the required information. Data must be gathered to:

- Identify and describe processes
- Identify process owners
- Identify units and unit owners
- Complete process and/or unit profiles

Data-gathering plans should be developed for all phases of the process review.

To obtain the necessary information, meetings must be held with the process owners and unit owners. It usually is best to start with the highest-level owners and work down. Joint meetings, at which a number of owners at various levels are present, can be very beneficial in ironing out differences in everyone's understanding of the process basics.

A large amount of information is required, but once the basic processes and their owners are established, some of the most important issues are:

- Business objectives (What is being accomplished?)
- Business risks (What can stop this from being accomplished?)
- Key controls (How are these risks mitigated?)
- Measure of success (How do they know they are successful?)

The reviewer must get agreement on these basic areas before proceeding.

Because there is so much information to be gathered, the following data-gathering tools should be used to document background information about the processes, units, tasks, and actions:

- Process Description Overview: An overview of all processes identified along with a brief description.
- Process Owner/Unit Owner Chart: A visual representation of all processes along with their owners and unit owners.
- Process Profile Worksheet: A single repository of critical information regarding processes and units.
- Workflow Surveys: An employee's synopsis of the work he or she accomplishes and the tasks he or she has completed.

Key Analysis Points

Conflicting Business Objectives

If you are analyzing multiple processes, you may immediately see that the objectives of one process are in direct conflict with the objectives of another process. Even more critical, you may see that the objectives of one process are in conflict with the overall objectives of the company. Your maps can help show how conflicting objectives are affecting the overall company performance.

Unknown Business Objectives

Another important aspect of business objectives is that they may not have been communicated clearly. Individual process or unit goals are often passed on to employees without letting those employees know how the goals fit to strategic objectives. In those instances, goals are often followed too literally, which can result in processes that focus on the wrong area or less important areas. Determine whether people understand why their goals exist and make sure that their actions match the company's strategic direction.

Absence of Process Measures

The reviewer may find an absence of success measures. Maybe the process has always existed in isolation, without any real measure of success. If there is no success measure, maybe this process is not even necessary. The reviewer will need to spend some additional time understanding what value is being added by the process. The success measure for one process may also be defined by the input and output of the process or by the gap it fills between processes. Process owners may not recognize this dependency relationship. As the pieces of the whole puzzle come together, the reviewer may begin to see clear measures of success that were not obvious to any of the owners.

Existence of Key Controls

Once risks are identified, it is a great time to go through the exercise of identifying key controls that help mitigate or eliminate the risk. This is the time to establish the process owners' ownership of controls. The

(Continued)

reviewer can show them how the control may specifically address a risk. If no controls exist, the reviewer can begin looking for areas where controls are needed and determine how best to add them with the least effect on efficiency.

Clear Start and End Points

Try to identify very distinct start and end points and agree upon these with the process owners and unit owners before proceeding. If you do not, you may end up with overlapping processes that are hard to isolate. Furthermore, if the client has not made that distinction, there may be duplication at the process transfer points.

4

Interviewing and Map Generation

Maps encourage boldness. They're like cryptic love letters. They make anything seem possible.

—Mark Jenkins

Creating the Storyboard (Finally)

Let the fun begin! This is truly the most exciting, rewarding part of any Process Mapping engagement. This is the point at which all the information really begins to come together. While working with employees, you will see their excitement as a picture of the process evolves around them, their ideas are taken seriously, and they learn that someone cares about what they do for a living. In addition, you will find yourself inundated with ideas and solutions. Working on the first project, you will feel swamped and a little intimidated—it is tough trying to sort through all that information. But you also will be amazed by how much you learn. And when all is said and done, you will feel exhilarated but wrung out—it is tough to learn and synthesize the tons of information you are about to receive!

The key to successful Process Mapping is the interview, and the key to a successful interview is creating an environment in which information can be openly shared. This type of environment comes from being prepared, being willing to spend some time talking to people in a nonthreatening environment, and being ready to listen.

Interviews for Process Mapping are not particularly different from any other information-gathering interview. It is all a matter of planning, talking, and, above all, listening. But many Process Mapping projects fail for lack of these very things. It is important to revisit some of the basic rules of interviewing and see how they relate to Process Mapping.

Ground Rules

Buy-In

The mapping project must have buy-in from the very top to be successful. Upper management must understand why the project is being completed and agree that the benefits outweigh the costs of employees spending "unproductive" time on the project. During the preliminary information-gathering phase of the review, the project should be explained to everyone you contact. Process owners and unit owners must understand who supports the project, why it is being done, what it is expected to accomplish, and how the project will be conducted. If any of the interviews must be handled at a site away from where the process owner resides, always have an individual meeting with site management before conducting any of the interviews. Treat that individual as you would any other process owner.

If possible, it is an excellent idea to have a floor meeting with the entire office before the project begins. This provides the opportunity to explain exactly what the project is about, why it is being done, and what it intends to accomplish. We also like to use the time to explain exactly what employees should expect when we interview them. This helps alleviate some of the fears that are inherent when an outsider comes in.

Setting Aside Adequate Time

The detailed map interview can take anywhere from 15 minutes for an individual involved in limited processes to 3 or 4 hours for key individuals involved in multiple processes. Be perfectly honest with people about the amount of time the interview could take. Longer interviews can be broken up, but be sure you set these meetings relatively close together. If there is too large a gap between the meetings, there may be a lot of time wasted while you catch up to where you were.

There is a tricky balance between the time to spend on each interview and the time available for the entire project. If you learn that interviews are taking longer than you first thought, you may find yourself forced to make a choice between more interviews with less information or fewer interviews with more information.

In one review, we had no more than an average of two hours with each person. There was one section in which each employee handled a large number of different types of transactions—each interview easily could have taken five hours. The decision was made to ask each person what he or she thought the highest risk transactions were. Our maps then focused on those transactions. It was interesting to note that most of the employees identified the same area, resulting in us spending our time in the most valuable area. However, the interviews were still not long enough to get to some important aspects. In particular, we were unable to ask the employees what they specifically thought should be changed. This is a crucial question, because employees can usually tell you exactly what is wrong with a process and how it can be improved. A number of significant opportunities were probably lost, but we accomplished what we could with the time available.

What this ultimately means is that time availability will dictate the interview process. Remember that, as a reviewer, you are trying to fit into the employee's schedule—not he or she into yours. It is usually best to try to get one contact person in the department to act as a coordinator. This will usually be a manager or supervisor, but there may an informal leader to whom management will direct you. We will give them the list of people to be interviewed and ask them to bring them in as they are available.

Secure a Private Interview Area

If you want people to be candid, provide them with the privacy to speak without someone looking over their shoulder or listening to every word they say. Some people like to perform interviews at people's desk. They believe this is an area where the interviewee feels comfortable and can get to any information they may need as the interview progresses. However, this is usually counterproductive. First, working on the floor lends itself to far too many interruptions.

We already talked about how scarce a resource time is, and setting yourself up for more interruptions will only make it worse. People also have a tendency to show you every piece of paper they touch as they perform their work. Part of the job of the interviewer is to sift through all the details the interviewee will provide and determine what is really important. Therefore, the interviewer must control the information that is received.

However, the most important reason for setting an interview session away from the floor is the feeling of privacy and intimacy. It is important that the interviewees feel they can tell you almost anything. They will know that the information is being used as part of a project that goes to management, but a private setting for interviews will help them feel that what they are saying is being held in some confidence.

Set a Friendly Tone

Set a friendly tone when conducting the interview. This should go without saying, but we have seen many people go into these interviews as though they had something to prove or had a big secret to discover. The participants should not be adversaries—they are working with you to make the process better.

Start with some small talk—how long they have been with the company; anything personal you may know about them; or even chat about sports, the weather, or something that will put the interviewee at ease and let him or her know you are human. Spending five minutes talking about someone's children or grandchildren may return a wealth of information in the future.

Give them an overview of what the interview will be about. If Process Maps are already on the walls, use them as an example of what the project is about. Let the interviewees know that they are the experts and you are here to learn from them.

Once the interview gets into the actual processes, maintain an objective demeanor. When someone reveals an issue that may be a major problem, sometimes it is very difficult not to react to the information instantly. Just take the information in stride and move on with the discussions. Later you can verify what you have just learned.

We have been involved with individuals who literally told the interviewee, "Well, that is totally wrong," or "You're *not* doing that, are you?" Instantly, the interview becomes useless. Any additional information that might have been obtained during the interview is lost. Ultimately, maintain a professional but friendly atmosphere and you will be amazed at what people will reveal.

Actively Listen

This may sound very basic, but we cannot tell you how many people we have seen conduct interviews as if they had a preset script—never listening to what the interviewee is really telling them. If that approach is used, they might as well have sent out a survey and tallied the results. Many people go into these interviews with a long list of questions to be asked. They do not think their work is done until every question has been answered. We find that the best approach is to have a very limited list or no list at all. The list should include some of the key points we want to include, but never include more than four or five. This is a conversation with people about what they do for a living. Quite simply asking, "What do you do next?" is often the best approach and will keep most people talking for hours.

The people you are interviewing are the experts. If you listen, they will tell you about the issues they are facing. As a result, they will tell you about the control issues, efficiency issues, and management issues that are keeping the process from accomplishing its objective. They probably even know how to fix the problems—all you have to do is sit back and listen. You still need to control the conversation, because it will often go places you definitely do not want to go, but you also have to let people say what is on their minds. Active listening involves spontaneous questioning based on responses you are hearing. You must have a good feel for the "right questions" to ask in order to get complete information.

You must also maintain an objective viewpoint. This means never arguing with the interviewee. You are gathering facts—hold the opinions for later. You, as a reviewer, should have a good idea of how the process works, but it is not up to you to give the answers. Interviewing is not reading a list of questions and recording the answers. It is maintaining an active conversation with people—an exchange of ideas. It is taking a true interest in what they are saying.

Select the Right People to Perform Interviews

A Process Mapping project may involve a team of several people, but each interview should have two people involved—one to act as the primary interviewer and one to act as the primary recorder. Selection of the members for this team is critical to the success of the project. The primary interviewer should be someone who has a good knowledge of the processes under review and an ability to actively listen and set an appropriate tone. A significant amount of detailed information must be obtained in a short period from a wide variety of people. The interviewer should be someone who can think on his or her feet and has a friendly, professional demeanor. The interviewer must also be capable of directing the information-gathering process.

The second person is assigned the job of recording the information obtained during the interview process. This person is responsible for identifying the significant portions of the conversation between the interviewer and interviewee and recording the information in a document for future reference. Accordingly, this person must be able to process information quickly, but also must have sufficient technical skill to input data directly into a document while the interview is progressing. The information recorder can still participate in the interview process (neither one of us can help ourselves—we always have to participate in the interview), but he or she acts mostly as a recorder of information.

The review team is trying to capture the major actions, the major shots in the movie. The interviewee will want to tell you about each action he or she takes and each paper he or she touches. The team must be able to process the detailed information that is received and determine how it fits into those major actions. The recorder should capture the details. The interviewer, as the map producer, must synthesize the information as the interview is going on, classifying the details into major actions. If there are problems with a particular part of a process, the interviewer must be ready to drill down into specific areas of the process and create a more detailed chart on a targeted area. The right combination of skills and people makes a successful interview team.

Sticky-Note Revolution

When we attempted our first real process analysis project, we went to a smog-filled valley in southern California (you literally could not see across the parking lot to the mountains a few miles away). We spent a week talking to people about their processes. We sent out preliminary surveys, recorded the information in detailed notes, and learned about major issues. We had private interview areas, learned (more than we wanted to) about what was and was not working at the site, and got plenty of suggestions on how to improve the processes. We left the office after one week with reams and reams of information and began the daunting task of creating maps based on the interviews. At this point, we realized that the project could last another couple of months before we finished maps of everything. We had only two weeks.

We had a lot of information, but no way to quickly organize it. Plus, as we constructed the maps, we realized that we had all our notes but, since we had no further access to the employees, there was no way to get additional questions answered. We had some successes—when people tell you how to fix things, it is easy to have successes—and we did produce some maps, but we were not happy with the time it was taking after the field interviews were done to produce a final product.

Six months later we were both at a seminar where the presenter was creating Process Maps in real time using yellow sticky-notes. That idea revolutionized our approach to Process Mapping. It was the solution to our problem—instead of creating maps after fieldwork, we could create maps in the field while we were doing the interviews. Using sticky-notes to document actions and poster-sized sticky-notes to record the various tasks, we set out on our first sticky-note adventure.

We arrived at an Arizona claims office with sticky-notes in hand. We even bought some special colored ones so we could color-code areas of the maps. As the interviews began, giant Post-it® notes with yellow badges of courage (yellow sticky-notes) were hanging from every possible wall surface in a small, closet-sized interview room. People were thrilled as they saw the processes unfold before their eyes. The only negative comment we got was that we did not get to everyone and some individuals felt left out because they did not get to be interviewed. This simple process of visually displaying the process as we conducted the interview created a curiosity that helped promote a positive atmosphere. It also allowed us to change maps as information changed and provided for a fast, easy method to input results into a flowcharting software package for more detailed analysis.

We have often been asked if the same effect would be achieved by inputting information directly into a flowcharting package.

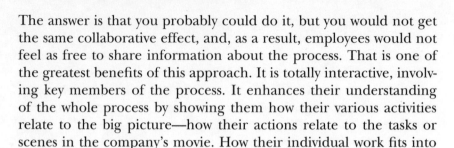

The answer is that you probably could do it, but you would not get the same collaborative effect, and, as a result, employees would not feel as free to share information about the process. That is one of the greatest benefits of this approach. It is totally interactive, involving key members of the process. It enhances their understanding of the whole process by showing them how their various activities relate to the big picture—how their actions relate to the tasks or scenes in the company's movie. How their individual work fits into the larger picture is something they may have never seen before.

Basic Rules

Before sitting down and beginning the Process Mapping interviews, there are some supplies you need to have on hand and a few basics you must know.

Supplies

Have a lot of posterboard-size paper on hand. (At a minimum, you will probably need one poster for every task you will review.) Flip charts are fine, but we have found that among the most useful products are two- by three-foot sticky-notes (yes, they really do make them that big). As you begin each process or task, you will need another sheet. You will find yourself working on a lot of the sheets at the same time. Even when you think one is finished, you will need to keep it handy in case someone else you interview wants to add something about the process. If you use a flip chart, you will constantly find yourself going back and forth, losing track of where you want to be. To make every chart easily accessible, we stick them right to the walls of the room in which we interview people. If you tape up your charts, you never know what effect the tape is going to have on the walls. You will also find yourself retaping the sheets as you constantly move them around the room. The poster-size sticky-notes solve these problems.

Have a lot of smaller sticky-notes (three by three inches). Every action will need a sticky-note. Every task will have a number of actions. And you will find a need to rewrite a number of these as you misunderstand and reunderstand the process. So let us repeat that point—have *a lot* of these sticky-notes on hand. Feel free to explore the various color selections available. These can be used to identify certain phases of the process or different individuals.

One individual we worked with started by outlining each sticky-note to make it look more like a flowchart symbol and then tried to find a way to have them preprinted with flowcharting symbols.

Use bold, felt-tipped pens. The darker they are, the easier they are to read. And you cannot write upside down with a ballpoint pen (there will be times you need to write upside down while constructing a map). It is usually good to have a combination of ink colors available, also. Much like the different colors of sticky-notes, this allows you another opportunity to color-code different aspects of the processes (e.g., blue for controls, red for risks, and black for basic processes). Do not use the very smelly kind of markers. This is an aspect you really want to check out before you begin the interviews. You do not want to be in that first interview, open the pen, and find yourself suddenly understanding all those old 1960s songs!

The Process

As mentioned before, use a separate sheet for each major task. It is not necessary to have every sheet prepared before the first interview. In fact, it is probably a better idea not to do so. You want people to understand that you have no preconceived ideas, that you only know what people tell you, and that they are the experts. Prepare each sheet as you go along. When interviewing people, prepare another sheet if a new task emerges. Sometimes you may find that you prepare a sheet and the task only has two steps. That is not a problem. Paper is inexpensive, and it is better to err on the side of being prepared for that simple task that turns into your worst nightmare.

For each new sheet, note the task name as a title across the top of the page, and then list the individuals involved in the process horizontally below the title. These names become the headings of columns that will show the action completed by that individual. It is usually best to list these in chronological order of involvement from left to right. However, you may not learn who the first person is right away, so there are three options. The first is to recreate maps later in the interviews. With the use of sticky-notes, this is a fairly simple process, involving only moving the notes to a sheet updated with the individuals in the correct order. The second approach is to list individuals as you hear about them. This may result in a more complicated initial map, but it often provides the same information and helps the interviewer quickly see where the information was obtained. The final approach works if you have a basic understanding of the process before you start out. The principal person in the task is listed in the center. Others involved in the task are listed to either side, but the action always comes back to the center character.

Maps are constructed so that time runs down the page from top to bottom. While it is a simple concept to understand, it is often hard for people to put into practice. But it is a key concept in creating the maps. The first action in the task should be the first sticky-note on the chart. If employees are being listed chronologically, the task starts in the upper left-hand corner with employee A. If employee A handles the next action, it is listed below the first action. As employee A handles each action, they are listed going down the chart. If employee B handles an action, it is listed horizontally (under employee B's title) next to the prior action. If B handles the next action, it is listed below the prior task. If an employee beside B handles the next action, it is listed horizontally from B unless there is already a task in that location. Then the action should be listed below the last task handled by that other employee. All the actions in the task are to be documented this way—process boxes under the appropriate employee, moving down the page as the events occur over time. If you get to the end of the poster sheet, either stick another one below it or use a connector to a new sheet. You may also find that subsequent discussions reveal an earlier starting point to the task than originally thought. If it is one action, just squeeze it in. If it is more than one action, add a sheet or make a connector.

Use the small yellow sticky-notes to denote actions taken by employees. Each sticky-note should include a symbol denoting the type of action and a description of that action. This should be stated in its simplest terms. Try to stick with a verb–noun format to help limit your description of the action. For example, if an employee says, "I look at the form and check to see if the person who signed the form is on my authorization list," the yellow sticky would say "Verify authorizations." In this example, the interviewer might have a tendency to want to add information about the authorization list. However, that should be done some way other than including it in the action description. For example, the interviewer can make a separate note on the Process Map, or the recorder can put it in the notes. Ultimately, the more you can stick with the verb–noun format, the more succinct your Process Maps will be. If you find yourself straying from this format, you probably are trying to put too much information in that particular action.

The symbols you use on the sticky-notes should be fairly straightforward. Process Mapping is not a document flowchart, so we use only a few basic symbols to keep the maps simple and readable. Sticky-notes already make a good representation of a box, so we use them for most actions. The diamond shape is used for decisions, and this is easily accomplished by turning a sticky-note on its corner. If we see an action that is causing a delay in the process, we use a shape that resembles a big D.

When a task goes directly from one action to another, there usually is little problem in keeping it straight. However, decisions and the resulting loops make it harder to construct a Process Map that is truly chronological. If the decision leads to two completely different sets of tasks, connectors to the new sheets are the best solution (see Example 1 in Exhibit 4.1). In many situations, one choice in a decision will lead to a series of actions that eventually lead to the action that followed the other choice (e.g., does the work sheet include the code? Yes—send to employee B. No—enter code and send to employee B). To keep the tasks in chronological order, the extra tasks should follow the decision and the second choice item should follow next (see Example 2 in Exhibit 4.1). If a hold-file is used more than once for the same documents, there may be a resulting series of decision trees. In that situation, either the number of times checked or the time in the hold-file should be used as a decision. Each referral back to the hold-file should (if possible) return to that part of the map, and a subsequent action should exist after the first decision (see Example 3 in Exhibit 4.1).

Remember that time flows down the page. Therefore, there should be connecting lines and arrows all flowing down the page, with only an occasional instance in which an arrow goes upward. In general, Process Map actions should not refer back to actions above them. This is very common in flowcharts—document flowcharts in particular—but a Process Map serves a different purpose. It is a visual representation and, as such, it must be as uncomplicated as possible. Maintaining the linear flow of actions helps keep it simple. Connectors can be used if you need to continue to another page.

As the map is developed, additional measures should be included to keep track of various aspects of the process. The first

Exhibit 4.1 Examples of Decision Trees

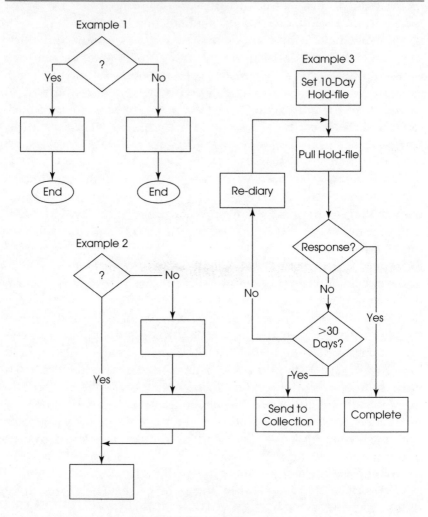

is the cycle time. For each action within the map, try to get an esti-
mate from the employee of how long it takes to accomplish the
action. If you get this information for every action, you will eventually have a feel for how long the entire process takes. It will also
show the actions that take up the most time. These are the ones
that are ripe for change.

The next measure to record is holding time. Any time an item
is batch processed or sits in a bin, there is a resulting delay in the
handling of the item. Intuitively, this means that someone took a

look at the process and determined that, overall, time was saved in processing all items at one time at the expense of delaying the single items a short time. This assumption is seldom correct. Even if someone made this conscious decision, it was probably made a long time ago, and things have changed since. Every time an item is held for any reason, the D-shaped symbol (*D*) should be used. Any time the *D* is used, ask the employees to approximate how long the item will sit. When this amount is added to the cycle times already recorded, there will be a more true approximation of how long a process takes.

For any decision symbol, try to get an idea of the percentage of items going down each path. For example, the decision may be "Is there an attorney involved?" (Using the verb–noun format, the action should read "Attorney Involved?") The interviewer should try to get an approximation from the employee of how many items need attorney involvement and how many do not. From this it can be determined how often processes related to attorney involvement are used and how often non–attorney involvement processes come into play. This percentage should be entered directly on the map.

These percentages are especially important when dealing with rejected or error items. Any time an error that requires rework is identified, there is a resulting loss of efficiency. In some instances, you will find whole departments whose sole purpose is to correct the errors of another department. Any rework means there is a process that should be reviewed to determine whether the errors could be reduced or eliminated. Enter the error percentage directly on the map also. Those areas with the highest error rates are the ones where the reviewer may want to spend additional time. Another flag that can be used by the reviewer to help identify these areas on Process Maps is an R-shaped symbol (for rework).

Conducting the Interviews

The beauty of this methodology lies in the fact that you can interview people in any order, even if they are involved in multiple processes, and still document their piece of the puzzle accurately.

It may be helpful to start with a supervisor or manager who oversees several major aspects of the process. There is a chance you already spoke to this individual as a process owner, unit owner, or subordinate owner. In fact, you may have already begun to obtain some information about tasks and actions during those meetings. But now it is time to start the documentation in earnest.

Use the information you gain from these individuals to start creating shells of maps for the major tasks. They should be able to provide not only the tasks, but also the names of the individuals involved in the tasks and where those tasks start and end. Interviews with these individuals may take a while, so we try to conduct them first. This tactic helps prepare them for how long other interviews may take. Also, by getting the managers' and supervisors' perceptions first, we can determine how well their understanding matches reality.

From this point on, you will probably interview employees haphazardly throughout the processes. That may mean key person #3 is interviewed before #1 or #2. And key person #3 may not have any idea what #1 and #2 do. Just record the actions for each person as you interview them; connections can be made after you get the entire picture. Additionally, each individual will probably be involved in multiple processes. Just keep adding them to the appropriate maps as your discussion proceeds.

If you circulated preliminary surveys, the information contained in the survey responses will give you an idea of the processes in which people participate and, for each process, the actions with which they are involved. If you have not done a preliminary survey, you will need to spend a little time in the interview going over the interviewee's basic job duties.

When you begin discussing a particular process, try to get the interviewee to go through the basic sequence of events—from start to finish—of his or her particular aspect of the process. The interviewer should control the dialogue without stifling the flow of information. If an employee can only describe a task by including actions in other tasks, you will have to work with that. You will probably find yourself having to create new maps as the discussion progresses and working back and forth between a couple of maps during the interview. If either the interviewer or the recorder needs clarification about the discussion, clear it up immediately.

You need to know from whom the interviewee receives work, what happens to that product when received, and where it goes when the transformation is done. If things are sitting for some time before processing, use the D shape to indicate a delay. Be sure to note the cycle times, error rates when applicable, and the percentages with decisions. One question to always fall back on is "What is the next action you take?"

At the end of each interview, walk the person through the maps you have created. Repeat each action, where it comes from, and where it goes. Get agreement that the map represents the process as it is understood by the interviewee.

There should then be three final questions you ask. First, "What would you change about this process/your job if you could?" There are times you will get nonsense answers such as "Get a raise" or "Work fewer hours," but more often than not you get a well-reasoned response. Again, these are the people who know their jobs, and they know what needs to be done to make them better. Often, this interview is the first time anyone has really asked them for their opinion. Some of the best solutions we have provided to our customers came directly from the suggestions of their employees.

The second question is "What do you wish I had asked you?" This is a little like the first question, but with a different slant. You are less likely to get an answer to this question, but when you do it may be more valuable. By asking this question, we have learned about morale problems in departments, supervision issues, and even ethical issues leading to fraud investigations. People in these situations are looking for someone with whom they can talk. If you have built the right kind of rapport during the interview, they will want to talk to you.

The final question is "Is there anything you would like to add?" Again, this is really a different way of asking the preceding two questions, but it is one more opportunity to solicit additional information. The best use of this question we ever saw was actually as part of a statement between a claimant and a claims adjuster. The typed statement had taken up 20 to 30 pages before the adjuster thought he was done. He asked if there was anything the claimant wanted to add. The claimant said he just wanted to mention that he had not been driving the car. The adjuster asked, "You weren't driving?" The claimant replied, "No, I was too drunk to drive. My friend was driving." Although this question led to another 30 pages of statement, asking it helped ensure that the interviewer had all the necessary information.

Creating a Final Map

You should try to finalize your Process Maps only after all interviews are completed. Each conversation has the chance of adding another action. Sticky-notes are easy to change; finished maps are a little tougher to amend. This is the point where you can straighten out any portions of the map that may not be constructed correctly. When we create maps, we have a tendency to stick things wherever they fit (sometimes sticky-notes go off the charts and onto the walls). But you will find that in your haste to create maps on the fly, the rules discussed previously are often bent. Putting the final map together is like the final proofreading of a report—it is the opportunity to make everything right. It is also a chance to see what may have been missed or what questions did not get asked. Take this opportunity to ask them.

Once the maps are finalized, have some of the key employees review them. It is one last chance to make sure everyone agrees that the content is correct. It also is one more opportunity to show these employees that they are an important part of the process. If anything is wrong, correct it immediately and let them see the revised product.

Example

To get an idea how a Process Map is developed, we take a closer look at the claims settlement process described in Chapter 2. Imagine you are at the company's claims office interviewing people and creating maps. Could Process Mapping have helped identify why the service they were delivering was less than satisfactory for the customer? Could it help the company pinpoint the "moments of truth" gone wrong? Let us work it through and see.

We want to look in depth at the claim reporting process and the claim assignment process. Workflow surveys were received from the following: an agent, the receptionist at the claims office, the claims loss assignment clerk, the auto claims adjuster, the medical claims adjuster, and the claims supervisor. Interviews were held with all six individuals.

Surveys and Discussions

The survey and discussions with the agent show that the agent is primarily involved in one task—receiving the claim. When the phone call comes in, the agent completes a "report of claim." This form contains all information necessary to report the claim in the company's system. After getting the information, the agent inputs this information into the company claim system. This information is input on the day the claim is reported or, if it is late in the day, on the following business day. When the office is closed (from noon to 1:00 P.M. on weekdays, all day Saturday and Sunday), voice messaging is used. The message states that the caller should leave a number and that the agent will get back to the caller as soon as possible. The message has no additional information about what to do if the client has had an accident. The agent also indicated that one of her staff might handle the entire process.

Reading the receptionist's workflow survey response and talking with her indicated that her main contact with individuals who have a claim is by phone. When she gets a call from a claimant, she looks on the computer to see whether that claimant has a claim number. If he does not have a claim number, she tells him to call his agent to report the claim. She knows that the claims supervisor assigns claims to adjusters every afternoon at 3:00 P.M. If someone calls and says he reported the claim in the morning, she tells him that he will be assigned to an adjuster in the afternoon and the adjuster will call him back the next day. Occasionally, the computer system will be down and assignments cannot be made. The office staff lets the receptionist know when this has occurred. If the system is down, she advises clients about the cause for the delay and explains that they may not receive a call from the adjuster for two or three days.

Discussions with the supervisor and his workflow survey response show that the supervisor is responsible for reviewing the loss reports input by the agents and assigning them to a claims adjuster. For claims involving only auto damage, the assignment is made to an auto claims adjuster. If injuries are indicated on the loss report, an assignment is also made to an injury claims adjuster. This process is done from 1:30 P.M. to 3:00 P.M. daily.

The loss assignment clerk's discussion and survey match much of what was indicated by other employees. After assignments are made (normally from 3:00 P.M. to 4:00 P.M. daily), the loss assignment clerk prepares files for the claims adjusters. The files are placed in the adjusters' in-bins. Adjusters usually pick up their files after 4:00 P.M. every day. If there is a particularly heavy volume of claims into the claims office on a specific day, the clerk may not complete all the assignment files until the next morning.

The auto claims adjuster states he goes into the office every day at 4:00 P.M. to pick up his assignments. He contacts all customers the next morning and goes out in the field on inspections after making all customer contacts. If he learns about injuries in his initial contact with the customer, he writes up an injury referral and drops it off at the office when he picks up his assignments.

The injury claims adjuster's story is much like that of the auto claims adjuster. The adjuster picks up assignments daily at 4:00 P.M. He contacts customers the following day. Many times, these assignments are generated by the auto claims adjuster's initial contact with the claimant.

Overview and Drill-Down Maps

An overview map is a high-level map that summarizes the major tasks in the process and those individuals or departments involved in those processes. Drill-down maps are completed to dig into each task as needed. When we first started Process Mapping, we assumed that it would be easy to create the overview maps at the beginning of the project and then go on to the drill-down maps. In practice, we learned that it is usually easier to create an overview map after you have created detailed Process Maps. In addition, creating detailed maps helps you learn about processes that were not visible to you before you began your review. However, to help get a handle on this process, we start with a high-level look at the process.

Overview maps should be created for every project. They are like a table of contents for the Process Maps. A systematic numbering process is used to tie the overview maps into the detail maps. If we use the previous example, an overview map might only have three entities—the customer, the agent, and the claims office. Then there would be five major tasks. Each would receive a unique number: Report Claim 1, Input Loss 2, Assign Claim 3, Investigate Claim 4, and Settle Claim 5. This representation is shown in Exhibit 4.2.

The map for a process then includes the number, for example "1.0 Claim Reporting." Each box on the map is labeled with sequential numbers—1.1, 1.2, 1.3, and so on—throughout the chart. This is an example of drilling down from the overview map.

As is discussed in one situation that follows, you may also find it necessary to drill down into just one area of concern in a particular process. If you maintain the numbering sequence on the maps, creating a new detailed map is the same process outlined previously. Use the number of the box in which the detail is being exploded for the title of the new detailed chart. For example, if you need more detail on how auto claims are assigned by the supervisor, you

Exhibit 4.2 Claim Process Overview

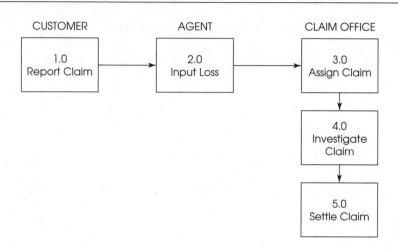

may explode out box 3.3 on the claims assignment Process Map (see Exhibit 4.3).

This technique is very useful. It helps you avoid too much detail on one map, but it allows you the freedom to explore any area in as much depth as is necessary. This technique can also be useful for assembling training materials, as you can really drill down into a step-by-step process, even to a narrative if necessary.

Claim Reporting Process

Turning to the processes, the key individuals in the claim reporting process are the customer, the agent or agent's staff, and the claims office receptionist. Three columns are used to represent the process, one for each key individual. The customer actions start with a box to represent reporting the accident. After this there is a decision—does the claimant call the claims office or the agent? If the answer is the claims office, the next actions lead to the receptionist. If the response is the agent, the actions relate to calling the agent.

Because all subsequent actions relating to this process will eventually lead to calling the agent, the receptionist's actions are shown next. The first action is to get the claim number from the claimant. Then there is a decision for the next action—is there a claim number in the system (Number Exists?). The next decisions do not relate to the claims settlement process, so a terminal symbol is used.

Exhibit 4.3   Drill-Down Example

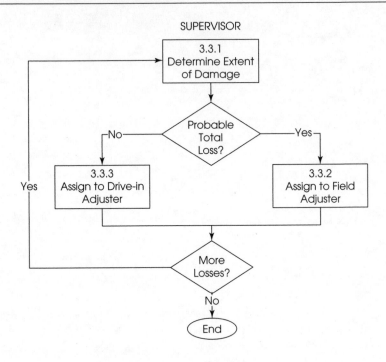

Up to this point, elapsed time has not been an issue. However, any action that leads to the report being made to the agent can result in a delay if the customer cannot reach the agent. Since time is beginning to elapse, it becomes important to start noting minimum and maximum elapsed times. As stated before, use the *D* shape if you immediately recognize that a delay may occur in a particular area. The action of inputting the report of the claim has the potential to result in a delay, because this is also a place where action may not occur immediately. Work could stack up here and delay the entire process. You should note the minimum and maximum elapsed times in the box or on the chart. In this case, it may be anywhere from five minutes to one day.

See Exhibit 4.4 for the final map of the claim reporting process. There are a number of important aspects to consider in this map. First, we started with the first event—reporting the claim.

Exhibit 4.4   Claim Office XYZ

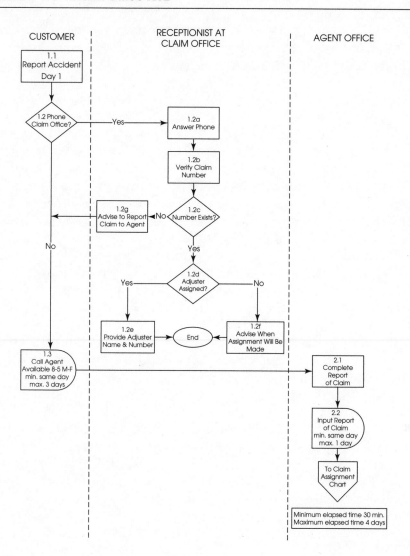

Because the customer generates the process, he is listed first. The action is put in the upper left-hand corner. This first action leads to the first decision. The results of this decision lead to one response resulting in the claimant continuing to work with the agent, or another response resulting in the claimant working with the claims receptionist.

Second, notice how time is moving down the page. To help facilitate this time flow, the two decisions the receptionist makes are placed in the order in which she would normally ask them.

Finally, notice that there is a handoff from the receptionist back to the customer if a claim number has not yet been assigned. If we want to make our moment of truth more positive, the company may want to consider having some means for the customer to report the claim to the first party contacted—either the agent or the claims office. When you visually review a Process Map, you should look for these handoffs back and forth between key individuals. These hand-offs can often point to inefficiencies in the process.

At the bottom of the chart, we summarize the minimum and maximum elapsed times for this particular process. As processes are added, you can add together the minimum and maximum elapsed times to determine what range of time can be expected for the entire process.

Also note the use of the numbering hierarchy. This is particularly important because, although we have one map, it includes information about two processes—the *Claim Reporting* and *Loss Input* processes. Realizing that you have two processes in one map is the type of discovery you may make after having already gone deep into the mapping process. Accordingly, just adapt the map and move on. For numbering purposes, 1.0 has been assigned to the first overall process—*Claim Reporting*—and 2.0 to the second process. Answering the phone (by the receptionist) has been identified as a task and been given the number 1.2. The drill-down is accomplished on the same map, so actions related to answering the phone have numbers 1.2a to 1.2g. For this last drill-down, we could have also used 1.2.1 to 1.2.7, much like in the previous discussion about drilling down.

Claim Assignment Process

The *Claim Assignment* process begins when the loss has been input and ends when the adjuster picks up the assignment. There are three key individuals in the process—the supervisor, the loss assignment clerk, and the adjuster. The first step in the process is the supervisor's review of the loss. This is entered in the upper left-hand corner of the report and is followed by a decision regarding the type of claim.

The next actions are placed under the Loss Assignment Clerk column. A box is completed for obtaining the loss reports. A diamond is used next to reflect the different actions for losses with and without an injury. It is important to record minimum and maximum elapsed times for both the supervisor's and the loss assignment clerk's processes, because potential delays could occur here. The adjuster has only one action at this point, but it is important to note the time the assignments are picked up because this will also help identify minimum and maximum elapsed times. All elapsed times should be added together to determine the maximum elapsed time.

See Exhibit 4.5 for a completed map. You will notice that the *D* shape has been used twice, and that these notations actually come one after the other. The first relates to the loss assignment clerk batching files before taking them to the adjusters. Since assignments are made at the end of the day, this delay may mean that the adjusters hold claims an additional 24 hours before making contact. The second delay relates to assignments sitting in the adjusters' in-boxes before being handled. Because adjusters are coming in or out of the office, this delay can be anywhere from zero to one full day.

Notice that we have made a decision to keep this map at a high level. There could be numerous steps involved in review loss report or assign claim. For example, review loss report might include the supervisor's looking to see whether injuries are reported or looking at the loss report to see the potential extent of damage before making a determination of potential injury. Assigning the claim could involve reviewing available personnel or accessing the computer to complete the assignment. If needed, the detailed information can be charted in drill-down maps. But you should only map the level of detail you need, even if the people you are interviewing give you drilled-down details. If, for example, significant delays were occurring in this portion of the process, you might want to do a drill-down map on the supervisor's *Claim Assignment* process to determine exactly where the delays are occurring.

As the reviewer prepares the chart, it becomes obvious that if the assignments are not completed by 4:00 P.M., the customer may experience a delay of another 24 hours in the process. Issues that are readily apparent, either control issues or efficiency issues, should be noted directly on the chart. You may use a special color, an open-ended box, or just a text box.

Exhibit 4.5   3.0 Claim Assignment Process

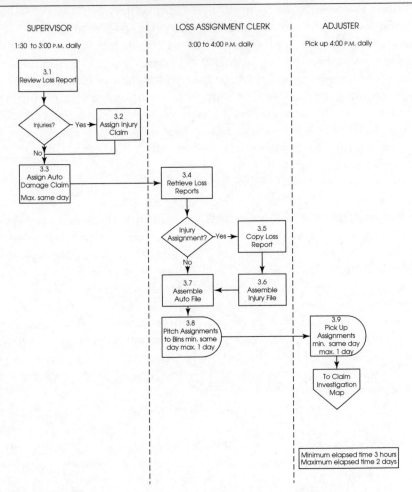

Map Implications

Looking at the maximum elapsed time on the two charts, a total of six days could go by before the adjuster receives the assignment. (This is all assuming that the agent actually responds to claimants' voice mails.) The adjuster always phones the customer the day after the assignment is received, so it could take up to a week for the client to receive a call from the adjuster. The best-case scenario would be receipt of the loss by the adjuster on the same day it was reported, and then the client would be contacted the next day (24 hours). However, if an injury claim was not originally identified, it could take up to 10 days from the date the customer reported the accident for the customer to be contacted by the injury adjuster. The original assignment could take a maximum of six days to be completed; there is an additional day for the auto adjuster to contact the customer and forward information on the injury assignment; another two days (maximum) could be used before the injury adjuster receives the assignment; and then contact with the customer would occur one day (24 hours) later.

By viewing the process through the eyes of the customer, you can see where service improvements can be made. In this example, what if the customer could call into one central number to report the claim and the claim was electronically assigned and received immediately by the claims adjuster? The company could go from a maximum of six days to receive an assignment to receiving the assignment the same day the claim is reported. Looking back at the questions we asked at the beginning of this example, it is easy to say that we would quickly identify why services are creating customer dissatisfaction and help the company pinpoint the "moments of truth" gone wrong.

Recap

The interviewing and actual mapping of processes can be the most fun and rewarding part of the Process Mapping project. It is the opportunity for you to see the fruits of your work and the opportunity for the interviewees to learn the value of theirs. But it can only succeed with the right preparation and the right approach.

The basic ground rules should be followed to ensure this success:

- *Get the buy-in of all senior clients.* Without their approval and support, very few people will be interested in helping to make the project succeed.
- *Set aside enough time.* To get all the information you need, you will need all the time you can get.
- *Set aside a private area for the interview.* Privacy will ensure fewer interruptions and help build a feeling of trust with the interviewee.
- *Set a friendly tone.* This establishes the rapport needed for a full exchange of information.

- *Actively listen.* The interviewee needs to believe that you are genuinely interested in what is being said. Sit back and let him give you his ideas.
- *Select the right review team.* Special skills are needed to conduct an effective interview. Make sure that the people on the team have those skills.

Once everything is in place, you can begin building maps. These should be built in real time using the sticky-note technique. This allows for a very interactive session that results in more information and further ensures the accuracy of the final product. The top of the page should show the individuals involved. Time should progress as you move down the map.

Keep the maps and the symbols simple. You are not trying to impress anyone with how much information you can get on a page. Instead, you are trying to make an easily understood visual of the process. Use drill-down maps when you need to explore more detail, and create overview maps to summarize the processes under review.

Key Analysis Points

Follow the Ground Rules

If you obey the basic ground rules, suggestions will come pouring in. In particular, providing people with a situation in which they feel comfortable talking will result in more openness. While this is not really an analysis tool, you will receive enough information to make it look like you spent forever in analysis.

Maps Flow in Chronological Order

By creating maps that flow chronologically, disruptive actions will show more easily. Look for obvious "blips" in the process. These are the tasks or actions into which you should drill down. This may also be an indicator of actions that can be eliminated.

Pay Attention to the Symbols

Look for the two symbol shapes that show there is a problem—D (delay) and R (rework). These are indicators of significant problems.

Batch processing slows down every process. When real-time processing can be accomplished, the process will run more smoothly. Rework means something has gone wrong. Look for what is causing the rework and see if the process can be improved to eliminate it.

Ask the Right Questions

You are talking to the people who know how things are done and know how to correct the problems. Ask them how to make things better. Give them every opportunity to tell you the solutions. Take these ideas and compare them to the entire process to determine if they are feasible. Ultimately, the answers will come from every discussion.

CHAPTER 5

Map Generation: An Example

Un bon croquis vaut mieux qu'un long discourse. (A good sketch is better than a long speech.)

—Napoleon Bonaparte

Try It—You'll Like It

It is time to take a very close look at our check request process. By taking a step-by-step approach to determining the units, tasks, and actions, you should get a good idea how a map is developed. Before we jump into this, however, take a look at the example and obtain a full understanding of what is going on. Next, try your own hand at building some of the maps. In the previous chapter, we walked you through part of an example. Now it is your turn.

Before you go on, let us repeat—try your own hand at building some maps. It is only through practice that you will get better, and only through practice that you will gain an understanding of the points we have been discussing. Take a look at the expense process and start thinking through the various levels. Then build your own maps. We will go on now, assuming you took our advice.

Unit Level

The first step is to drill down to the first level and determine the units. In Chapter 1, we discussed the appropriate units for this process. The easiest way to break this process down is by using the geographic locations of the field office and the home office. Each has a specifically identifiable purpose and the process flows well between them. The first unit (1.0) is Prepare Request, the second unit (2.0) is Prepare Check, and the third unit (3.0) is Deliver Check. (See Exhibit 5.1.)

A simple unit-level map can be drawn with units 1.0 and 3.0 under the Field Office and unit 2.0 under the Home Office. While this is very rudimentary, it serves as the basis for the work to follow. Notice that we are already using the basic traits of a Process Map: simple process diagrams, each function a column header, and time runs down the map. In addition, the beginning is shown with the input item (Receive Bill), and termination of the process is also

Exhibit 5.1   Payment by Check Request—Unit Level

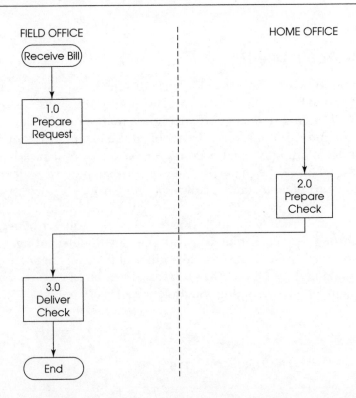

identified. Finally, note that we have begun our numbering system and have documented it on this high-level map.

Task Level

Prepare Request Unit

Exhibit 5.2 shows the drill-down from the unit level for unit 1.0, Prepare Request, to the various tasks involved in this process. As mentioned, the units were defined based on their geographic areas, which also correspond to different high-level departments. These were also chosen to show significant changes between sets of activities.

Exhibit 5.2   Prepare Request (1.0)—Task Level

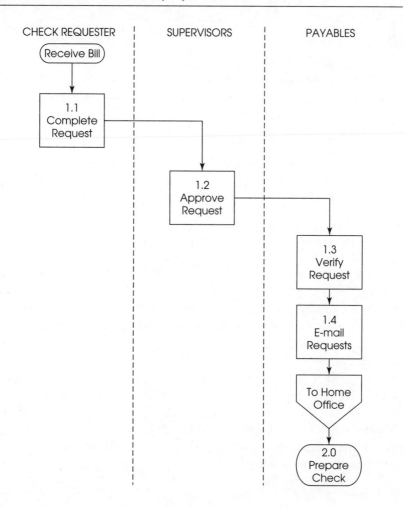

This approach should be used for the task level, also. For the Prepare Request unit, all actions occur within the field office. However, it is still easiest to break the tasks down based on departments. There are three involved in this unit—the requester, the supervisors, and field office disbursements. Therefore, drilling down into the unit reveals four tasks.

The first department is the one that actually receives and pays the bill—the requester. (Note that we are already moving away from department names in the headers and using titles that refer to a single person.) The next department is the employee's supervisor or, depending on the size of the request, supervisors. The final stop is at the field office payables department.

The first task, *complete request,* is done by the requester. The second task, *approve request,* is completed by one or more supervisors. The next two tasks, *verify request* and *e-mail requests,* are performed by field office payables. *E-mail requests* is a relatively simple task, and when we go to the action level you will see that there are few associated actions. However, because this shows the transfer of information from one unit to the next, it is an important step and should be emphasized at this point. Also note that the map ends by showing the connection to the next unit—Prepare Check (2.0).

Prepare Check Unit

In Exhibit 5.1, the next unit is Prepare Check (2.0). Exhibit 5.3 shows the task-level activity in this unit. Exhibit 5.1 shows that there is only one department involved in this unit—home office disbursements. However, there are two primary functions that occur: (1) check issuance and (2) check retrieval. Because these represent distinct sets of individuals in the department, and to help show the control structure established by the department, the two functions are listed as separate on the task-level map in Exhibit 5.3.

In Exhibit 5.3, the map begins by showing the unit providing the input (Prepare Request—1.0) as well as an indication of the source of the input (From Field Office). For the check issuer, the first task involves a number of operations, including initiating the printer, getting the requests, and reviewing the requests. We do not want to drill down to that level yet, so a more general task must be developed.

Exhibit 5.3 Prepare Check (2.0)—Task Level

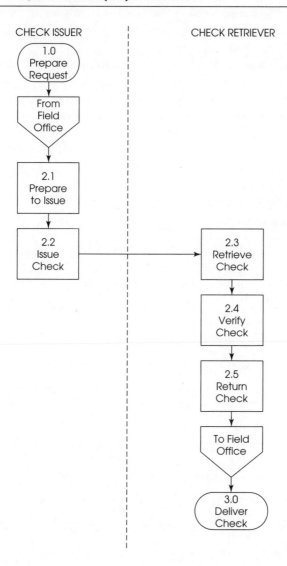

In this case, *prepare to issue.* This encompasses the many actions the issuer must complete before the check can actually be issued. The next task is to actually *issue check.*

The next tasks relate to the check retriever. The first task is the most obvious—*retrieve check.* Next is the review process—*verify check.* Finally, just as we did with the prior unit, we want to emphasize the transfer of information. Therefore, the relatively simple task *return check* is included. Finally, the task-level map shows the transfer back to the field office and the connection to the next unit, Deliver Check (3.0).

You may have noticed that the process description includes a lot of detail about what is done when things are not exactly correct. Some of these review and hold-file systems may even be tasks. However, even at the task level we are trying to be fairly simple. The intent is for these maps to provide an overview, and complicating them now will only make the final mapping more complicated.

Deliver Check Unit

In Exhibit 5.1, the Deliver Check unit (3.0) revolves around one department (field office payables) and one primary function—getting the checks to the appropriate individual. However, in Exhibit 5.4, rather than just show the one department in the map, the customers of the process—payees and requesters—are also shown. In that manner, the actions directly related to these individuals can be emphasized if necessary.

In Exhibit 5.4, the Deliver Check task map again starts with the source of input by listing the previous unit (Prepare Check—2.0) and the source of the input. Notice that in constructing this map we have put the initial department in the center rather than on the left-hand side. This is done to mirror the structure of the other maps. Previous maps started with the requester on the left-hand side, so this is continued whenever possible.

The first task in Exhibit 5.4 is *review check* and is listed under the Payables heading. The next operation is a decision. If the check goes to the payee, there is one distinct set of actions. If the check is returned to the requester, there is another set of actions. Therefore, they are set up as individual tasks. Notice that no number is assigned to this item. It is not really a task, but a split-off point that sends the process in one of two directions, depending on the answer to the question. As such, no real actions are assigned to it. In general, the actions that lead to a decision are reflected in previous tasks or actions. Therefore, if there are no actions associated with the actual decision, it does not need a reference number.

Exhibit 5.4   Deliver Check (3.0)—Task Level

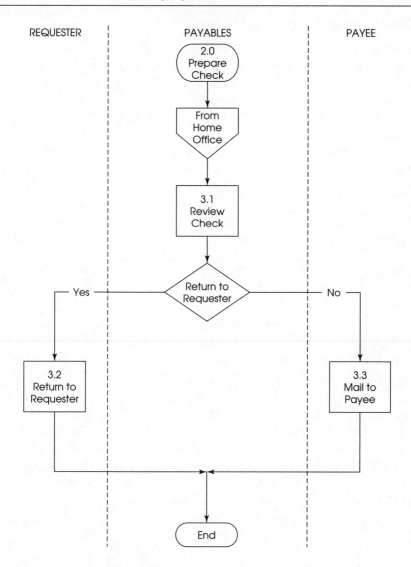

However, some decisions will include tasks. In those instances, a number should be assigned.

Once the decision has been made, one of two tasks is performed. These are listed under the appropriate headings—*mail to payee* under the Payee heading and *return to requester* under the Requester heading. At this point, the entire process is complete, and the termination is illustrated on the map.

Action Level

Prepare Request: Complete Request Task

After all this preliminary discussion, it is time to build the actual detailed map of the specific actions. The map in Exhibit 5.5 shows the *complete request* task. This is a drill-down map starting from Exhibit 5.1, the Prepare Request (1.0) unit, to Exhibit 5.2 and the *complete request* task (1.1). Let us start at the very beginning. Each mapping level (unit, task, and action) begins with the identified input and trigger. Therefore, this map in Exhibit 5.5 also starts with the requester receiving a bill. Once it is received, the first action is preparation of the check request (1.1a).

You will note that, at the action level, we have begun providing additional details as notes. There are no hard and fast rules regarding such notes—you should enter as much information as needed to help the user understand the map. In this example, even before getting to the first action, there is a note regarding cycle times. In this case, there are many types of bills and any number of requesters. Therefore, it is almost impossible to determine the elapsed time between receiving bills and preparing requests. This should be noted for analysis. Also, because there is quite a bit of information required in completing the request, this has been included as a note to the side of the action.

If the check is to be mailed to the payee, the requester must prepare an envelope and include it with the request. If the check is to be returned to the requester, a Return to Requester form must be completed. This is illustrated with a decision point and the option of the additional step necessary when the check is to be returned to the requester. Both options then converge on the next action—the requester submitting the request. The requester then faxes the support to the Documentation Center. The final step is notifying the supervisor that the request is ready.

At the end of the map is a connector to the next actions. The letter A is used as a reference to the next page. Depending on the circumstances, you may want to reference the next task, *approve request*, much as we did between tasks.

Prepare Request: Approve Request Task

Exhibit 5.6 is another drill-down map of the Prepare Request task-level map shown in Exhibit 5.2. This set of actions begins where

Exhibit 5.5   Complete Request (1.1)—Action Level

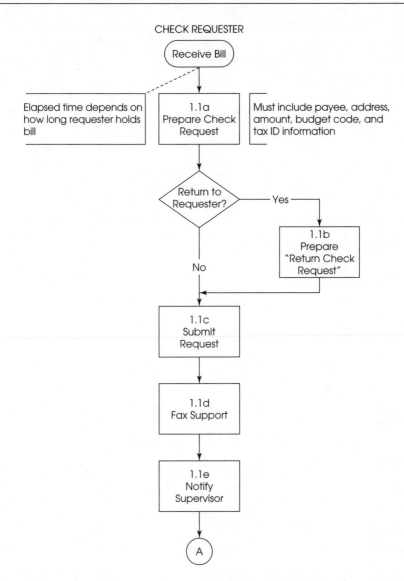

the last set left off in Exhibit 5.5. This is indicated by the connector marked A. Since the last map ended with the requester notifying the supervisor that the request is complete, we begin Exhibit 5.6 with the supervisor. In an effort to keep the order of personnel consistent between maps, the supervisor is listed in the middle. It may be easiest to think of the whole set of maps being one big map. In that case, the first name to the left would be the requester. You should try to maintain such order throughout all maps.

The first action in Exhibit 5.6 is the supervisor's review of the documents. This situation is similar to that faced when trying to determine how long bills remain on requesters' desks. Because of the number of supervisors, we cannot determine how long items

Exhibit 5.6   Approve Request (1.2)—Action Level

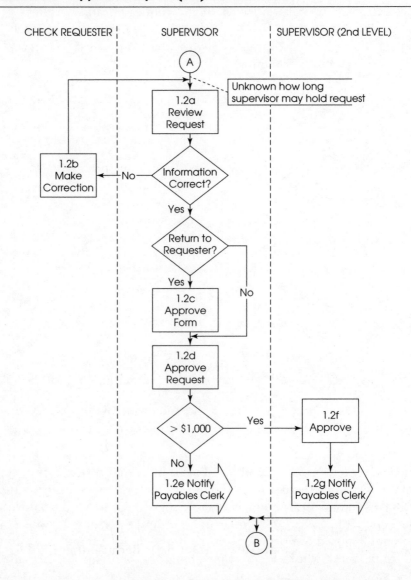

are held before review and approval. The note regarding this situation is referenced to a point in the process just after corrected requests are returned. This may indicate that delays exist every time a request is returned for correction. There are no further references to cycle times in this particular map, because the time to handle an individual item is very short.

If something is wrong with the request, it is returned to the requester for correction. This is illustrated with a decision, an action that is the responsibility of the requester, and a return to the beginning of the task. If the check is being returned to the requester, the supervisor must input a separate approval. This is represented by an additional decision. Notice that, to keep time flowing down the page, the next action listed is the one that requires additional steps—in this instance, the signing of the forms. This is followed by the next action required by both choices—approving the request.

Finally, the supervisor determines whether an additional signature is required. If not, the supervisor notifies payables that the request is approved. However, if additional approval is needed, the supervisor will notify the next-level supervisor, who approves the document and then notifies the payables department. Notice that although the actions are fundamentally the same, they are done by different people with different priorities. Therefore, different index numbers are used for each action. In addition, the second-level supervisor's actions could easily include the decisions shown at the start of the map—sending the request back to the requester. Because it is the same process, the decision was made to not include that detail.

The task ends after the last approver notifies the payables clerk. Although separate actions are used for the supervisor and the second-level supervisor, the same connector leads to the next page. This is intended to show that, once out of these individuals' hands, there is no significant difference in the way they are handled.

Prepare Request: Verify Request Task

Exhibit 5.7 again drills down from the *verify request* (1.3) task in the Prepare Request map (see Exhibit 5.2). Because there are few details to the *e-mail requests* (1.4) task, it has been included. This map continues from the *approve request* (1.2) map in Exhibit 5.6. A connector is used to show the input into the system. All requests wind up in the payables clerk's incoming e-mail, so the task begins there. Because batch processing is an indication of a delay, the *D* shape is used. This delay includes the amount of time the paperwork may sit, as indicated by the times the batch is processed. Notice that even though there is nothing really happening to the paperwork, it is still assigned an index number.

Exhibit 5.7 shows that when the clerk begins working through the batch, the first thing reviewed is to see if the request is complete. If not, it is sent back to the requester. The decision on the map shows the requester correcting the problem and then sending it back to wait for the next batch.

If everything is okay, the clerk approves the form. Because this is an important control detail, it is included on the map. Once these two actions have been completed, the request is set aside until all requests have been reviewed. The delay here shows the reason for the delay and an indication of the maximum amount of time the requests may be held waiting for the batch to be completed.

The next step is to print out all the requests. This can take up to 30 minutes. The printouts are put in a five-day hold-file. Notice that the document flowchart symbol was used. This highlights how the documents are handled. In addition, the hold-file is represented by the manual file symbol. It is not necessary to use these—process boxes will work just as well—but a few different symbols can help highlight certain situations. The requests are then e-mailed to home office disbursements.

As was mentioned while discussing the task-level flowcharts, there is not a lot of detail regarding mailing the requests. However, it is important enough to be considered a separate task. On this map, it is indexed as Action 1.4.

Exhibit 5.7 completes the drill-down maps of the Prepare Request (1.0) tasks shown in Exhibit 5.2. Exhibit 5.5 showed the drill down of the *complete request* (1.1) task. Exhibit 5.6 showed the drill down of the *approve request* (1.2) task. Exhibit 5.7 showed the drill down of the *verify request* (1.3) task. Exhibit 5.8 included the drill down of the *e-mail requests* (1.4) task.

Exhibit 5.7   Verify Request (1.3) and E-mail Requests (1.4)—Action Level

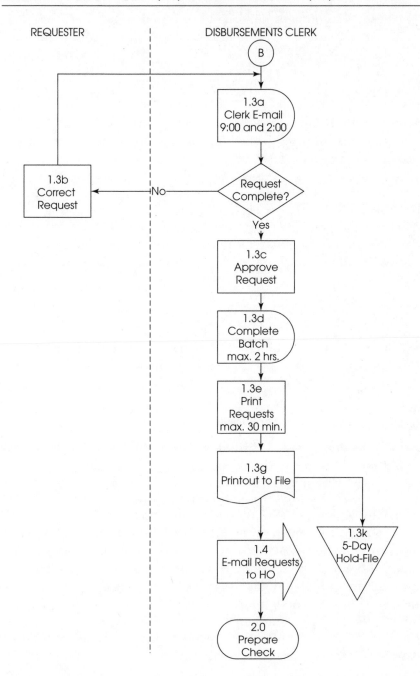

Prepare Check: Prepare to Issue Task

The next series of maps will drill down into the Prepare Check (2.0) unit. The task-level map in Exhibit 5.8 drills down from Exhibit 5.3 and the task *prepare to issue* (2.1). Since we have started a new unit, the map begins with a reference to the source of the input—the first unit from Exhibit 5.1, Prepare Request (1.0). Exhibit 5.8 shows that the requests are held for issuance until 1:00 P.M., so the *D* shape is used and the appropriate information is input.

After this, the steps follow in logical order. One of the clerks notifies the supervisor (2.1b), the supervisor turns on the printer (2.1c), the supervisor relocks the cabinet (2.1d), the clerks print out the e-mail (2.1e), sign on to the system (2.1f), and then access the checks (2.1g). For each check, the clerks are reviewing to see if they are appropriately approved by payables. This is shown as a decision on the map. Because the clerical staff does different things in this situation toward the same end, they are both represented in a single box.

The task ends with a connector to the next page. We have used the next letter in sequence from the one used in the prior unit (see Exhibit 5.7). This is done to help reduce confusion regarding which sheet goes with which process. The more unique the connectors, the less likely it is that there will be any confusion.

Prepare Check: Issue Check Task

Exhibit 5.9 continues the drill down from the Prepare Check tasks in Exhibit 5.3 with the *issue check* (2.2) task. This is a relatively simple process. Only one section within a department is involved (the check issuers), and other than one batch process and one handoff of the documents, everything is a simple action.

After using a connector from the prior task in Exhibit 5.8, there are two straightforward actions—entering the check information and printing out the requests. The completed requests are batched until all are completed. The maximum amount of time these are held is included. There are two more actions—printing the checks and signing off from the system. The final step is to hand-walk the forms to the check retriever. The arrow helps emphasize this transfer. Another connector leads to the next task.

Exhibit 5.8   Prepare to Issue (2.1)—Action Level

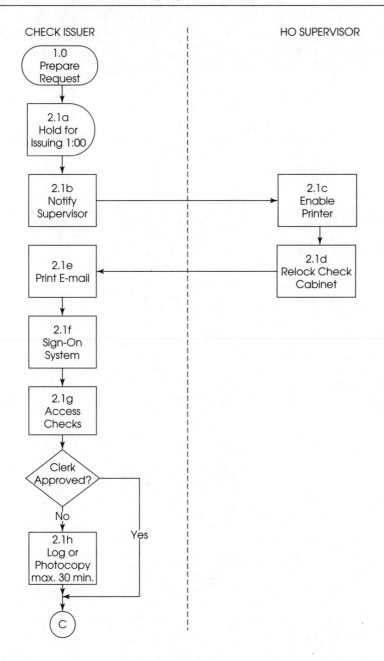

Exhibit 5.9   Issue Check (2.2)—Action Level

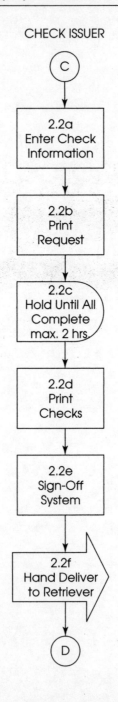

CHECK ISSUER

C

2.2a
Enter Check
Information

2.2b
Print
Request

2.2c
Hold Until All
Complete
max. 2 hrs.

2.2d
Print
Checks

2.2e
Sign-Off
System

2.2f
Hand Deliver
to Retriever

D

Prepare Check: Retrieve Check Task

Exhibit 5.10 shows action taken on the *retrieve check* (2.3) task. After another connector from Exhibit 5.9, we have another task that starts with a delay caused by batching work. The maximum amount of time the batch may wait is listed as one hour. The next series of actions goes back and forth between the check retriever and the supervisor. The retriever notifies the supervisor, the supervisor

Exhibit 5.10 Retrieve Check (2.3)—Action Level

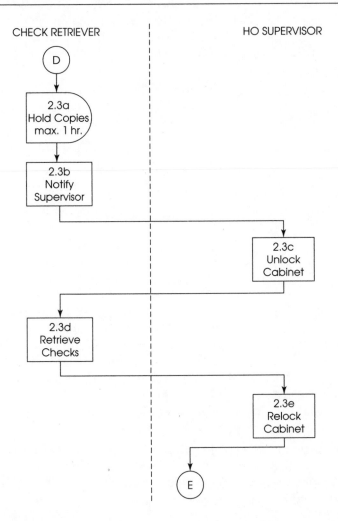

unlocks the cabinet, the retriever collects the checks, and the supervisor relocks the cabinet. This ends the retrieval process.

Prepare Check: Verify Check Task

Exhibit 5.11 combines the final two tasks, *verify check* (2.4) and *return check* (2.5), from Exhibit 5.3. These tasks are handled entirely by the check retriever. The first action is to match the checks and requests to ensure that everything has been completed properly. If they do not match, they are held until all checks are matched and mailed. This potential delay is represented by the *D* shape after the decision. However, the process for rectifying nonmatching items is fairly complicated and requires additional drilling down. Therefore, a reference is made to the detailed map—the HO Non-Match Maps—that will be constructed.

If everything is in order, the retriever enters the check number on the copy of the request and initials it. The requests are filed by date and check number ordered. The checks are held in a bin until each office is done. Some items may remain in waiting for up to four hours. Once an office is completed, the checks and photocopies are overnighted to the field office. Once again, although the only action within the task is overnighting the checks, it is important enough to isolate. Also, since this is the end of this unit, the connector shows the output going to the next unit, Deliver Check (3.0) (see Exhibit 5.4).

Drilling Down: HO—No Corresponding Check or Request Action

Exhibit 5.12 is a drill down from action 2.4b in Exhibit 5.11. In the previous map, we mentioned that the process involved when checks and requests do not match was too intricate to explore at that time. Instead, a connector was used to reference another map (see Exhibit 5.11). Drilling down into this process in Exhibit 5.12 is important, because it is a key control point and, as mentioned before, it is a little more complicated.

Exhibit 5.12 shows the first of two alternatives—that there is a request, but no check. We start by showing that situation as the beginning of the map. From there, the retriever searches the system to determine whether a check was actually entered. If not, the decision shows that the request is returned and the check is issued in the normal issue process (as shown by the connector). If a check

Exhibit 5.11   Verify Check (2.4) and Return Check (2.5)—Action Level

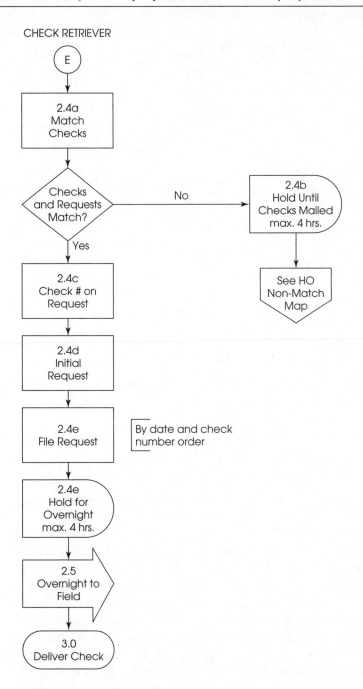

CHECK RETRIEVER

E

2.4a
Match
Checks

Checks
and Requests
Match?

No

2.4b
Hold Until
Checks Mailed
max. 4 hrs.

Yes

See HO
Non-Match
Map

2.4c
Check # on
Request

2.4d
Initial
Request

2.4e
File Request

By date and check
number order

2.4e
Hold for
Overnight
max. 4 hrs.

2.5
Overnight to
Field

3.0
Deliver Check

Exhibit 5.12   HO Non-Match—Request/No Check (2.4b)—Drill Down

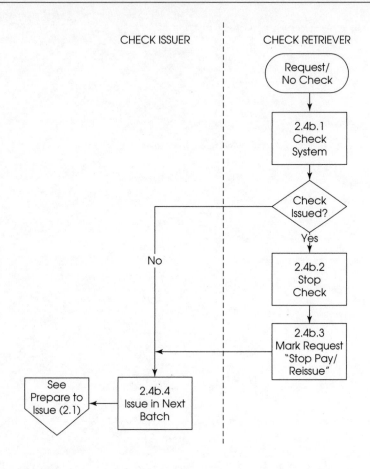

was issued, it is stopped in the system. The requester marks the check "Stop Pay/Reissue" and, again, the normal issuing procedures are followed.

Notice that the numbering system used relates to tasks and actions that lead to this process. The entire activity results from task 2.4 (*verify checks*) and from action 2.4b (hold until checks mailed). Therefore, a numbering system relating to those activities is used—2.4b.1, 2.4b.2, and so on.

Exhibit 5.13 shows the second alternative, in which there is a check but no request. Again, we show this situation to start the map. The retriever will verify with the issuer that the request cannot be found.

Exhibit 5.13   HO Non-Match—Check/No Request (2.4b)—Drill Down

CHECK RETRIEVER

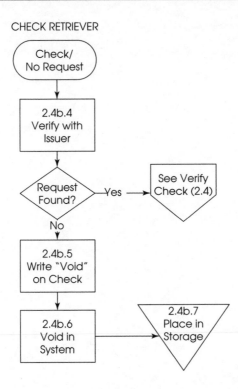

If the request is found, a connector splits from the decision and shows a return to the *verify checks* map. If the request is not found, a series of actions follows: writing "Void" on the check, voiding the check in the system, and storing the void check. The storage point represents the end of the process.

The numbering system is continued in these processes. Note that the numbers continue the series started with the previous actions.

Deliver Check: Review Check Task

Exhibit 5.14 starts the drill down into the Deliver Check (3.0) unit shown in Exhibit 5.4. As with the previous tasks, this task begins by showing the unit that preceded it, Prepare Check (2.0). Since all items are held until 10:00 A.M. for processing, a *D* shape is used to indicate the potential for delay. The hold-file is pulled, and all requests are matched to checks. If the checks and requests do not

Exhibit 5.14   Review Check (3.1)—Action Level

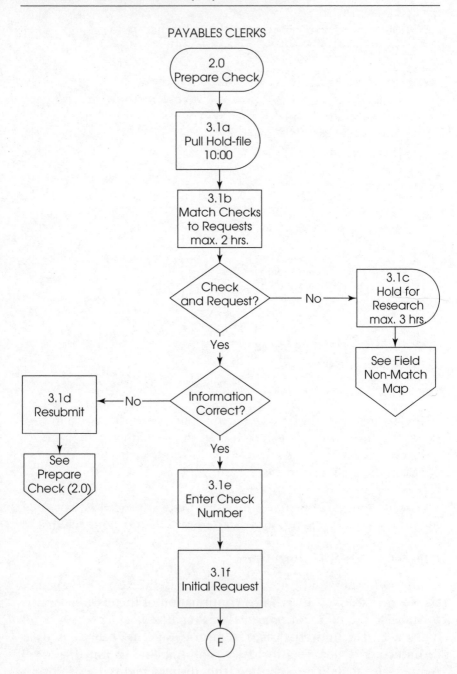

match, they are held to process later. Again, there is a fairly complicated system used to clear these items, so there is a reference to a separate map. In this instance, the reference is to a field map, to differentiate it from the home office drill-down map completed as part of the Prepare Check unit.

If the check and request match, the clerk verifies that the amounts and the payees are correct. If they are not, the request must be resubmitted. The map refers the reader to the Prepare Checks maps. If everything matches, the clerk enters the check number and initials the request. A connector is used to refer to the next set of maps. Again, the letter used for this connector continues from those tasks completed previously.

Drilling Down: Field—No Corresponding Check or Request Action

Exhibit 5.15 is the first map in this series of drill downs from Exhibit 5.14, action 3.1c. This map relates to the situation in which the payables clerk has a check but no request. The check is marked "Void," and a "Void Check" form is completed. An arrow is used to indicate overnighting the documents to the home office. The check issuer voids the check in the system and places the supporting documentation in storage.

Exhibit 5.16 is the next map in the drill-down series from Exhibit 5.14, action 3.1c. It represents the beginning of the drilled-down process when the disbursements clerk has a request but no check. The request is put back into the hold-file. This may delay handling the missing check by up to five days. If the check does not come in, a Check Locator form is completed. A copy is printed and put in a hold file. The original is e-mailed to the check issuer, who holds it for processing the following day.

The next action is to determine whether the check has been issued. If it has not been issued, the check is issued using the process shown in the *issue check* map. If it has been issued, additional information is added to the form that is e-mailed back to the field office. The connector to the next map is slightly different. Because this is a drill down rather than a continuation of the existing maps, use of the existing lettering system might become confusing. Instead, "DD1" is used (this stands for drill down one).

Exhibit 5.17 is the last half of the drilled-down process from Exhibit 5.14, action 3.1c, when the disbursements clerk has a

Exhibit 5.15   Field Non-Match—Check/No Request (3.1c)—Drill Down

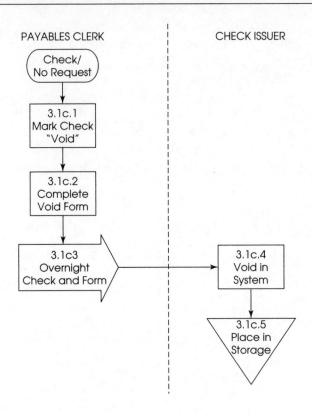

request but no check. The "DD1" connector starts the map. The clerk will verify that the check has not yet been received. At this point, a series of additional actions could be included to show the steps taken if the check had been received. However, because the focus of this process is on the situation where it has not been found, there is no particular emphasis placed on that situation. If the check has not been received, a "Stop Pay Form" is completed and a new request prepared. Both are e-mailed to home office.

When the check issuer receives the form, the system is checked to see whether the check has cleared. If it has not cleared, payment is stopped and a new check is issued. While this could be considered two separate actions, there is no particular need to separate them in this analysis. Therefore, they have been combined into

Exhibit 5.16 Field Non-Match—Request/No Check (3.1c)—Drill Down

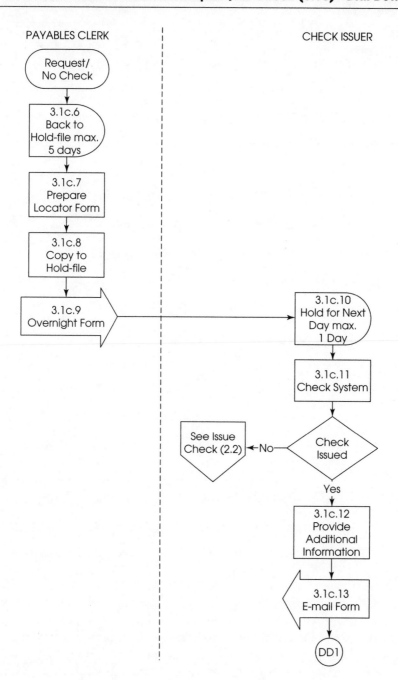

PAYABLES CLERK | CHECK ISSUER

Request/
No Check

3.1c.6
Back to
Hold-file max.
5 days

3.1c.7
Prepare
Locator Form

3.1c.8
Copy to
Hold-file

3.1c.9
Overnight Form

3.1c.10
Hold for Next
Day max.
1 Day

3.1c.11
Check System

Check
Issued

See Issue
Check (2.2) ←No

Yes

3.1c.12
Provide
Additional
Information

3.1c.13
E-mail Form

DD1

Exhibit 5.17 Field Non-Match—Request/No Check (3.1c)—Drill Down (Continued)

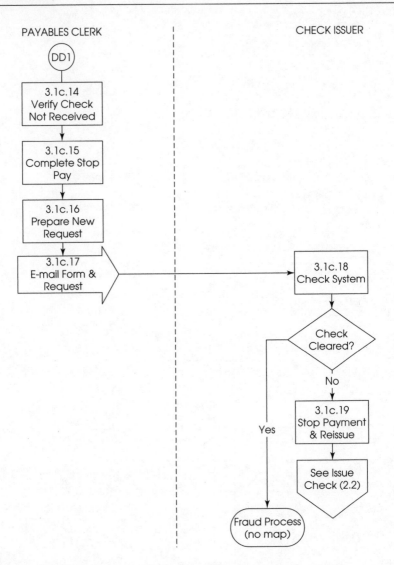

one step. The map references the *issue check* tasks. If the check has cleared, the processes that relate to fraud are implemented. Notice that the termination of the map shows this process with an indication that the process has not been mapped. This often happens as you work through a process; additional processes interact with the one under review. However, there is never enough time to look at

Exhibit 5.18 Field Non-Match—No Corresponding Check or Request (3.1c)—Task Level

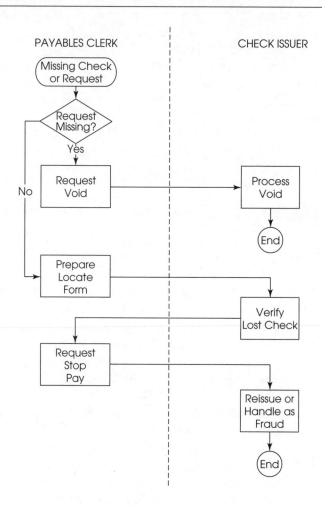

all of them. Therefore, the map can reference these situations with an indication that it is outside the scope of the review.

Because of the complexity of the process for unmatched items, it is a good idea to raise the map a level. Exhibit 5.18 represents this bird's-eye view of what is occurring. This is also an example of how you may wind up working from the details to the overview, rather than the other way around.

The process starts by determining whether the situation is a check with no request or a request with no check. If there is no request, the request to void is prepared in the field office, and the actual voiding of the check takes place in home office. If the check is missing, there are four higher-level steps that occur between the two offices. The field office prepares forms to have the home office locate the check. The home office then verifies that the check was issued. The field office then processes a stop pay. Finally, the home office begins lost check procedures—either issuing a new check or handling the situation as a fraud. This high-level view helps document how the process jumps from one location to another.

Deliver Check: Return to Requester Task

Exhibit 5.19 is the last of the drill-down maps for the task Deliver Check (3.0) shown in Exhibit 5.4. Notice that this map combines two tasks, *mail to payee* (3.2) and *return to requester* (3.3), because they are closely related and relatively straightforward. The final map starts with the connector F, which ended the prior map.

There are two routes that can be followed, depending on how the payment is to be handled. These correspond to the two tasks. If the check is to be mailed to the payee (3.2), the envelope is stuffed with the check and any necessary correspondence. The documents are then routed to the mailroom. The end of the process is shown by the mailroom mailing the check. If the check is to be returned to the payee (3.3), the information is recorded on the delivery log. All items are held until check processing is complete. This is shown as a delay in the system. This is an excellent example of a delay that may be necessary. If the clerk were to deliver each check as it was processed, the entire system would slow down. However, even if this appears to be the best system, it is still better to use the D shape to identify all batch-processing systems.

Once all checks are processed, the clerk hand-delivers checks to the requesters. When the check is delivered, both the clerk and the requester sign the log to show transfer of the document. The process ends once the check is delivered.

Note that, in building this map, rather than showing the processes side-by-side, we have listed them sequentially. The order doesn't matter, but this approach helps the user understand the difference.

**Exhibit 5.19   Mail to Payee (3.2) and Return to Requester
(3.3)—Action Level**

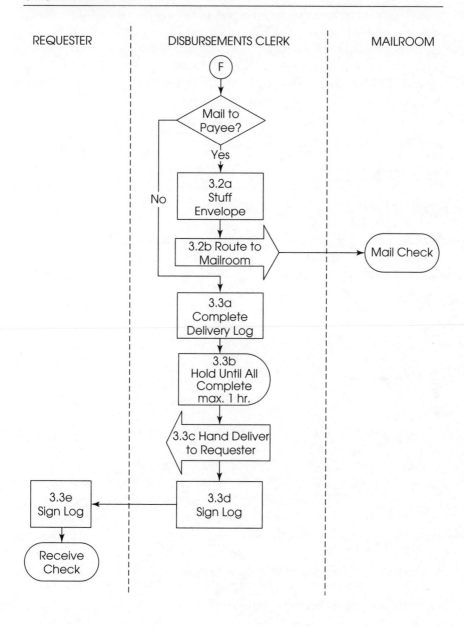

Recap

In general, the best way to learn Process Mapping is to do it. This example should have provided you with just that chance. If you completed your own maps before looking through our examples, you probably found that yours are very different. That is to be expected. No two people will build a map the same way.

If you did not try your own hand at Process Mapping with this example, you probably should go back and try anyway. The chances are you are looking at the maps now and thinking that although there are a lot of them, there does not seem to be anything tough about them. That is the great part about Process Mapping—the final product looks deceptively simple. Almost anyone can understand it, and people who are involved in the process recognize it instantly. Process maps are not easy to produce, and it is only by working on your own that you will learn how to make it look easy, too.

Key Analysis Points

Know the Process

While it is true that one of the purposes of Process Mapping is to learn about the process, that does not mean that you should go in completely clueless. By knowing the basics of how the process works, you will have an insight into what should be documented. In the expense example, knowing that there were a number of transfers between departments meant there should be extra emphasis on this part of the process. Accordingly, these transfers were highlighted by using large arrows.

Begin Visualizing Controls

A corollary to knowing the process is having a rudimentary understanding of the controls that exist in the process. By understanding these controls, you will have a better chance of accurately showing them in the map. This emphasis will help you isolate breakdowns during the analysis phase. In the expense example, one instance of this is specifically breaking out the check issuer and check retriever duties into separate columns. This separation highlights their roles in two-party controls.

Use the Levels to Understand the Process

Units, tasks, and actions are intended to give varying depths of understanding to a process. They should be used accordingly. Starting from a high level gives the broad overview that helps define the purpose of actions. However, starting with the actions makes it easier for the reviewer to build an initial map. Then the understanding of the broad units can be built from there. Ultimately, the approach that provides the best understanding should be used.

CH A PTER

Analysis

There is a natural hootchy-kootchy motion to a goldfish.
　　　　　　—Walt Disney on the fish ballet in *Fantasia*

Into the Editing Room

By now, you should be acutely aware that true analysis for a Process Mapping project occurs from the first moment you take the project to the moment you walk out the client's door for the last time. If you have been waiting until this point to begin analysis, it is far too late. To show this, we have been including analysis tips and techniques that should have been going on from the project's initiation. However, once the maps are close to completion and the interviews have been done, it is time to try to tie all the pieces together.

When the shooting is complete, the actors go home, the extras get their little checks, and the miles and miles of film go into the editing room. While the editing of a film really starts when the writer has that first glimmer of an idea, the real nuts and bolts of developing the finished product—of analyzing the acts, scenes, and shots to develop a coherent product—occurs in the editing room.

So it is with a Process Map. In some instances, you may have a room that is wallpapered with white sheets of paper and yellow sticky-notes. In that case, you have the Herculean task of translating these notes into a graphic picture that everyone can understand. Other times, you may have dutifully recorded the map information at the conclusion of each interview, changing information as you needed to and maintaining a pristine picture of processes as you went along.

But even if you are able to faithfully duplicate the images you have captured with your sticky-notes and arrows, there is still an important task ahead of you. You must transform those units, tasks, and actions into a coherent product that shows not only how the process is done, but also how it should be done correctly. There are clues in the maps themselves that will help you determine what is right and what is wrong. But before you dig into the maps, it is a good idea to take a step backward.

Go back to the Process Profile Worksheet. Look back to see if what you were told matches what really happens. In developing these worksheets, you have been given someone's perception of what starts that process, what ends that process, who owns parts of the process, what the business objectives are, what the business risks are, what the key controls are, and what the measures of success are. Look to see if that initial understanding is true.

Triggers and False Triggers

In the beginning, you identified the triggers that initiate each part of the process. If you discussed this in depth with the owner, you probably made sure that the trigger was truly initiated from customer needs. Now, make sure that the *right* trigger has been found. In some instances, you may see that the true trigger for the process occurs earlier or later than first thought. If that is the case, there are a number of things you must review.

First, make sure that you have covered everything you need to cover. If the trigger actually occurs sooner than was first thought, you must take a look at more of the process. In the expense example, it would be very easy for a reviewer and an owner to come to an agreement that preparing the check request is the trigger for the process. It is easy to see this as a precise point in time, and it is the first document created. However, this would result in an important part of the process being missed—the time between receipt of the bill and paying it. If significant delays in the payment of bills came about because of a delay in the mailroom getting bills to the requester, that part of the process might be missed. Because timely payment of bills is a measure of success, it is important not to leave out any part of the process; therefore, the proper trigger should be receipt of the bill *by the company*.

However, setting the trigger too early can cause just as many problems. Primary among these is that too much information might be gathered, resulting in a morass of information that obscures the analysis. Again using the expense example, a reviewer and an owner may come to agreement that the payment process cannot begin without some action being taken that causes the expense—the janitorial service cleans the office, electrical expenses are incurred during a month, the CEO orders a new magazine, or making a profit results in taxes being owed. In that case, it might be thought that the trigger is incurring the expense. However, setting the trigger too early in this case has resulted in a process that is too broad and complex. The reviewer cannot be expected to look all the way back to how electrical expenses are generated. While this is a problem for the analyst, it is also a problem for the company being reviewed. If the company thinks of its expense process in this manner, it may have unreasonable expectations about timeliness and what it expects of its accounts payable group.

Second, make sure that a company's misconceptions regarding the trigger do not cause problems with interrelated processes. The more a process needs to be completed in a "just in time" manner, the more important this is. An example of misidentifying the trigger—developing a "false trigger"—can be shown from our earlier example of making breakfast. We talked about the trigger for all the tasks for cooking ingredients (cook bacon, cook eggs, toast bread, fry potatoes) being the same—prepare ingredients. However, if this is the actual trigger used for all four areas, part of the breakfast is going to be cold. If the bacon takes longer to cook, the trigger for it may actually occur during the ingredient preparation unit. If the toast is done fairly quickly, the optimal trigger may be somewhere in the egg-cooking task. Therefore, if the cook uses "pan hot" as the trigger for bacon (even though all other ingredients are not used) and "egg cooked for one minute" as the trigger for heating the toast, the final result may be a complete breakfast with all items served at the same time, piping hot.

Inputs and Outputs

Inputs

Closely related to the trigger is the concept of inputs to the process. Make sure that people involved in the process recognize all inputs and their sources. If people do not recognize the source of an input, they will not know where to go to rectify problems when they occur.

When evaluating outputs, it probably is more important for you as the reviewer to approach outputs differently than the company does. In the classic definition of output, it usually is easy to understand the resulting product. That information should be recorded on the Process Profile Worksheet. At the same time, you have identified the customers receiving that output. You have also tried to determine whether value has been provided to that customer—whether the job's output satisfies the need of the customer.

Later, we will discuss approaching the mapping project by analyzing the job the customer is trying to accomplish. However, it is important to take a broader look at what outputs can be produced. In his book *The Competitive Power of Constant Creativity*, Clay Carr dissects outputs and allows us to take a better look at what really comes from a process.

Outputs

Begin by thinking of each process creating results rather than output. There is an input to the system, a transformation occurs to that input, and there is some result to the company. Carr defines four different types of result. The first is the most obvious and the concept that is normally used—output. This is the result the company anticipates and wants—it is what the company expects to make.

Waste

The next result is waste. The classic definition of waste is product that is thrown away as useless. However, for our purposes it needs to be broader. For example, it should include scrap. Many companies think of scrap as an achievement—waste for which value is found. But it is waste nonetheless. It is a result that does not provide the value expected. Anything produced that does not result in full potential is waste, and a good analysis focuses on how these wastes occur and what is done with them.

One area that often comes under scrutiny during a Process Mapping project is the system in place to correct errors. Very often you will see maps that spend a lot of time focusing on error rates and rework items. However, it is always less expensive for a company to get things done right the first time than to have to go back and fix them. Therefore, it is better for the analyst to understand why errors occur rather than how to fix them more efficiently. Although streamlining the correction process is fine, it is just as important to look upstream in the process to see where the errors occur.

It is also important to point out that you cannot understand what waste is until you actually know what it is you are trying to produce. Even something as easily defined as a cog needs a prototype to ensure that the correct items are produced. Without knowing what is required up front, the entire production may be nothing but waste.

Surprises

Now we move into less obvious results. As stated a number of times, processes are designed to do something (ideally, to provide value to some customer). However, it is a rare process that always does what it is expected to do. These unexpected results are surprises.

New processes are the most susceptible to surprises. When a process is established, everyone has a good idea what they think it will accomplish. But there are too many variables, and there will always be surprises. And it does not take a new process to produce surprises. All it requires is a small change to the input or process itself—maybe even something as simple as an employee going on vacation. One company had a process for accepting payments from independent contractors. Cash collections were deposited to a local bank. The independent contractor would write a check from the account and send it in to the servicing office along with any checks received. For one independent contractor, the process was going fine until the bank clerk he normally worked with went on vacation. Because they were good friends, she would always call when his account was about to be overdrawn. However, when she went on vacation, the temporary clerk did not warn him, and his check bounced. This was a surprise for the independent contractor. It was also a surprise for the servicing office, because it was the first indication of a $20,000 embezzlement.

It is evident that surprises can be either pleasant or unpleasant. This was a pleasant surprise for the company—it discovered and stopped embezzlement. However, this was an unpleasant surprise for the independent contractor.

Another example of surprises can be seen with the expense payment example. In this case, there are a number of unpleasant surprises. The most obvious may be increased costs because of missed discount dates or fines from missed payments. A less obvious surprise might be an increased workload, because the designers misunderstood the volume of work that would be experienced.

Invisible Consequences

The final result is invisible consequences. These represent the forest most companies cannot see for the trees. The difference between surprises and invisible consequences is that surprises are quickly seen, whereas invisible consequences lie in the dark waiting to strike. Surprises cannot be ignored. Eventually, invisible consequences cannot be ignored either, but it is that "eventually" that is the killer.

There is a joke that a consultant is someone you pay to tell you the time off your own watch. There is some truth to this, because the consultant comes in with fresh eyes. A good reviewer (even if working from within the company) has the ability to be naïve in the ways of the department and ask the questions that have "obvious" answers. He or she should be able to come in and see the invisible consequences about which other people are not naïve enough to ask.

In the *Expense Payment* scenario, there could be any number of invisible consequences. These might include the company's loss of reputation within the community because of delayed payments, employees looking to work for a company that respects its employees enough to ensure that their word to suppliers is honored, and the eventual destruction of morale as workloads increase.

In a review we recently completed, we made a major suggestion to the executive in charge of the department; it provides an excellent example of an invisible consequence. We were called in shortly after the executive took over. He had been put in as a developmental assignment and knew almost nothing about that line of the business. His prior experience had been in one of the support services.

On top of that, the prior two executives in that position had also been on developmental assignments. They both had some marketing experience, so they understood a little more about the department, but not enough to instill any confidence in the workers. In addition, each had left the department for new assignments within two years. It was apparent in our discussions that the employees were tired of the revolving door. Other companies were hiring in the same line and hiring away the department's good employees. Those who were left behind (including some of the top managers) felt disenfranchised and overlooked. The solution we presented could not solve the entire problem, but it would address some of it. We suggested that the executive spend part of a day with each employee and learn what he or she did. Not just a gratuitous "I'm part of the team" type meeting, but a meeting to actually learn what the nuts and bolts of these jobs were. In this way, the executive could show that he cared about his team while he also showed that he cared what was really occurring. At the same time, by admitting that he did not know as much as anyone else, he was able to show them some of the leadership skills the CEO had seen when he gave him this appointment.

Process Ownership

Once the maps are complete, it is a good time to review the self-declared process owners for each process. At the outset, you tried to determine these owners, and in some instances, this was relatively easy. However, there may have been portions that remained unclear—in some instances, you even may have walked into turf wars.

This is the point when you can determine who the process owners are and possibly make your own decision about who would be the best owner. This can be a tough recommendation to make, but if your map shows that the process is best handled by someone else, then by all means make that recommendation. In one situation, a collection center was overseen (owned) by the accounting department. This seemed to make sense, because the collection of cash is normally an accounting function. However, it became apparent that while the majority of the work was counting and depositing collections, there was also a lot of coordination required with the billing department. This billing department was part of a larger administration department and could not be separated. The result was that the collection department changed its reporting to the administration department. With the new "ownership," the processes between billing and collection became more transparent and customer service was improved.

Beyond determining whether the right owners are in charge, you should make sure that everyone understands who the owners really are. And, possibly more important, you should make sure there is an owner who will really take responsibility. In an amusement park, responsibility for various areas was defined by what the people did. Food servers were responsible for preparing and serving food; ride personnel were responsible for getting people on and off rides safely; janitors were responsible for seeing that the walkways, chairs, and tables were clean; and gardeners were responsible for the plants and shrubs and other outdoor accoutrements.

In the middle of one large building was a fountain. It was becoming the disgrace of the park. The food servers did not think it was their job to keep it clean because, although it was in the food court, it had nothing to do with serving food. The ride personnel did not think it was their job to keep it clean because, even though there were rides on either side of it, it had nothing to do with running the rides. The janitors did not think it was their job to keep it clean because, although it was surrounded by walkways, chairs, and tables, there was a definite planter surrounding the fountain. Gardeners did not think it was part of their job because, although there was a planter surrounding the fountain, the fountain itself was not a plant.

No one wanted to be the owner. The solution was an interesting one. Rather than try to force any one department into being the owner, a new arrangement was established. Instead of there being a manager of food service and a manager of ride personnel and so on, one person was put in charge of each area of the amusement park. Suddenly, everyone who worked in that particular building not only had responsibility for the fountain but also had responsibility for everything that went on in the building. The ride operators were responsible for the food court, the food servers were responsible for the walkways, and everyone was responsible for the fountain. By redefining the owner of the process, fewer processes slipped through the cracks.

Business Objective

There is no one single thing more likely to be lost in the hustle and bustle of getting things done than remembering why you are doing them in the first place. The same is true of a process. By the time you have mapped and talked and analyzed, you may have forgotten what the process was trying to do in the first place. And many of the employees (if they knew in the first place) have forgotten also.

So this is the point when you look back and re-evaluate whether that process is still hitting its mark. Look at the overall process and make sure it is addressing the primary objective. Take a look at parts of the process and see if they are also supporting those objectives. If not, determine whether they are supporting some other objective. This may mean that part of the process must be realigned or even transferred to another process. It may also mean that potentially a big objective is being missed, and more emphasis should be placed on it.

In a check issuance process we reviewed, there were two major objectives—to issue checks for the correct amount and to ensure that no fraudulent checks were issued. One of the key controls relating to fraudulent check issuance was a systematic managerial review of payments. A listing was printed showing all check numbers for the selected time period. Managers selected ten per week for review.

However, the manager did not understand the objective of the process. He delegated the review to a supervisor (one who had check issuance authority and would be reviewing his own checks), and he allowed the supervisor to replace checks for the sample when he could not find support for one in the original selection. The result was that the control was totally ineffective. Once the objective of the process was explained, the manager took control of the operation and completed the reviews (with no substitutions) himself.

Business Risks

A set of risks was identified at the outset of the project. These were discussed with everyone involved in the project, and agreement was reached on the major risks. So, at this stage, there is a chance you have already helped them recognize risks they did not see themselves.

Now that you have seen the full process, how it fits together, and what it is truly accomplishing, you have an excellent opportunity to determine whether new risks have been identified. Usually, this does not focus on changing broad risks, but on the portions of those broad risks that may be a concern.

The first situation is that in which an employee has made you aware of a condition no one recognized. Just as we have talked before about employees giving us the best ideas, they have also warned us of some of the largest problems. While reviewing a claims process, one supervisor informed us that original documentation was not always available when the claim was being settled. This would result in portions of losses being covered that were never intended to be covered. Obviously, there was a resulting increase in claims costs. In some cases the documentation was lost, but in most cases it was never prepared or submitted. We told the supervisor we were a little surprised about this, because over the last year we had tested this very item and found that everyone currently understood the requirements. Our testing showed that everyone was doing a very good job of following these requirements. The supervisor agreed, but then mentioned that the problem was happening in policies that were more than three years old.

We had the right risk (the exposure of incorrectly paying claims because of improper documentation), but we were focusing on the wrong part. We had focused on the current understanding of procedures and the resulting requirements. Everything was fine in this area—recent training had brought everyone up to speed and our tests showed a good track record. However, we had forgotten the full risk. Complete documentation means more than getting it right from now on—it also means getting things right in the past or making them right. We realized that we had to let our customers know that there was an additional unidentified risk—past documentation was incomplete.

Some new risks may become apparent from the structure or content of the maps themselves. This is really based on the input of employees also (what in Process Mapping is not?). This situation usually occurs when there is a part of the map going in a direction no one anticipated. It usually comes from one employee who handles the miscellaneous operations where so much hides.

One company we worked with was thinking of making changes to its purchasing processes—primarily streamlining approval processes and the resulting paperwork. Purchasing is one of those areas that no one seems to want to change because it is very susceptible to fraud and contains many sacred cows. Everyone had recognized risks regarding fraud, overpayment, and even misstatement of assets. In talking with various employees, it looked like the new process would work well, everyone's concerns could be addressed, and the process would be significantly streamlined. Then we spoke with one of the accountants, who mentioned that the information from the furniture and fixtures listing went into a certain report. As we dug deeper into the report, we found that it was the basis for part of the company's state taxes. We immediately had a new risk—compliance with tax regulations. And it was a very important risk to identify, because the new process had not addressed the situation at all. We raised concerns about the new risk, and there was instant agreement to make changes necessary to comply. The process was still streamlined (with a few extra steps), the company had a fuller understanding of the risks it was facing, and the company had fuller assurance that risk was being properly mitigated.

Key Controls

This is sometimes the easiest issue to identify while reviewing (and even while completing) Process Maps. The initial discussion with owners usually identifies the primary controls. If the controls do not exist, that is usually discovered before the actual mapping begins. In those cases in which the owners are not sure whether a key control exists, the mapping can prove whether it does or does not.

However, the most likely scenario is that the process owner, senior management, or even local management states that there is a good control in place. Procedure may back this up. But when you speak with the people performing the work, you sometimes find that they either never heard of the control or do not bother completing it.

A perfect example is the one discussed previously, where the accounting section supervisors were not completing file reviews for payment support. Everyone knew what the procedure was, but they did not think they had the time to do it. The process owners knew there was a procedure and thought it was being completed, and even senior management knew there was a procedure and thought it was being completed, but they all were wrong.

In some instances, everyone may understand the control and be doing their best to comply, but miscommunication results in a breakdown of the control. During the review of processes for a significant unit of a company, we began looking at accounts processing. The accounts clerks handled many transactions, and we completed a number of maps that headed in many directions. We then had to track down those different directions. One account (a collections account) included a task where the monthly numbers were sent to an individual in the company's home office. The clerical staff indicated that there was no further work needed—balancing and adjustments were not their concern. Speaking with the person who received the reports, we found that he was a programmer who had originally written a software program to store and report on the information. He had requested the information four years ago to test the new program. He had been receiving the reports ever since. He threw out any reports he received and, in spite of often asking them to no longer send the reports, still received them.

It is vitally important to follow up and verify all paths in a Process Map. As is discussed in a little bit, it is the dangling ends that may indicate problems. In this case, it showed that a key control did not exist.

Measures of Success

Measures of success, too, are relatively easy to see when maps are completed. Primary measures are often a function of elapsed time—issuing checks within 48 hours or returning phone calls within 20 minutes. The cycle times on the maps may instantly provide evidence that a measure is unreachable. In those instances, a determination must be made—either to change the process or change the measure.

While reviewing a call center, we learned that the measurement was answering 80 percent of phone calls within 20 seconds. In developing the maps, we learned that every call was logged in a call management system. Because of system utilization, the time between entering the information and going to the next screen could often take up to a minute. Based on the volume of calls and the time spent working within the system, it was impossible to meet the goal. There were two choices available to the process owners. The first choice was to change the goal. A more realizable goal was to answer 50 percent of the calls.

This goal was unacceptable to the client, because it thought that the objective of customer service could only be met by answering more calls in less time. The second alternative was to change the procedure. That is the choice management accepted. Rather than logging all calls, procedures were established regarding which calls to record. By not logging all calls, the objective of completely documenting calls was not going to be met. However, this streamlined the process enough so that the more important goal of customer satisfaction was accomplished.

Analyzing the Actual Maps

So now we return to the actual Process Maps. There are basic actions you can look for in every map that are indicators of problems— either inefficiencies or control breakdowns. These should be isolated and examined in depth, because they represent golden opportunities for improvement.

Remove Approvals

Business has passed through the golden age of empowerment. It was one of the buzzwords of the 1990s, and it seemed that everyone wanted to give everyone more authority. Despite that, companies still find themselves mired in layers and layers of approvals. For every authorization requirement that was removed, 10 or 20 must still exist.

Do not misunderstand. We are not advocating the removal of every level of approval that exists. But in most companies, authority levels are usually a sacred cow that deserves to be slain.

In *At America's Service,* Karl Albrecht repeats a story told to him by Dick Scott, CEO of Longs Drugs stores. Scott was standing at one of his stores when he noticed the store manager approving customers' checks. The cashier would stop the line, walk over to the manager, and obtain the approval. In general, the manager would be talking to someone else, and Scott noticed that the manager was not even looking at the check. Instead, he would initial it and just hand it back to the clerk.

Later, Scott talked with the manager. He suggested that the cashiers just approve the checks so the customers would receive better service. The manager was horrified and thought there would be a significant rise in bad checks. Scott asked him, "When she brought you the check for your approval, what thought process went through your mind as you approved it?" The manager answered, "Well, no thought process, really. I didn't give it much thought to tell the truth." Scott replied, "If you didn't have any thought process going on in *your* head, don't you think we could teach her not to have any thought process going on in *her* head?"

Approvals are extremely time-consuming, and they take up the time of people whose time is most valuable. Look at the example of an approval process in Exhibit 6.1. First, the paperwork can wind up going through many hands. If it is more than $1,000, it is touched by two employees, a supervisor and a manager. And that is

Exhibit 6.1 Journal Approval

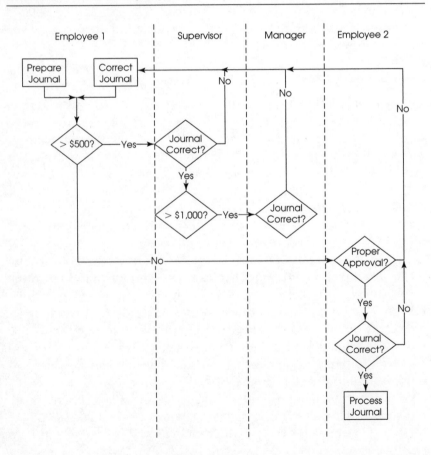

only if it is all done correctly. If there are constant errors, one piece might go through that same loop a number of times. Also notice that the phrase *Journal Correct?* is used three different times. That means three different people are required to ensure the correctness of this journal.

It may well be that this is a perfectly legitimate need. It all depends on what the journal is for or what the process surrounding it is. However, these are the kinds of tasks that must be identified to determine whether they are necessary, and the need for the control must be weighed against the additional time this takes. What is not included on this particular map are the cycle times and the holding times. Usually, the higher the individual's position, the longer a request for authority will sit in an in-bin. Once again, elimination of approvals or setting higher authorities for low-level employees may make for quicker customer service.

Looping Errors

In computer programming this is known as an infinite loop—a situation in which the programmer has inadvertently set up criteria that force the computer to process the same commands over and over. This results in the program fatally crashing. Likewise, looping errors can make a process fatally crash, even if the loop is not infinite. Exhibit 6.1 is also an example of this.

As mentioned in the previous section, constant errors could cause the document to go through the same loop a number of times. When these types of loops are encountered, there are two things that must be determined. Are all these decisions really necessary? If so, does everything have to feed back to the beginning? We discussed the need for the decisions in the previous section. But sometimes a better question is whether the information needs to go back to the top of the Process Map. In our example, the journal is going back to the person who first wrote it. Then it falls back through the same filters to either pass muster or be returned again.

In general, these type of loops stem from a "do the crime, do the time" mentality. In other words, because the employee did it incorrectly, it is up to the employee to fix it. However, this sometimes arises because the company is attempting to help employees learn how to process information correctly by showing them when something is wrong. No matter what the situation, it is important to determine if there is an appropriate feedback loop to help ensure that people learn how to complete processes correctly. If not, the same errors will occur, and the process will never be streamlined.

Isolate Delays, Rework, and Handoffs

If you have been using the symbols suggested in Chapter 4, this should be very easy—look for the D or R shapes. If you have not been keeping up on this, there will be a little more work.

Delays exist for various reasons, but some are more apparent—and more easily eliminated. One of the main delays to look for is when documents sit in incoming mail (or, even worse, in an in-basket). Although not identified as such, there may be significant delays in Exhibit 6.1 at both the supervisor's desk and the manager's desk. There is a good chance journals are set aside until "I can get to them." Or they may be held until there are "enough worth doing." While doing reviews of small businesses—usually two- to four-person operations—we have found situations in which the days' collections are held in a desk drawer because the owner "does not have time to make the deposit."

For these types of situations, you must determine two different aspects of the problem—is it something that should be corrected? And what is causing the delay? It is important to think of them in this order, because the answer to the first question may eliminate the second—if it is not worth correcting, no one cares why the delay exists. In the case of depositing collections, it is obviously a problem that must be corrected. Collections sitting around are collections that can be stolen, and a key control over a significant business risk is not operating as intended. That means the reviewer would need to determine whether the delays are the result of misunderstanding (or not caring about) procedure, or if there is a problem in the process. For the situation in which journals are delayed, it is less obvious whether this needs correction. In previous sections we talked about eliminating delay by eliminating approvals. However, if the approvals are needed, it may be an education issue with management. Ultimately, though, it may well be that, although the approval is necessary, it does not need to occur for a couple of days. In that case, there may be no need to improve the process.

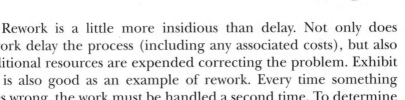

Rework is a little more insidious than delay. Not only does rework delay the process (including any associated costs), but also additional resources are expended correcting the problem. Exhibit 6.1 is also good as an example of rework. Every time something goes wrong, the work must be handled a second time. To determine whether this is a significant problem in the process, the error rates should be entered. Much like the analysis done for delay, determine whether the rework should be eliminated and what is causing it. If an error rate is very low, there may be no need (or it may not be cost-effective) to eliminate the errors. However, it is always worth determining whether the errors are based on a lack of education. A little training can solve many problems.

Handoffs occur whenever a product or paperwork (or even a computer file or e-mail) is going from person to person and sometimes back again. Exhibit 6.1 is also one example of a problem with handoffs. The approval process requires that paperwork go from the employee to a supervisor to a manager to a second employee. Four people handle a virtual piece of paper that may only require being handled by two. Since employee #2 is performing a verification, there may be no need for the handoffs to the supervisor and the manager. In fact, if the proper computer systems are put to work, employee #1 may be able to handle the journal without any assistance.

There may be an opportunity to streamline the process anytime a physical transfer exists. This may mean something as simple as replacing memos with e-mail. It may also mean getting people to handle their part of the process at one time rather than spreading it over time. Exhibit 6.2 is loosely based on a process we reviewed a few years ago, and it is constructed at a fairly high level. Two departments were involved in accepting or rejecting input received from the field. Department 1's function was primarily clerical, whereas Department 2 was a professional-level function. The information could be received by computer or on paper. In talking with the people, it seemed a fairly straightforward process. If the field input the information into the system, it went directly to Department 2. If not, Department 1 input part of the information and, barring immediate rejection, input the entire form. Department 2 then reviewed the information, determined what other data were needed, reviewed the data, and then made a final decision.

Exhibit 6.2 Accept/Reject Process

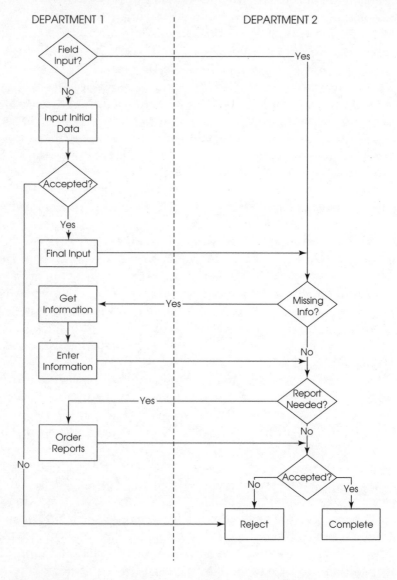

However, as the map shows, information was being passed back and forth at an alarming rate. These handoffs were hidden in the process and only became apparent when the map was completed. When the process owner was shown these maps, he instantly realized the heart of his problem. The number of times actions cross from department to department becomes painfully obvious. And it was not until it was shown graphically that the people involved in the process understood how they could combine tasks to gain more efficiencies in the system.

This is also an example of how decisions sometimes hide a problem with handoffs. Most people we spoke with in Department 2 thought their process was very streamlined. They spoke of how they would receive the work and handle it to conclusion. They believed they had a "one and done" process (handle it once and be done). The people in Department 1 also thought they were handling things efficiently. When they got the work, they completed the task they were supposed to and passed it on. They had never seen the connection that some of the work was being handled two, three, or four times.

People tend to think of decisions as an important step in a process. So when they complete a decision, they often think they have reached a milestone that marks the end of a process. This causes an artificial termination in their minds. Therefore, they may not see the connection with the full process. That was the situation in this example. Because the decision was completed and a resulting process was started, employees thought they had an efficient process. By graphically representing these decisions in the overall process, they could see that each decision was only one step of many.

Follow the Forms

In completing Process Maps, be sure you are keeping track of the actual forms that are being used, including knowing exactly where they go. Although it was not mentioned specifically in Chapter 4, another useful symbol is the document symbol. You do not necessarily want to go into a lot of detail about individual forms in your Process Map, but it may be useful in some situations to create a document flowchart. These are usually constructed with the departments across the top. It is not a bad idea when creating this type of flowchart to follow the Process Mapping rule of having events move chronologically down the page. Each form should be represented, along with how many copies there are. Each copy should then be tracked through the various departments it visits. Exhibit 6.3 is a very simple example of a document flowchart for the beginning of a purchasing process.

Exhibit 6.3 Document Flowchart—Purchase Order

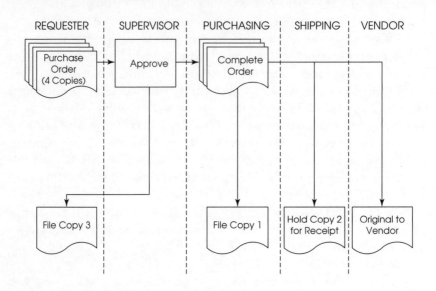

In some situations, document flowcharts can be analyzed much like Process Maps. The most obvious situation is when forms are moving back and forth between departments. The situation is much like that described in the previous section. If you see forms flying between departments, there may be a serious problem.

Whether you keep track of the forms through a document flowchart or by some other method, once the maps are completed it is time to take a close look at what happens to the form. Elimination of forms (whether they are paper or electronic) is a quick and easy way to reduce costs—not only by reducing the time spent handling the forms, but also by eliminating the costs resulting from producing the forms in the first place. Make sure the form is actually needed. Look for situations in which forms are filed, but no further action is taken. Often, these may show up as dead ends on the maps. Also look for situations in which multiple forms are going from one person to another. This may represent a situation in which forms can be combined. If the information on the form is needed, see if there is a way the same information could be transferred electronically. Finally, even if you cannot eliminate a form, see if you can get rid of some of the copies. That is one of the primary reasons for ensuring that you track all copies of the form through the system in the document flowchart.

Although reports are not strictly forms, the same approach can be used for reports. We have spent quite a bit of time talking about making sure information is available to measure success. Well, the other side of the story is just as important. Track where reports are going and see if they are actually used. Often, a report has been generated for as long as anyone can remember, but no one remembers why. However, because it has always been generated, everyone assumes that it is necessary and someone must be using it. The Process Maps should show the same indicators for unused reports that it does for unnecessary forms. And your review of reports should be much like that done for forms—make sure the reports are used; if they are used, determine whether they can be distributed electronically; and make sure all copies are needed. If necessary, you can prepare a document flowchart that follows how reports are used.

Incomplete Maps: Dangling Actions and Unanswered Decisions

Somewhat related to the idea of unnecessary forms and reports is the concept of "dangling actions." In a complete map, every action should lead to another action, a connector, or a process termination. If there is any part of the map that shows an action that leads nowhere (or contains the dreaded words "to file"), it should be explored further. It may be that the reviewer has not asked enough questions to fill in this area. In that case, the reviewer must decide whether to look deeper or just drop it. If you are far into the project and time is running out, going back and asking the questions may not be an option. However, often these unimportant loose ends show a backwater area that needs attention.

We previously cited the example of reviewing purchasing procedures to determine whether they could be streamlined. It was only by following up on a dangling action that we learned of the tax ramification of the change. The original map had shown that information was provided to the tax accountant, but there was no indication of any further action. We went back and spoke with the individual and found out that a serious violation could have occurred if we had continued as planned.

Another aspect of this type of problem is the unanswered decision. Every decision should have two arrows leading from it—one for yes and one for no. If not, additional information is needed. As with the dangling action, this may lead to the discovery of a new area that needs to be included. However, it may also mean that a review is either unnecessary or unused. When we have seen this happen, it usually means that someone is completing a review, but the results are not used. For example, we have spoken with clerks who tell us that they check for correct information (coding, signatures, matching documents) and then complete the process. When we ask more, we learn that they do nothing with the information— they do not correct the information, they do not refer it to anyone, and they do not create a log of errors. This can either mean that they are completing the process without understanding why or that they have decided to do the review on their own. Surprisingly, we have come across this type of situation a few times.

Question Hold-Files

Apparently the world would come to an end if there were no hold-files. Every process you review will seem to thrive on them. That is not to say that hold-files are a bad thing. However, it does mean that people may be relying on them too heavily. Look closely at each hold-file established in the process. Determine what goes in it, how it is used, and why it exists.

Verify that the time frames established for the hold-files are correct. If an individual sets a short hold-file, but then just refiles the information for the future, time may be wasted pulling this information unnecessarily. In addition, if the information is pulled too late, it is useless. Determine what situation caused the need for the hold-file. It may be that another portion of the process is not running efficiently and the hold-file had to be established to ensure that work was received on time. Also look at the success rate of the hold-file—how often is there a problem with receiving the information on time? While this can help establish the reason the hold-file was established, it can also be an indication that timeliness requirements for some departments are not effective.

Cycle Times

We have often mentioned keeping track of the cycle times for all events. Implied in this is the understanding that the reviewer is watching for events that seem to take too long. It may seem obvious, but take a good look at those actions that take the longest. Reducing these times can have the greatest effect on the overall process.

Besides focusing on the individual actions, attention should be paid to the overall process and the associated cycle times. In particular, the critical paths should be determined for the overall process. Once established, the timing for the critical paths can be used for a number of approaches.

The first is to determine where delayed actions are also causing delays in associated actions. As shown in the breakfast example, it is not necessary to wait for every part of some tasks to finish before other tasks can be started. As mentioned in our breakfast process example, if we wait for all the ingredients to be ready and then cook them at the same time, we will wind up with some cold food. In that situation, a critical path chart would show that the cooking task that took the longest time (e.g., cooking bacon) was holding up all other tasks. It is then necessary to determine whether the processes can be streamlined, new triggers should be established, or no change is necessary.

The second approach is to determine the length of time related to the entire process and verify that the measures of success based on time can actually be achieved. This approach can also be used for units or tasks that represent measurements. As mentioned before, analysis of the time taken to issue checks in the expense payment example shows that the 48-hour turnaround cannot be met—it is physically impossible.

Another approach is to determine the minimum and maximum cycle times for each action. From this you can determine the minimum and maximum cycle times for the critical path. This is important to understand, because standards are often set based on the minimum critical path time. However, the reality is that the maximum time will be experienced more often. The claims experience discussed in the beginning of Chapter 2 is a good example of this. If everything happens perfectly, the claims representative will speak with the claimant within the required one day. However, it is highly likely that the experience will have a few glitches and result in a time frame closer to the maximum. When reviewing this area, determine how often the minimum times and the maximum times are reached. If the maximum time is more prevalent, the area should be reviewed and the criteria should be re-examined.

Ultimately, time is one of the major resources a company is trying to conserve. In doing any assessment of risk, a major component is financial volume. The idea is that the larger the financial volume, the higher the risk that there will be a financial loss. Including and analyzing cycle times will show where time is being used the most and where the greatest risk of wasting time exists. Accordingly, the cycle times show where the most effort should be spent finding solutions.

Finalizing the Project

After all the discussions and all the interviews and all the maps and all the frustration, it is time to finalize the project. While not actually an analysis process, it is what the analysis has led to. Plus, every time you talk about the maps, you will be learning a little more. Each discussion may lead to another discovery. Analysis is never finished.

Finalizing the project entails a number of reviews of the maps. As you talked with people, you should have been reviewing the final maps with the employees to ensure that your understanding was correct. A number of miscommunications may occur, and you want to have these cleared up before you go farther in the project. An interesting point about these reviews is that it may be the first time the employees really recognize that what they have said was taken seriously. Most employees will be glad about this, but you may have a few who suddenly panic about the information they may have shared. There is no good answer for these individuals, but it is a good idea to be prepared for them.

Once the whole project is done, it is time to review the maps with the owners. They may well have seen bits and pieces before the meeting, but it probably will be the first time they have seen the entire package. Give it to them ahead of time. No one should be expected to absorb the information contained in all these maps in just a few minutes. This will often be the point when they first discover that their understanding of the process is incorrect.

Once they have reviewed the map, get their input regarding correctness. Ask for their questions and concerns first. They will not be interested in your comments until their issues are addressed. Also, it may give you additional insight or issues you want to include. Remember that this is still a part of the analysis process. Go over any questions that remain open. There should be very few, but there will also be issues that only the owner can answer. Finally, begin talking about the findings. The intent of this part of the meeting is to prepare the owner for the content of the final report. It is usually a good practice to keep the owner up to date regarding issues as the project continues, but this is the point where all those issues should be summarized. It is also an opportunity for the owner to start thinking about solutions to the issues that are raised. Even if you have worked with the staff to come up with viable solutions, the owner will want time to take ownership of them.

In some instances, the maps may have pointed out areas where additional research is needed. Depending on the circumstances, you may want to do additional testing. Even if you do not have the time, it is a good time to suggest that the owner initiate a similar project. In a recent review, we recognized that the processes over account controls were faulty. We talked with the owner, who requested that we determine how big the problem was. This resulted in our looking at a large number of files to support our understanding of the problem. Because we had the time available, we were able to expand the Process Mapping project and provide additional value.

The actual report will vary widely, depending on your individual needs and circumstances. However, there should be a final report that spells out what was reviewed, what was found, and, if possible, how things have been improved. The report should also contain copies of all maps. Make sure the owner gives copies of the maps to all employees involved in the project. Managers and supervisors should get all maps; employees should get copies of the processes they are involved in. This is one final opportunity for the reviewer and the process owner to show employees that they were part of this project and that their participation was appreciated.

Recap and Key Analysis Points

We have been providing key analysis points at the end of each chapter. However, since this entire chapter is about analysis, the recap provides the same information.

Once maps are completed, it is time to get into the real analysis. There are two separate approaches that should be completed—revisiting the Process Profile Worksheets and searching through the maps.

The primary approach to revisiting the Process Profile Worksheets is to ensure that your initial understanding is still correct and to make sure that the final analysis ties in with the major categories of the worksheet. These include triggers, inputs, outputs, process ownership, business objectives, business risks, key controls, and measures of success.

Most of these reviews are based on the same information contained in the worksheets when they were originally completed. However, outputs should be viewed in a different light. It is important to think of outputs as results and to recognize that there are four different types of results: outputs (what you expect the process to produce); wastes (items produced that do not meet the expectations of outputs); surprises (offshoots from the process that can be favorable or unfavorable, but were unexpected); and invisible consequences (long-term effects that are not recognized until after the process has been in place for a while). Recognizing and analyzing these results will help identify areas that may warrant additional attention.

While analyzing the actual maps, the reviewer should be aware of indicators that represent areas that warrant further review. Removing extraneous approvals helps empower the workers to complete their actions in a more timely manner. Looping errors, situations in which the process tends to go back through the same loop a number of times until restrictive conditions are met, should be resolved. Delays, rework, and handoffs should be eliminated or streamlined. Forms and reports should be reviewed closely to see whether they can be eliminated or reduced. Situations in which maps are incomplete, (e.g., dangling actions and unanswered decisions) should be identified to ensure that all avenues have been properly reviewed. Hold-files should also be reviewed to see whether they are necessary and, if so, that they have been established correctly.

Also look closely at cycle times. For the individual actions, identifying those that take the longest will show where streamlining may have the greatest effect. The overall cycle time for the processes, units, and tasks should also be reviewed to determine whether measures of success based on time can actually be met. Finally, the critical paths based on cycle times should be reviewed to determine where restrictions on timeliness might occur.

Before meeting with the owners to finalize the project, individuals interviewed for the maps should have a final look at the maps to ensure that they are correct. The same should be done with any supervisors and managers involved. Finally, the process owner's buy-in should be obtained. This discussion should help identify any problems with the map and prepare the owner for the final report. The structure of the report will depend on the needs and constraints of the situation. At a minimum, it should include what was reviewed, what was found, any known solutions, and copies of the map.

CHAPTER 7

Map Analysis: An Example

*When you make the finding yourself—even if you're the last person
on Earth to see the light—you'll never forget it.*

—Carl Sandberg

This Is Only an Attempt

We have seen the basic process of expense payment and have
developed the majority of the maps. In addition, we have developed
the fundamental Process Profile Worksheet. With this information,
it is time to do some preliminary analysis on the process.

We will approach this analysis by reviewing only the worksheets
and maps, but that is only part of the job. As mentioned earlier, the
entire Process Mapping approach actually leads to the best results. By
looking only at these bits and pieces, we will not be involved in a true
holistic approach. However, there is enough information available at
this point to show many of the fundamental aspects of analysis.

Process Profile Worksheet

The first step is to revisit the Process Profile Worksheet. Exhibit 7.1
is the Process Profile Worksheet we completed for the *Expense
Payment* process in Chapter 3 (Exhibit 3.5). This provides the basic

Exhibit 7.1 Process Profile Worksheet—Expense Payment Process

Process Name—Number	Process Owner
Expense Payment Process—EP	J. Doe, Treasurer M. Bucks, Mgr HO Disbursements P. Change, Mgr Field Accounting

Description
The process of paying for incurred business expenses other than travel and purchase order.

Triggers
Event beginning: Receive bill
Event ending process: Distribute check to employee or mail to payee
Additional events: Complete check request, obtain approval, submit request, issue check

Input—Items and Sources
Bill/Invoice or other support — employee

Output—Items and Customers
Disbursement check—vendor

Process Units	Process Unit Owners
Check Request	Field Disbursement Supervisor
Check Issuance	Home Office Disbursement Supervisor
Check Retrieval	Home Office Disbursement Supervisor
Check Distribution	Field Disbursement Supervisor

Business Objective(s)	Business Risks
Prompt and accurate payment of valid, properly approved business expenses	Fraudulent payments Delayed payments—missed discounts Customer dissatisfaction

Key Controls	Measure of Success

Segregation of duties
  Requester and approver
  Requester and issuer
  Issuer and retriever
	All checks issued within 48 hours
	Utilization of early pay discounts
	Complaints about delays
	Absence of duplicate payments

information we require for beginning our analysis. To complete some of this analysis, we will make assumptions about what was discussed or learned during other phases of the project. In this way, the basic approach to analyzing the worksheet should become evident.

Triggers

Some of the concerns about triggers for the *Expense Payment* process were discussed in Chapter 6. By defining the trigger as "Receive bill," the process owners have shown a good understanding of what starts the process. As already mentioned, setting the trigger later could mean that an integral part of the process is missed: The time from receipt of the bill to the time the request is prepared might not be properly analyzed. This trigger might show a fundamental misunderstanding of one of the major objectives of the process—timely payment of expenses.

A review of the "Other events" defined in the worksheet shows a fairly good understanding of the process. However, there could be a disconnect between the events listed and those used to define units. Although it is not necessary for these to match, it is important to ensure that everyone is in agreement. Discrepancies between these two areas may indicate the need for additional discussion. In this example, there is evidence that agreement has already been reached based on the list of process units included in that section of the work sheet. These same units closely match the final unit-level map.

Finally, the event ending process is defined as "Distribute check to employee or mail to payee." This may be an incomplete definition. The objective of the process includes the timely payment of expenses. In our review, we have identified two basic situations that will bring the process to an end. The first is distribution of the check to the employee and this correctly represents final completion of the process (the customer has received payment). However, the second situation—mailing the check to the vendor—does not perfectly complete the transaction; it does not mean the expense has been paid. It may be better to define the event ending process as "Vendor receives check." If this is the true termination point, the maps are incomplete. While it is impossible to take into account all aspects of delivering the checks to vendors, the maps could, at the very least, take into account the company's mail service or methods used to ensure receipt of the payment. If the termination point is redefined, there is more work to do.

Inputs and Outputs

The input items (bill or invoice) are properly identified. The reviewer might want to ask a few questions to determine whether there are any other documents that can generate expenses, but the major documents seem to have been included. The stated source of the input (employee) shows there may be some confusion internally. We already discussed how identifying "Receive bill" as a trigger shows a good understanding of the customer involved in the process. However, that customer is also the true source of the document; identifying the employee as the source may be inadequate. A more accurate source is the vendor. If the focus of the review is to stay within the company, the employee can be the correct source. However, if a broad focus (a truly customer-focused approach) is used, the person supplying the bill actually generates it. Since we ultimately want to focus on customer satisfaction, the external approach of including the customer in the process may be the correct one. In our example, this redefinition only means that additional discussions may need to be held with the process owner to ensure a complete understanding of the customers, the triggers, and the inputs.

The basic output is the check, and the ultimate customer is the vendor. However, there are deeper concerns with the outputs. Remember that the actual output is only one of the four types of results that may occur from a process. The second result is "waste." Looking at the maps, there are a number of situations in which inaccurate or incomplete output can result. One obvious example is the "Verify Request (1.3) and E-Mail Request (1.4)—Action Level" map, which is repeated in Exhibit 7.2. At the start of this part of the process is a review, which is intended to ensure the request is complete. If there are problems, this action will end up causing waste, a result that does not provide the value expected. Additional examples are evident in the two "Field Non-Match—Request/No Check" drill-down maps and the "Field Non-Match—No Corresponding Check or Request" map. These are shown again as Exhibits 7.3 through 7.5. Each of these represents a specific process intended to identify and correct errors. Any time spent on these processes represents waste, both in the time spent to produce a flawed product and to correct that flawed product. We look at this more closely when we begin to analyze the maps.

The next result is surprises. In Chapter 6, we discussed three potential surprises that might exist with the *Expense Payment* process: missed due dates, increased workload, and increased mailing costs. The final result is invisible consequences. This, too,

Exhibit 7.2   Verify Request (1.3) and E-mail Request (1.4)—Action Level

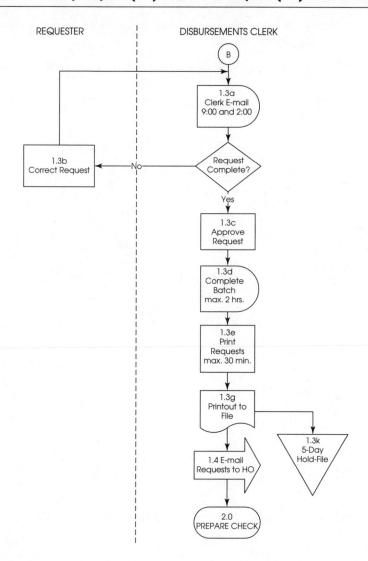

was discussed in Chapter 6 and includes loss of reputation and decreased morale.

Process Owners

Based on the discussions documented in Chapter 3, the process owners have been properly identified. Ultimately, the treasurer is the primary owner. The two managers—home office and field

Exhibit 7.3   Field Non-Match—Request/No Check (3.1c)—Drill Down

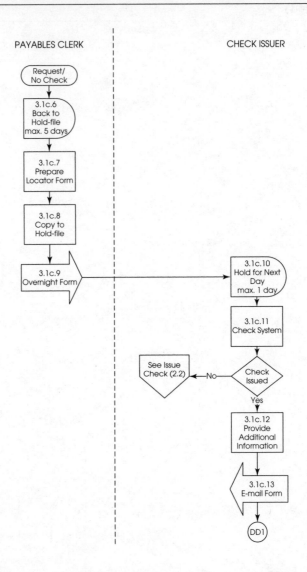

office—own the underlying parts of the process. This helps reinforce ownership of the interchanges between the two departments
throughout the process. In addition, as the Process Mapping project
progresses, these distinctions will also help determine each individual's involvement in final decisions regarding suggested changes
to the process. Individuals at the manager level will be probably be

Exhibit 7.4   Field Non-Match—Request/No Check (3.1c)—Drill Down (Continued)

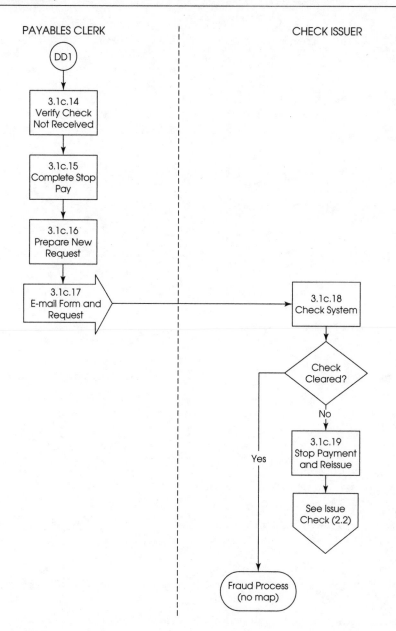

Exhibit 7.5 Field Non-Match—No Corresponding Check or Request (3.1c)—Task Level

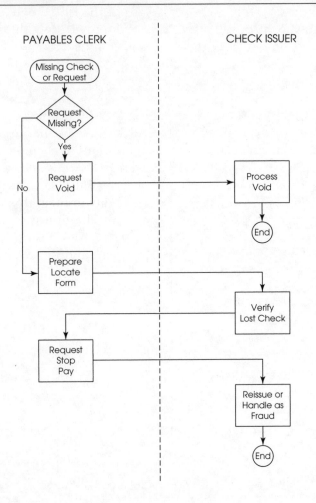

used to enforce the implementation of actions; the Treasurer will be used to provide final authority and to resolve any disputes that may occur.

Business Objective

The business objective has been identified as "prompt and accurate payment of valid, properly approved business expenses." The objective itself seems well defined—including timeliness, accuracy, and

propriety. It is important to verify that all steps in the process help
support these objectives.

As an example, it is already apparent that the timeliness objective is not being met. We previously discussed how the delays in
processing (the numerous holding bins, transfers, and batch processing) make it impossible to meet the promise of a 48-hour turnaround. A deeper look reveals that the emphasis on the other two
aspects—accuracy and propriety—may contribute to the inability
to ensure the first—timelines. The number of approvals and reviews
are indicative of this problem. We look at these further when we discuss the actual maps, but it is always important to keep the objective
of the process in mind during the analysis. In the final assessment,
it may be that the company's approach to centralizing the payment
process is the ultimate culprit in its inability to meet the timeliness
requirements. This is not to say that centralization is good or bad
in itself. Rather, that the company's approach to this centralization
may be contributing to the problems we are finding. We will discuss
this in more detail at the end of this chapter.

Business Risk

The original business risks identified—fraudulent payments,
delayed payments, missed discounts, and customer dissatisfaction—
are still applicable. They tie in with the objectives and explain the
need for certain steps in the process. In addition, there have been
no new high-level risks identified that might have been missed.

Key Controls

Everything we have learned about this process's problems leads us
to suspect that key control identification is incomplete. Currently,
only one control has been identified—segregation of duties. This is
followed by a list of some of the segregations—requester/approver,
requester/issuer, and issuer/retriever. It is becoming apparent that
the accuracy and propriety objectives are the only ones the process
owner has focused on. Despite the owner's protestations that all are
of equal importance, key control identification shows that this is
not correct. If timeliness were truly important, the process owner
would have advised the reviewers of any key controls over that area.
Since there are none, the owner is sending an unspoken message
that this is not important.

There are measurements in place (as discussed in the next section), but no way to ensure that these benchmarks are met. In fact, some of the actions in the process show a decided lack of interest in achieving timeliness. In the description of the check matching process, the point is made that all checks are held until all checks for that office are completed. There is no evaluation to determine rush items. There is no accommodation to send partial groups of checks if the overnight deadline is approaching. In general, completing the tasks is more important than timely delivery of checks. Consideration of either one of these suggestions would show that the owner had some concern for timeliness issues.

Ultimately, there must be a key control that deals with the timeliness objective. None is apparent from the existing maps, and that provides evidence of the problem we are seeing. Discussions should be held with the process owner to develop these key controls, possibly including a rush payment process, an online tracking system, or a daily report on timeliness. However, the best solution will be one developed within the department. It is possible that the process owner might disagree and believe that such controls are unnecessary. In that situation, the final report may need to indicate the disconnect between the objectives of the process and the reality, allowing the reader to reach the necessary conclusions.

Measures of Success

Analysis of the measures of success continues to reveal some of the disconnects between objectives, controls, and measurements. Three of the measurements relate to timeliness—issuance within 48 hours, use of early pay discounts, and complaints about delays. However, there is no control to ensure that these occur. The last measure of success—absence of duplicate payments—has to take on the duty of measuring success related to accuracy and propriety of payments. And it is obvious that it is insufficient to properly measure such success.

The lack of measurements over accuracy and propriety provides some understanding as to why there is a preponderance of controls over them. Because there is no way to measure success, there is no assurance that controls are effective. In response, management has developed more and more controls. In its quest to completely mitigate risks associated with these objectives, the objective of timeliness has taken a backseat.

There must be extensive discussions with the process owner regarding this area. The first task should be development of a measurement system. Something as simple as keeping track of the error ratios might provide sufficient information. The second task should be to see if some of the approvals and reviews can be eliminated. We discuss this in more detail when reviewing the maps, but it is important to note that until we know how successful certain tasks and actions in the process are, we cannot determine which to eliminate without compromising controls.

Analyzing the Maps

Now it is time to dig into the actual maps. Rather than explore each map individually, we will analyze them using the basic approaches discussed in Chapter 6. As we have frequently stated, the best analysis comes from looking at the process as a whole. However, benefits can also be found in these individual reviews.

Remove Approvals

It is apparent from the previous discussion that the high reliance on segregation of duties (including approvals) in this process may be related to the disconnect between objectives, controls, and measures of success. Approvals are an important part of that segregation. Obviously, not every approval can be eliminated, but removing or reducing some approvals is one step that might be taken to help alleviate the bottlenecks we are seeing.

In going through the maps, the first approval process we see is the one related to the initial approval of the request (see Exhibit 7.6, formerly shown as Exhibit 5.6). This is a basic control and a sacred cow to many people, but it warrants immediate analysis. One place to start is by asking how the budget process is used in expense control. A well-designed budget can be a control in itself. If the company uses the budget as a detective control—identifying when expenses are out of compliance—approvals may not be needed. In that situation, the ultimate control is how well the department meets its budget.

At the very least, verify that the approval levels are accurate. Why do all expenses have to be approved? Can this requirement be changed to approval only on items over $250? Why do expenses greater than $1,000 need a second approval? There may be legitimate

Exhibit 7.6 Approve Request (1.2)—Action Level

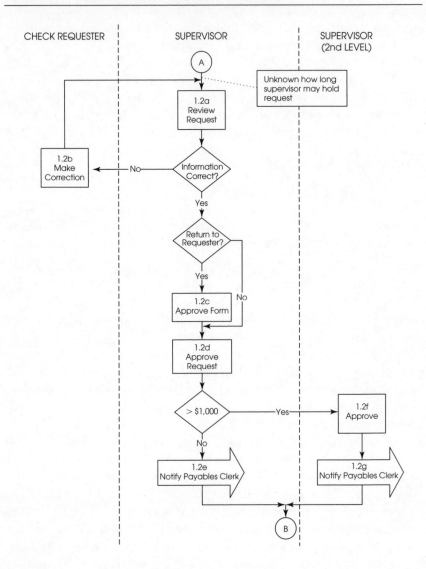

answers to these questions, but they must be asked to see if the approvals can be modified or removed.

In reviewing the need for approvals in this process, there is an important issue that should be addressed. This relates to one of the reasons approvals exist—assurance that requests are completed correctly. If this is a major problem in the company, the approval process might not be the answer. The real solution is training. In addition, a backup process exists to ensure correct completion—the disbursements clerk's review.

Another excellent example of an approval that needs further analysis is the one required for checks returned to the requester. What is the objective of this approval? Is there a compensating control? Is the risk associated with that control high enough to warrant delays in the process? These are the questions that should be asked regarding every approval found in a process. An approval may be the right choice, but be willing to question its value.

Looping Errors

There are a number of major loops in the *Expense Payment* process. Some of these relate to the way the drilled-down processes work within the *Expense Payment* process and are discussed later in this chapter. However, one of the first loops is shown in Exhibit 7.2—the requirement that the request be returned to the requester to correct errors of completeness. In some instances, this may be necessary. However, there are at least as many times when the disbursements clerk already knows what the correct information is. By allowing the clerk to make those changes, the elapsed time might be reduced by days.

As discussed in Chapter 6, there is a tendency to want to force the individual who made the mistake to correct that mistake. In addition, there is a concern that, if the individual does not understand that he did anything wrong, he cannot correct it. Rather than delay the process by forcing instruction or punishment, it is much better to facilitate processing and provide instruction at a later date. This is one loop that might be eliminated.

Isolate Delays

The *Expense Payment* process is rife with these types of situations (as well as rework and handoffs). There are 11 different instances in which the *D* shape is used to indicate a delay. (Note how easy it is to identify these when the shape is used.)

While it is true that the first instances of delay might occur when the request is waiting for approval, the first two instances on our maps are shown in Exhibit 7.2. Like most of the delays in these maps, these are the result of batch processing. There may be good reasons for batch processing (as we will see in a little bit), but batches are often just as big a sacred cow as approvals. In the first instance, the clerk is waiting to process received requests. This makes some sense, in that batching these items probably allows the clerk to work on other projects at other times. If the clerk was required to handle each request as it came in, the interruptions might result in a decline in quality for other processes. However, this delay also means it takes even longer to get incorrect requests back to either the requester or the approver. By delaying the review, an additional day could be added to the reimbursement process.

The second delay occurs when the clerk holds the approved requests, preparing to print out copies to be filed. It is not necessarily a bad idea to wait and print them all out at one time. But this raises the question: Why do they need to be printed? The answer—because copies need to go into the hold-file—is not completely satisfying. We will talk about hold-files later, but the need to establish one may point to the problems inherent in centralized processing, as practiced in this example. In this situation, the batch itself is not a problem, but it points to the broader problem in the process.

Another delay is shown in Exhibit 7.7 (formerly shown as Exhibit 5.9). Once again, the printed requests are held until all are completed. Approximately two hours later, the checks are printed out. A review of this process indicates that such a delay may be necessary. This will occur very often during analysis—something identified as a potential problem cannot be eliminated and is necessary. It is important to remember that the purpose here is just to take a second look, not to eliminate everything.

A delay warranting additional analysis exists in Exhibit 7.8 (formerly shown as Exhibit 5.8). The check issuance actions begin at 1:00 P.M. However, it is readily apparent that the requests are available much earlier in the day. We may be unaware of the reason such a delay has been put in the system. However, with the information we have, this delay seems unnecessary. This is particularly important, because overnight mail is picked up at 3:00 P.M. Depending on the volume of requests, it may be unreasonable to expect this entire unit to be completed in less than two hours. Yet that is exactly what must happen to achieve the 48-hour

Exhibit 7.7   Issue Check (2.2)—Action Level

turnaround. Beginning the action earlier in the day could allow as much as an additional three hours for completing the check issuance process.

These same types of analyses should be done on all 11 delayed actions. It is also a good idea to complete another review of the maps to see whether any delays exist that were not identified the first time

Exhibit 7.8   Prepare to Issue (2.1)—Action Level

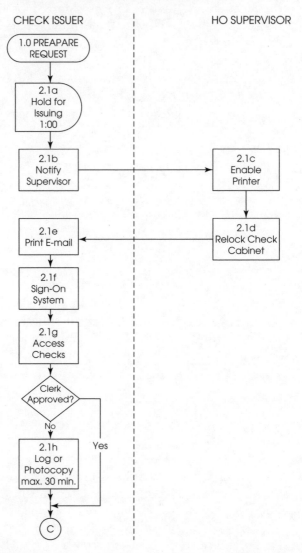

through. (For example, the transfer of the request from the requestor to the supervisor may be a source of delays. We will look into this as part of our discussion on isolating handoffs.) Again, all delays cannot be eliminated, but they should all be reviewed. And when we are completing that analysis, we begin to look at the broader issues, just as we did with the first delay.

Isolate Rework

Identifying these situations in the Process Maps is a little more difficult than identifying the delays. While the *D* shape was used for delays in constructing the maps, the *R* shape was not used for rework. Trying to isolate these instances in the current maps shows how use of these shapes can facilitate this analysis. However, there are some other obvious signs to look for. One example is the upstream flow of the process. This usually means items are going back to their source for additional work. The example we have already looked at a number of times is Exhibit 7.2. We have also discussed many solutions to this situation.

Another telltale sign of rework is connectors to maps that are not part of the normal process flow. In the expense report system, these are usually represented by drill-down maps. Prime examples are Exhibit 7.9 (formerly shown as Exhibit 5.12) and Exhibit 7.3. Exhibit 7.9, the situation where there is a request but no check, shows an example of rework. If the system shows the check was already issued, the check is stopped and reissued. This requires inputting the same information a second time and is a good example of rework. It is obvious that, in the given situation, rework is required—the check must be re-entered. But in analyzing this rework, we are not trying to eliminate the step. Instead we want to identify it as a potential area for analysis. Rework is an indicator of problems in the system. In this instance, the reviewer should determine the error rate (something that could have been included on the maps) and then determine why these situations occur. Again, the intent is to determine what flaws in the process require this rework.

Exhibit 7.3 shows a similar situation—a request but not a check. However, this time the check cannot be located in the field office. As is evidenced by the map, this is a much more complicated process. Ultimately, the rework is also the same—inputting data for a new check. But, again, the purpose of identifying the rework is not so much to evaluate the rework task itself as to analyze the associated processes. The same steps should be performed, including determining error rates and the causes of these errors. However, in this instance, reducing the error rate will result in much more significant savings to the company. The more complicated the process that is eliminated, the greater the benefits.

Exhibit 7.9   HO Non-Match—Request/No Check (2.4b)—Drill Down

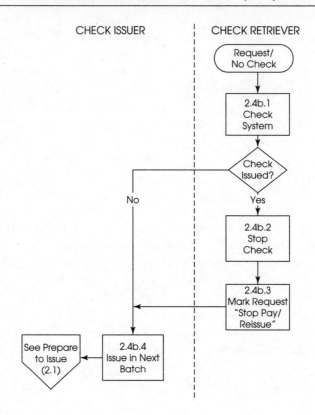

Isolate Handoffs

The purpose of isolating handoffs can be the same as that for identifying delays or rework. In some instances, just as we try to eliminate delays, we want to eliminate handoffs. In other instances, handoffs are akin to rework—an indicator of other problems. In the expense payment process, because it has been centralized, there are a lot of handoffs. The number is increased because of the focus on segregation of duties. Throughout these maps, the majority of these handoffs are shown with larger arrows. This was done to highlight those situations. However, in general, any time the map moves from one individual to the next there is a handoff.

Exhibit 7.10   Payment by Check Request—Unit Level

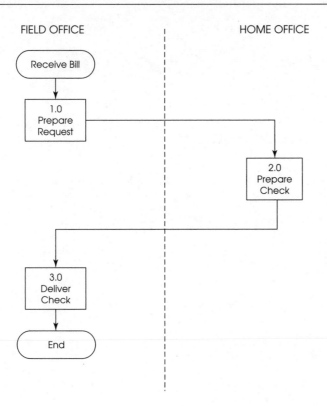

The existence of handoffs is shown in Exhibit 7.10, previously shown as Exhibit 5.1. The unit-level map indicates that the first unit exists in the field office, the second in the home office, and the final one back in the field office. The following task-level maps (Exhibits 7.11 through 7.13, previously shown as Exhibits 5.2 through 5.4) then show the handoffs between departments within each of these offices. This high-level cursory review does not reveal any particular problems; there is no real evidence that handoffs are going back and forth between offices or departments. It is important to point out here that no single handoff is necessarily bad. Problems begin to occur as handoffs pile one on top of the other.

Exhibit 7.11   Prepare Request (1.0)—Task Level

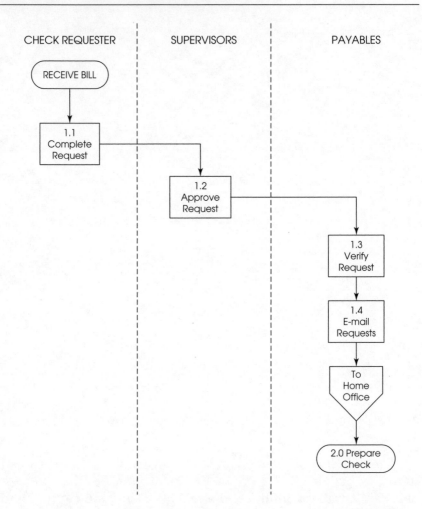

The first time large arrows are used to show a handoff is when the requests are approved (Exhibit 7.6). In these situations, the supervisor notifies the payables clerk that the request has been approved. While not a true physical handoff of the request, it does represent the transference of information from one person to another. These have been highlighted because the reviewer understood that this notification might result in a delay. A *D* shape could

Exhibit 7.12 Prepare Check (2.0)—Task Level

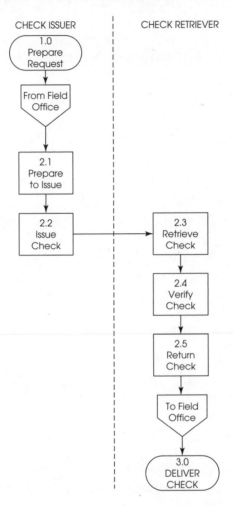

have also been used, but the arrow helps accentuate the handoff's attributes. This is an instance in which the problem may relate to the method of handoff. We have no indication of how the supervisors notify the payables clerk. If different methodologies are used, there could be inconsistencies in how the payables clerk moves forward with the process. In some instances, there may be no delay. In others, this could result in as many as two extra days being added to the process. There may not be an easy solution, but this must be evaluated to understand the impact.

Exhibit 7.13 Deliver Check (3.0)—Task Level

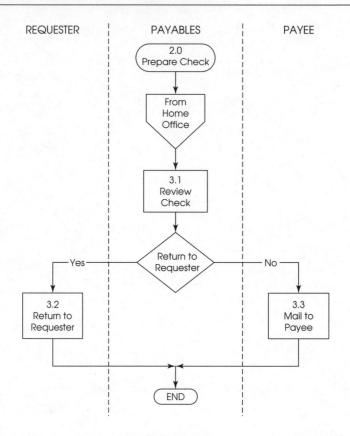

Another handoff worth looking at is not represented by large arrows. In fact, at first blush it might not be thought of as a handoff. This is shown in Exhibits 7.8 and 7.14. (This last was formerly shown as Exhibit 5.10.) Technically, nothing is handed off. However, the flow of the process goes back and forth, first between the issuer and the supervisor and next between the retriever and the supervisor. In some respects, the flow is handed off. Whenever this type of back-and-forth situation is encountered, the reviewer should take a look to see how much of it is really necessary. In this instance, there is an obvious concern for control over the check printer. The supervisory control over the check printer in these situations actually represents a kind of approval process (the type mentioned before that is not obvious.) It may be that this control causes no real delay and is not important. However, it does interrupt the supervisor's day and may cause delays for that

Exhibit 7.14   Retrieve Check (2.3)—Action Level

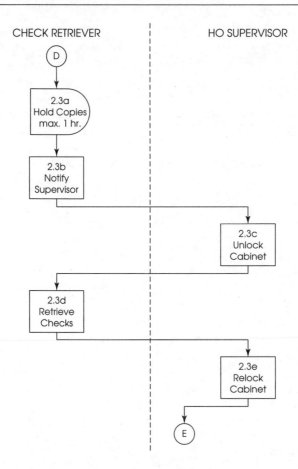

individual. The need for this control should be evaluated and weighed against the benefits of eliminating it.

The two most convoluted handoffs in the overall process are shown in Exhibits 7.3, 7.4, and 7.5. In these instances, documents are going from the field office (payables clerk) to the home office (check issuer) numerous times. There can be as many as three transfers between the offices, and these transfers take time (and money). Because these transfers relate to incorrectly processed items, the same analysis done for rework should be completed here. (What is the error rate, and why do errors occur?) But the analysis should also include ways to streamline the process. In Exhibit 7.5, for example, why does the disbursements clerk have to prepare the request for stop pay? If the check issuer completed the request, there would be two fewer handoffs. Keep in mind that there may be control issues requiring this, but, as has been mentioned before, it is something that should be reviewed to make sure it is the best process available.

•   There is another handoff that is not specifically indicated and could be the cause of significant issues. This is the point where the requester notifies the supervisor that the support has been faxed and the request is compete. This handoff actually occurs between the Complete Request map (Exhibit 7.15, formerly shown as Exhibit 5.5)

Exhibit 7.15   Complete Request (1.1)—Action Level

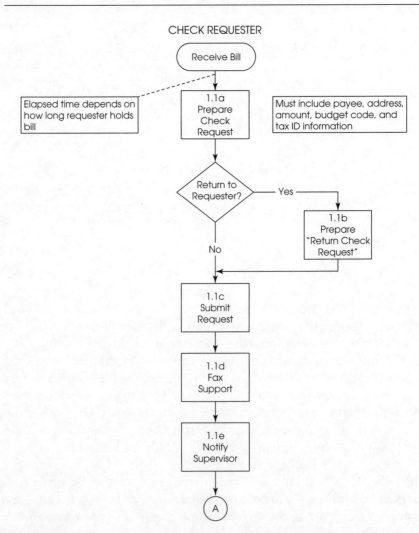

and the Approve Request map (Exhibit 7.6). Note that the two connecting tasks are *notify supervisor* and *review request*. Yet, there is nothing between those two tasks to indicate control over the transfer. In particular, there appears to be no control over the timeliness between notification and review. This point is emphasized in the maps with inclusion of the note indicating that the amount of delay is unknown. This represents something to watch for in the construction of Process Maps. In moving between these two maps, an important handoff may not be recognized.

Follow the Forms

No document flowcharts have been developed for this process, because the number of documents is not overwhelming. In addition, it is not hard to follow what happens with them. But there are a couple of points about the documents that become obvious as the maps are reviewed.

The first relates to the request itself (and sometimes copies of the request). It is the primary document, and it is at the heart of most of the process. It is used as a control in the field office when the original is e-mailed; the copy is used as a control in the home office when the check is issued. The maps show that there is a good understanding of this document's impact.

The second point relates to the Return to Requester form. Much is made about this form at the beginning of the process. There is an emphasis on it being prepared and approved. However, it completely disappears after the first action-level map. There may be a number of reasons for this. One reason might be that the maps did not go into additional detail on this area, with the assumption that any process the request went through included the return form. Another reason might be that the form is not reviewed after that initial request, because completing it serves the fundamental purpose of ensuring that the check must be returned to the requester. However, this is a form that should be closely analyzed. It may be that the form is not needed and can be eliminated (along with any associated processes).

Incomplete Maps: Dangling Actions and Unanswered Decisions

Looking at the maps, there are three instances in which the maps are not complete. The first occurs in Exhibit 7.8 and is not overtly obvious. At the end of this map, the issuer verifies the request has been approved. Depending on the issuer, the information is entered on a log or photocopies are made. However, there is no indication of what happens to the log or photocopies. As with any of these situations, it is possible that the reviewer purposely did not include that information on the map. However, there should be a reference to an unmapped process (as was done with the fraud process in Exhibit 7.4).

The more likely scenario is that there is no follow-up by the department on these items. (The primary evidence supporting this is that the clerical staff uses two different methods. If it were an important control, more standardization would be expected.) This means that one of two things should happen. The first is to develop a system that allows adequate follow-up. In this situation, it might be gathering statistics to determine which office has the highest error rate (non-approved items) or referring the items back to the servicing office to see if these are potentially fraudulent requests. The second solution is to eliminate the review entirely. Of course, that might mean eliminating the disbursements clerk's approval; if no one is checking to ensure an action is being taken, then that action might not need to be taken in the first place. As in all other situations, the need for a control must be weighed against the cost of that control.

The next two occurrences of incomplete maps are on Exhibit 7.16 (formerly shown as Exhibit 5.13) and Exhibit 7.17 (formerly shown as Exhibit 5.15). This is the situation in which the map is incomplete, because information goes into a file and never comes out. In this instance, it is most likely because the time period for retention of voided checks is based on statutory requirements. To make this more complete (and eliminate the questions that can come from dangling actions), the map could include the final disposition of items maintained in storage.

Question Hold-Files

There is really only one hold-file evident in the process maps. (This ignores any hold-files individual requesters may establish to ensure that the check is issued.) This hold-file appears in Exhibit 7.2 and reappears in Exhibit 7.3. The hold-file itself seems to be a necessity. It is the only way to ensure that checks are received. It also

Exhibit 7.16   HO Non-Match—Check/No Request (2.4b)—Drill Down

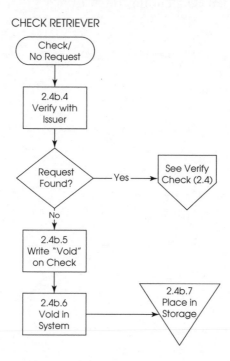

CHECK RETRIEVER

seems to be developed in a very logical fashion. What may need analysis is the time frame established. The company is promising a 48-hour turnaround, yet the hold-file is set for five days. This represents a very pessimistic attitude toward the objective. It may be a good indicator of just how long the process actually takes. However, our analysis of this process shows that it may be very slow. The five-day hold-file may be overly optimistic, and may result in the clerk pulling numerous items just to re-diary them. The analysis should include a recommendation regarding the adequacy of the length of the hold-file.

Another aspect of the use of hold-files may relate to how few of them there are. While it is true that the analysis is trying to determine which hold-files might be eliminated, it may be that the hold-file is the perfect control (as described previously) and its absence is as much a problem as anything. For example, there are a few situations in which the field office requests that a check be voided or a stop payment be placed on the check. There is no indication that they

Exhibit 7.17   Field Non-Match—Check/No Request (3.1c)—Drill Down

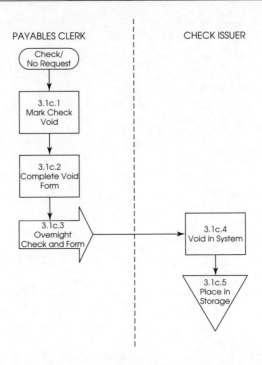

verify that these actions actually occur. The quickest and easiest solution is the establishment of a hold-file set for the appropriate number of days after the request is submitted. When the hold-file comes up, the system can be reviewed to ensure that the appropriate action took place.

Miscellaneous

The prior discussion has focused on the basic reviews that can be done to find problems in the process map. However, there may be many situations you face that do not fall into these categories. For example, it is interesting to note that the check request is completed online. However, the Return Check to Requester form is completed manually. The reviewer may want to take the time to analyze why this is required and how much additional time this takes the requester. It may be a simple reason; for example, it's possible the designers of the system did not know this form was required, or the form may have been developed after the mechanical system was put in place. (We have seen such things happen.) After the fact, this seems obvious. But such considerations are not always included as processes are developed, and the Process Mapping project may be the first time anyone has asked such questions.

Another example exists in Exhibit 7.8. We discussed the handling of nonapproved requests, but glossed over an important point. Some issuers are photocopying exceptions, while others are logging them. There should be one standard approach. While the analysis may show that either is unnecessary, if value is found in the action, everyone should do it the same way. The solution to this depends on what the process owner wants to accomplish. Logging items helps show trends that can be provided to the field offices. Photocopies can be used to determine the legitimacy of the request.

There are probably more flaws and problems with the system that you have identified, but this is intended to give you just a few ideas on how analysis can be completed. In fact, if you have seen additional problems, you are starting to get the hang of how to use maps for analysis.

The Bigger Picture

Looking at this entire process, there appears to be one fundamental flaw: The centralization of the expense payment process is not providing customer value. Because there has not been a full commitment to this approach, the overall result is bad. As with so many other aspects, the solutions depend on what the process owner ultimately wants to achieve. But the analysis completed through process mapping should help in the decision. Overall, these solutions fall into two different categories—full centralization or full regional operation.

The first solution is to take the middleman (field accounting) out of the process. This would require submission of requests directly to the home office. This cannot work if the layers of approvals and reviews are maintained. The process maps show the delays that are already occurring because of these hierarchies. If these are maintained, the problems will only be exacerbated. This solution only works if the requesters are empowered to spend as they see necessary and the home office is allowed to make corrections with as little help from the field office as possible.

The second solution is to move check issuance to the field office. This would require access to online systems and an increase in the number of issuance facilities. This approach would allow the maintenance of tight controls over accuracy and propriety, while increasing the timeliness of check issuance. The associated costs would have to be weighed against these benefits.

In general, the review has helped establish not only the smaller problems that are causing this process to fail, but also the large overriding problem. Implementing any of these solutions helps lead to the ultimate success of the process. But just addressing the large one still requires an understanding of the way the smaller parts work together.

Recap and Key Analysis Points

This chapter provided some practical application of the analysis techniques described in Chapter 6. As such, it covers much of the same territory but in a less theoretical way.

While analysis of the process should be done holistically, just as all other aspects of Process Mapping, following some simple rules may help. Start with the Process Profile Worksheets and then look through all aspects of the maps. Never forget that the focus of the process must be on the customer. Evaluating the worksheets and maps with this in mind will help ensure that the process adds value.

When analyzing maps, take a close look at the standards that have been established. Output is the normal result of a process, but waste is another. However, waste is defined by the user. Changing the standards (e.g., eliminating the need for an approval) may result in a reduction in the number of items considered waste.

Also remember that identifying individual items in the maps (e.g., rework, delays, and handoffs) is not necessarily meant to lead to solutions; it is determining what causes them to happen. In general, Process Mapping is not about the *what*, but about the *why*.

Ultimately, Process Mapping should help lead to the big picture of what is wrong. Despite that, it is the details from Process Mapping that provide the best results.

CHAPTER 8

Pitfalls and Traps

We're drowning in information and starving for knowledge.
—Rutherford D. Rogers, librarian, Yale University

Challenges

We were first introduced to Process Mapping almost eight years ago, and since that time we have had incredible successes, humiliating defeats, and everything in between. In this chapter, we share some of the things we have learned through our years of experience. Every project brings new challenges and every project is different. While the basic techniques remain the same, this approach requires constant refocusing on what is important. Your first project will be radically different from the one you will do in a year or two. And you will make mistakes—it takes a while to perfect your technique. Do not get discouraged, do not skip steps, and do learn from your mistakes.

Mapping for Mapping's Sake

Mapping projects are undertaken with some broader issue in mind. It may be to examine efficiencies, review controls, ensure that the efforts of employees support strategic goals, or isolate the root cause of a particular problem. But whatever that issue, mapping is a tool used to help answer those broader questions. The map is the means, not the end.

Reviewers sometimes forget this. They focus on the mapping effort—the drawings on the wall and the details of the process. They forget to look at what they are mapping and why. They are compelled to map every piece of information given to them and to produce more and more maps. By focusing on the map, they lose sight of the true purpose of the project. Instead of achieving results, such as efficiencies and goal-oriented processes, the reviewer has . . . well, the reviewer has a lot of maps. Despite tons of information, the project has failed.

We were involved in a project in which every employee in a very large department was interviewed. Detailed maps were created of each person's job activities. Many of the maps listed only a single employee and all the steps that employee went through in a day to complete the job tasks. The reviewers were busy for several months and created a multitude of maps. But in the whole time they spent developing maps, they never analyzed them. At the end of the project, all they had were maps of individual tasks. They had transcribed information, but they had not made any effort to interpret it. They had not matched the process to the business objectives to ensure the objectives were being accomplished. They had not summarized the details into an overview. It was as if they had created a bunch of single shots but had not put them together into a scene, much less organize them into the overall theme of the movie. They were mapping for mapping's sake.

When we first started using the mapping approach in our audits of claim offices, we performed quality assurance reviews on a large number of the maps completed by other offices. We looked at all the maps and the reports for these audits and provided feedback to the auditors on the mapping process. We often saw reports that indicated there were no control issues, although there were glaring control breakdowns obvious in the maps. The auditors had completed the assignment—creating the maps—but they had never stepped back and taken a good look at what they created. They thought the maps were the end product.

Merely creating maps is not what Process Mapping is all about. The reviewer must step away from the details (and you *will* be buried in details) and take a good look at the processes under review. The reviewer must examine the maps to see what the information is revealing about the process. Does the process work as everyone expects it to? Does the process accomplish its objective? Are sound controls in place to ensure that the business objectives are accomplished and risks are minimized? Are there bottlenecks and inefficiencies? Does this process hang up another process due to excessive delays? Are moments of truth revealed in the maps? How does the process look from the customer's perspective?

You cannot create only the border and call the puzzle done. You must fill in all the pieces and see how they relate to the whole. The goal of Process Mapping is a holistic view of the function under review. It is visualizing the process as it relates to the whole. It is seeing how the function or process affects the strategic efforts of the company. Do not forget the analysis phase.

Lost in the Details

Getting lost in the details can be fostered by a "mapping for mapping's sake" approach. However, this problem is often due to the inability of the reviewer to put the details into an appropriate context. When you interview people, they will tell you literally *everything* about their job. It is the interviewer's job to decide whether the information is pertinent and how much detail needs to be documented.

Assume that someone tells you, "First thing in the morning I open the mail, I unfold each piece, I stack the mail in a pile, I look to see whose name is on the mail, I start stacks for each person who has mail, then I put the mail in everyone's incoming mail bin." What is critical in this process?

To answer this question, it is helpful to think in the verb–noun format. If you mapped every detail of this person's morning, you would have boxes for "open mail," "unfold mail," "stack mail," "identify recipient," "sort by recipient," and "file in mail bin." Six boxes detailing how to open the mail. You could even drill down farther regarding what happens if the recipient cannot be immediately identified. This would lead down an entirely different path with even more details. However, unless there is a major concern about this area, we probably could document the process with two entries: "sort mail" and "distribute mail."

Making sense of the details is one of the hardest things to do when you start mapping. You must synthesize information very quickly. Someone may talk to you for five minutes, and you summarize it with one box. Another person may give you more important details in five minutes than you got from anyone else in one hour. Using the team approach to mapping is helpful. As described before, one person is taking notes and another person is interviewing while they create the process map in real time with sticky-notes.

The note-taker should be taking detailed notes that summarize the critical issues being discussed. The note-taker is not merely a transcriber—taking notes verbatim—but someone who is charged with summarizing the critical events in the process. Reviewing the notes should show a synopsis that provides all the details necessary to complete the map. That means the notes must have just the right amount of detail without bogging down completely.

The mapper should also be synthesizing information as the conversation is progressing. The mapper must listen to what is being said and summarize the information concisely in a verb–noun format on the sticky-note. The mapper need not create a box for every detail. Instead, the details of the map should reflect the necessities of the project. If additional information is needed after the interviewee is gone, the team can always refer back to the notes.

The mapper also must decide where the information fits. The people being interviewed are usually involved in only a small portion of a process. The interviewer must be able to take the details provided and determine whether they are important only to this small part of the process or to the process as a whole. Tasks must be related to processes, and the appropriate "bucket" for this information must be found. If you have done a good job in the preliminary information-gathering phase of the project, you should already have a good idea of what tasks are involved in each process. Inputs and outputs, as well as critical trigger events, should have been identified. These should help you determine where the random pieces of information you receive should be ordered. Go back to the Process Evaluation Worksheets if you are getting lost in the details. Review the objectives, risks, trigger events, inputs, outputs, and measures of success.

As a side note to getting lost in the details, it is also important to maintain a positive relationship with the interviewee. Although you want to avoid unnecessary details, you must find a tactful way to bring them back to the core of the discussion. Sometimes, even if you are not particularly interested in the information they are providing, you must make sure you are actively listening and acknowledging the contribution. We sometimes write sticky-notes with more detail than we ever intend to put into a final map just to let the interviewees know that we heard what was being said and that we realize it is important information to them. Just because it is on a sticky-note does not mean it has to be in the final map. When you translate from the sticky-note medium to a mapping software program, you again have an opportunity to synthesize information. Know your path, synthesize, synthesize, synthesize, and do not get lost in the details.

Penmanship Counts

This may sound elementary, but even the initial Process Maps—the sticky-notes you are slapping on the walls—must, at some point, be legible to the participants in the project. The intent is for the interviewee to see the process as it is developed. They are urged to become part of that development, moving the pieces around to result in the proper picture. But they cannot do this if they cannot understand what is on the wall.

The first point is that you should fully explain the process that will be used in building the maps. Outline what you are trying to achieve, provide information on the processes that are being reviewed, and explain how the final product will be built using their input and your sticky-notes. As you go along, make sure they understand each step you are adding and why you are adding it. This should be based on the information they have just provided, so it should not be hard to accomplish. But reinforcing it provides one more opportunity to ensure you have the right information.

The second point is that you should write as clearly as possible on the sticky-notes and try to keep the overall map in some kind of organized chaos. We both have very bad penmanship. And when we are involved in interviews, we find ourselves getting excited about the discoveries, excited about the maps, and excited about the entire process. This excitement means that we work faster building the maps, and neatness begins to take a backseat. At first, this is manifested when the information on the sticky-notes is not completely legible. Then it gets worse as we add notes so fast we lose track of our own requirements on how to build a Process Map. Lines start going across functions, extra notes are stuck to the wall, and it soon looks more like a flock of sticky-notes than an organized representation of a process.

In one particular instance, we spent approximately an hour talking with an analyst. She began describing her job and we followed up with questions. All through this we quickly scribbled verb–noun actions on sticky-notes and tried to throw them where they belonged. Arrows starting wrapping around actions, and names and positions were being added wherever they would fit. As we wrapped up the interview we were at the stage where we were ready to ask, "Does this look like the process?" We looked at our "map," we looked at each other, and we knew that, even though this made sense to us (after all, we can read our handwriting), it was gobbledygook to the interviewee. We didn't have to start completely over, but we did have to start with a clean sheet of paper.

Round and Round, Up and Down

Process maps should represent a flow of tasks over time. Some people, especially those trained in traditional flowcharting techniques, tend to make process maps look like traditional flowcharts. Numerous symbols may be used to depict different types of operations or documents. Lines and arrows are going up, down, and all around the page. A related mistake that is commonly made results from people being obsessed with keeping the map on one page. They violate the time rule and place sequential tasks at the top of the page with appropriate lines and arrows directing the reader back to the top of the page.

Remember that time is running down the page just like water over a waterfall. Water running over the waterfall drops straight to the bottom and then proceeds on its journey down a river or stream. The water may split as it falls, veering off on slightly different paths, but it all eventually gathers in the pond at the waterfall's end. There will be eddies and spray when water, for the moment, leaps up, but gravity and time always win, and the flow continues downward.

Just as water cannot run up the waterfall, sequential tasks should not be forced back up to the top of the page. Adhering to the sequential linear flow helps simplify the maps. When the process is laid out showing the appropriate time progression, delays in the process can be visualized and quickly identified.

Process maps should adhere to the KISS (Keep It Simple, Stupid) principle. When done correctly, process maps can summarize both high-level information on multiple processes and very detailed information on units or individual tasks. Use drill-down techniques and create additional maps as necessary. Avoid the temptation to cram everything onto one page. If it doesn't fit, it doesn't fit, and you will need to use a connector that allows the map to spread over multiple pages.

Generally, flowcharts are confusing to people who have not been trained in flowcharting techniques. A map may perfectly represent a process, but if it appears overwhelming, no one will use it. If symbols go up, down, and around, and arrows and nodes go every which way, only the creator will use the map. Process maps should provide value to the customer after the reviewers leave. Maps can be used to assist in re-engineering efforts, to help train employees, and to help educate employees on how their piece of the puzzle fits into the whole. However, if the maps are so complicated they require an interpreter; the customer will never look at them again. The goal is to produce maps simple enough that someone who does not know anything about the process could look at the maps and follow the basic flow of events. The average user should be able to easily identify who is involved in the process, the major tasks performed in the process, the duration of the process, and the duration of associated tasks.

A good process map is like a work of art. The lines should be aesthetically pleasing, flowing naturally from task to task. A map should be clear and concise, pleasing to the eye and mind. It should not be cluttered with too much detail or too many symbols.

Failure to Finalize

We generally try to finalize maps as we go, rather than waiting until the end of the project to do so. We already discussed our initial Process Mapping engagement, where we left the mapping until the end and were totally overwhelmed. Now, as soon as a sticky-note map is complete and has been verified with the interviewees, we try to transfer that map to a flowcharting package the same day.

Maps should be finalized while the details are still fresh in your mind and while you still have access to the people who were interviewed. Loose ends may become apparent as you start finalizing the map. You may have decision points that do not lead to a conclusion, or something that made perfect sense when the interviewee was speaking may now appear to be Greek. Finalizing the map as soon as possible results in less confusion and allows you the opportunity to clear up any unresolved issues.

Finalizing the maps means more than just completing them. It also includes reviewing them with the unit owner. The maps that have been created reflect how individuals involved in the process perceive, or want you to perceive, how the process works. This may be very different from how the unit owner perceives the process, or it might be different from how the process is actually working. (As discussed later in this chapter, testing may be necessary to validate the accuracy of the maps.)

We were in an office reviewing the procedure for paying rental car bills. This procedure stated that the bills should be paid as soon as they were received. The unit owner indicated that the procedure was being followed. Discussions with clerical personnel revealed a different story. There had been some turnover in the office, and the clerical staff was spread very thin. The staff told us that the bills were being placed in a pending file until they could get to them. They did not know how long it was taking to pay the bills, but they knew they were behind. They just kept filing them in alphabetical order to detect any instances of duplicate bills. If a vendor called, they would pull the bill and request payment the same day. If a vendor did not call, the bills stayed in the pending file for an undetermined time.

We reviewed the map with the clerical personnel, who agreed that we had properly documented the process. However, when we were reviewing the map with the unit owner, we got to the area where the bills were placed in a pending bin awaiting payment and the unit owner disagreed with us. He believed there was no way the process could have broken down this way. We then asked the clerk to pull the pending folder. There were more than 300 bills in the folder, with initial billing dates up to 6 months old. Needless to say, the unit owner was extremely surprised and had no idea the bills were being pigeonholed. By reviewing this map with the unit owner and verifying what was actually taking place, we were able to get corrective action immediately. Overtime was authorized to alleviate the problem, and the process was changed so that batch payments could be made to the vendor on a weekly basis, eliminating the need to issue a check for each individual rental car bill.

When problem issues are identified in the mapping process, it is a good idea to get the input from all parties on potential solutions to the problem. Ultimately, either the unit owner or the process owner is responsible for resolving the problem, but people doing the work may come up with some excellent ideas. Side notes can be included on the map to indicate where improvements could be made. You can use these side notes as a discussion point with the unit owners and process owners.

We think it is more effective to review the final maps face-to-face with the parties involved—interviewees and owners. While you may want to leave the map so the client has time to review it and develop questions, we find it beneficial for the reviewer to walk the person through the map, one step at a time, during the verification process. This should only take a minute or two per map, and provides much better results than leaving a copy of the map with the person and asking to be advised if anything is wrong. Sometimes you do not have the luxury of being able to review the maps face-to-face, and you may have to leave them for comments. If they must be left before they are finalized, you should follow up with a phone call to discuss any outstanding issues.

Letting the Customer Define the Process

The ultimate success of a Process Mapping project means total buy-in from all customers involved. It also means getting input from the people who know the process. Many times you will become involved in a process where you may have a good feel for the overall process, but underlying details are yet to be understood.

Despite this, you must facilitate discussions and help develop an end product that will give real value to all parties involved. The customer may be the expert on the process, but you are the expert on Process Mapping. We have spent a lot of time going over the terms and ideas that are fundamental to completing a Process Mapping project. These terms are common enough that everyone thinks they understand what they mean, but in a Process Mapping situation (as we have learned) there are subtleties involved in those definitions. That means that as you lead the group through discussions, you must tactfully lead them away from their own preconceptions.

This is true for almost any of the definitions—trigger, input, output, even customer. However, one of the biggest pitfalls usually involves misunderstanding what a process is. We were involved in a mapping project that the department head planned on using for developing objectives for the following year. This was a high-level review. To begin the project, we spoke with the heads of each section about risk structures and how controls affect final objectives. Eventually, we began discussing what processes they thought were involved in their department.

Many of the processes were basic and fell in line with the types you would expect to see in any company. But as we continued, the participants began identifying areas that were not true processes. Examples included areas such as decision making, customer service, and management. Now, each one of these might be thought of as a process, but they are not business processes of a type that can actually be analyzed. For example, decision making is actually a part of every function. Every input must go through a transformation, and there are usually decisions made regarding that input. So it is often impossible to separate decision making from other processes. Customer service is usually only a process if you specifically have a customer service department, and in those instances, the processes are usually better defined as complaint handling or order processing. However, these processes were apparently a concern to the department, and they wanted to bring that point forward.

Unfortunately, we did not help direct the customer to the correct processes. While it did not significantly sabotage the project, it did cause later meetings to become bogged down in irrelevant discussions. As new concepts regarding Process Mapping were introduced to the customers, the nonconforming processes did not match the model being described. This ultimately resulted in wasted time for the customers and for us.

At the end, the final product was still good, but there were areas where arguments and discussions were not as strong. Those were the areas where "non-processes" were forced into the process model. Always remember that you are the one who knows where the project is going, and it is important to help the customer get there based on your knowledge.

Leading the Witness

In a court of law, attorneys are prohibited from asking leading questions or putting words in the witness's mouth. When you are interviewing someone and you know the process very well, it is sometimes tempting to direct people to the right answer. The minute you start "leading the witness," though, you start getting responses that tell you what you want to hear rather than responses that tell you what is actually happening.

In the auditing world, every auditor eventually uses an internal control questionnaire at some point in his or her career. These questionnaires are designed to ensure auditors cover the important aspects of the control structure in a given function. Good internal control questionnaires use open-ended statements, such as "Explain how the process is performed." Less-effective questionnaires ask yes-or-no questions, such as "Are you reconciling the account?" People can figure out what the proper answer is to a yes-or-no canned question. Auditors are often surprised when someone answers "yes," and test work reveals the answer is really "no." Good auditors, even when faced with a set of yes-or-no questions, will use open-ended questions that encourage an interactive response on the part of the person they are interviewing. The auditors will then determine whether the question deserves a "yes" or a "no" based on the discussion with the interviewee.

The reviewer in a Process Mapping engagement must capture the process as it actually occurs. Yes-or-no questions do not lend themselves to the give-and-take necessary to effectively achieve this. Let us say the procedure states that all check requests over $500 must be approved by the supervisor. When you are interviewing the accounts payable clerk, she states that she inputs all of her own check requests. The interviewer could lead this person to the correct answer if she asks, "Do you get your supervisor's approval on all check requests over $500?" The better question would be, "Under what set of circumstances do you get approval before issuing a check?" To the second question, the person could answer, "There has never been a situation where I had to get my supervisor's approval," and still think she is answering the question correctly. Another response might be "Whenever a request is greater than $1,000, I get my supervisor's approval." Had the leading question that included the $500 amount been used, the interviewee might have seen the mistake and answered differently.

It is also important to remember that if the person does answer incorrectly, it is not appropriate to tell them that they are not following the proper procedure. As mentioned before, it is inappropriate to give a reaction that might make the interviewee think a horrible mistake has been made. Reaffirm the answer and go on.

The issue should be addressed with the unit owner, along with any proposed corrective action. The unit owner would then be responsible for educating and monitoring the employee's performance to ensure that proper approvals are being obtained.

Ultimately, the best question is always, "What is the next action you take?" or "Could you explain what you do?" This allows the interviewee the opportunity to expound on the work being done without the restraints of yes-or-no questions. Ask open-ended questions whenever possible, and try not to lead the witness.

Verifying the Facts

Even if you are careful to ask open-ended questions, and you create a great interactive environment, people may still misrepresent the facts—intentionally or unintentionally. If reliance is being placed on certain key controls, it is prudent to perform some limited testing to verify that the control is working as represented. For example, if you are relying on approval controls, pull a quick sample of transactions that should have evidence of the proper approval, and verify that the actions are being taken. If a receptionist tells you all calls are answered within three rings, phone the office a few times and see if the statement proves to be true.

A prime area for testing is the measures of success for the process. Is there hard evidence that shows the measures of success are being met? If not, you may need to review a sample of transactions to determine why the process is not accomplishing the intended goal. The maps you have prepared can help guide you through the process of reviewing transactions. You may find that some people told you what they know should be done, rather than what is actually being done.

Verifying the facts can often be done through simple observation. When we review a check disbursement operation, we want to make sure issued checks are properly safeguarded and promptly mailed. In one office we visited, interviews with employees indicated that checks were put in envelopes and mailed out immediately after they were issued. However, when we walked through the office, we saw two desks piled with issued checks, some with dates from five days earlier. No one had mentioned this obvious bottleneck. Further discussions revealed that the person normally responsible for mailing the checks had been assigned phone duty in the afternoon and was not able to keep up with her check distribution duties. Sometimes observation and additional testing are just intended to see what else to ask.

Determining what transactions to verify and how many transactions to review is always a tough decision. Critical transactions that pose a high risk to meeting key objectives are the transactions that should be verified first. Targeted samples of just those transactions can then be examined quickly to determine whether the process is working as intended. Sample sizes will often depend on the resources you have available. Volumes have been written on sampling methods and techniques, and we do not explore those issues here.

Another area that should usually be reviewed relates to any self-audits conducted over the area. It is best to select a small sample of those items to validate the results of self-audits. First, this will tell you the quality of those audits. Second, reviewing sample items will often bring out other areas of concern that may not have been covered in the initial mapping effort. Even a small sample of five to ten transactions or a casual observation of the process can provide the reviewer with some assurance that the maps reflect reality.

Do Not Forget the Customers

When you are heavily involved in analyzing processes, it is very easy to lose the customer's perspective. You can become so focused on the internal processes that you forget to look at how they are affecting external customers. Do not forget that the maps should help show where the moments of truth are occurring. Take a look at all of the areas where the business has some interaction with the customer. At each one ask the questions, "Is it easy to do business with this company? Why? Why not?"

The authors have had a standing disagreement on whether customer service orientation is a process. It may or may not be a process, but it is an attitude that permeates a department, a function, and the entire business. When you Process Map a function, you will get a strong indication of whether the entity has a positive customer service orientation.

In one of our first Process Mapping engagements, literally everyone we spoke with in the office mentioned that their first responsibility was to take care of the customer. This was from the highest level of management to the transcription clerk. The transcription clerk went into great detail explaining how important her work was because the letters she produced were seen by every customer. The office exemplified a positive customer service orientation. Conversely, in another office, it was clear from our discussions with employees that many had an adversarial relationship with customers. It was a classic "us against them" mentality from the top down.

Both offices operated under the same strategic guidelines and the same procedures. However, it was clear that management in one office fostered a positive attitude, whereas management in the other office did not. While these may be soft issues, difficult to quantify, they are critical to the success of the business. Whenever possible, we try to include these types of problems in our final report. It is not always well-received by the process owners, but we feel a responsibility to give them the complete picture. It is the reviewer's duty to look at the business through the customer's eyes and report any adverse findings back to upper management.

Recap

The fundamentals of Process Mapping are simple, but its application is as complicated as the processes you review. You will make mistakes, and it is important to learn from them. We want to share our mistakes to help you avoid them.

You are not being asked to make maps—you are being asked to assist in the analysis of a process. However, it is very easy to get so wrapped up in the actual development of the maps that the purpose of the project is lost. Every time you finish talking with someone, take a look at the map and start analyzing. Get in the habit of making analysis the objective of the project rather than allowing the maps to exist on their own.

As an offshoot to the prior pitfall, it is just as easy to become so wrapped up in the minutiae you are receiving that you lose sight of the big picture. As you are getting the details from interviewees, always try to keep the overall objectives of the process in mind. If the details are unimportant to either the process being mapped or the objectives of the Process Mapping project, they are not necessary.

One excellent way to help maintain this focus is by using two people—a recorder and a mapper—to complete each interview.

Speed is not of the essence. Take the time to explain to the interviewees what they can expect, and take the time to build a relatively coherent map when you first put the sticky-notes up on the wall. If they can't understand what you have developed when you ask them to verify it, it is of no use.

Maps are a very effective tool for the reviewer and for the process or unit owner. However, convoluted maps that only the reviewer can understand are useless. To help maintain the simplicity of Process Maps, remember they should be constructed so that they flow chronologically down the sheet of paper. There are rare instances in which a map references an earlier step and will momentarily flow upstream, but this approach should be used sparingly. An additional point related to this is that the reviewer should use as many sheets of paper as necessary. There is no requirement that a map be completed on one page.

There are two important steps in bringing the mapping project to a close—transferring the sticky-note maps to a charting software and talking with the process owners. Maps should be transferred to software as soon as possible. It should be done while the information is still fresh in the team's minds and the individuals interviewed are still available. Once maps are done, it is just as important to make sure that they are discussed with all levels responsible. This helps ensure that the information is correct and helps bring the process owners into the completed project.

While the language of Process Mapping is not based on unfamiliar vernacular, it does have nuances that may not be understood by the customers. Accordingly, it is up to you to help facilitate discussions in such a way that accurate information is obtained. That means helping lead the customers to the correct conclusions without leading them to what you think the conclusions should be. Ultimately, do not let the customers allow the project to get off track. You have been brought in as the expert on Process Mapping—use that responsibility to lead the project to a successful conclusion.

If you want a true picture of how a process works, you must allow the people involved in the process the chance to tell you how it is done. Questions should be expressed in a way that prompts dialogue—an exchange of information from the interviewee to the interviewer. Closed-ended and leading questions only serve to stifle discussions or, even worse, promote incorrect responses. Using open-ended questions may increase the length of interviews, but it will also increase the information obtained.

You will be given a lot of information. Some of it will be correct and some of it will be less than correct. In some instances, you will be able to verify this information through additional interviews. However, depending on the time available and the criticality of the information, actual testing may be necessary. Key areas for testing include measures of success, high-risk objectives, and self-audits conducted within the department.

As you dig deeper and deeper into a process, it is important to take a breath and remember the ultimate purpose of the process—satisfying some customers. These customers were identified at the beginning, and they should be considered throughout the project. As each map is constructed, look for the moments of truth and ask whether these are being used to their fullest example. In addition, look at the employees and determine whether they understand the importance of the customers to the process.

Key Analysis Points

While they are not true analysis points, keeping the following issues in mind while completing the Process Mapping will result in a better analysis of the process.

Why Am I Here?

Why was the project initiated, and what is the reviewer's purpose? Do not lose sight of what the project is all about. Do not get lost in the details.

Where Are We Going?

Is the process meeting some business objective? If the process is not accomplishing a business objective, does it even need to exist? Does everyone involved in the process understand what he or she is trying to accomplish?

Who Cares?

Ultimately, everyone's job depends on how the customer experiences each interaction with the company. Where are the moments of truth? Are they fostering a positive, caring customer relationship, or is anyone even paying attention to the customer's perspective? Walk through the business processes in the customer's shoes.

Who Is in Charge, Anyway?

The only person who truly cares about what goes on in a process is the individual who owns or has some responsibility for the process. The owner generally must authorize changes in the process. Know who the owner is and make sure he understands how the process is really working.

No Tool Is an Island

Process Mapping is more than just producing maps. It is a holistic approach to reviewing a business or a segment of a business. The maps are not the end product; the analysis of the operation is.

Information Is Power

Do not forget to gather data on the various measures of success. Gathering the data may lead you to areas where the process is breaking down or help you identify areas where it is working very well.

Keep It Simple

Chart the highest level possible, and if more detail is necessary, prepare a separate drill-down map.

CHAPTER 9

Customer Mapping

There is only one valid definition of a business purpose: to create a customer.

—Peter Drucker, *The Practice of Management*

Identify Jobs the Customer Wants to Get Done

As we have gone through a description of Process Mapping and the various actions that can lead to a full review of the process, you may have noticed a transition in our approach. When we first analyzed processes during the process identification phase, we spent a lot of time concentrating on trying to understand the process from the perspective of the customer. In fact, in our first attempt at understanding the actions within a process, we suggested viewing it through the camera eye of the customer.

But, as we progressed through the steps involved in a Process Mapping project, we began looking at internal processes. Our focus turned to the company: What does the company see as the objective of the process, what does the company see as the risk to the process, and how does the company measure the success of the process? Understanding the approaches involved in Process Mapping is easier when first approached from the company's perspective.

But now it is time to go back to that customer. It is time to think about objectives, risks, successes, and other aspects of the Process Mapping project in the customer's terms. As Peter Drucker has stated, a business is "defined by the want the customer satisfies when she buys a product or service." So we need to begin thinking in terms of what the customers want.

This "want" is a function of the jobs they need to get done. People ultimately choose to buy goods and services because they perceive those goods and services as being the ones that will best serve the purpose of getting the job done. Clayton Christensen, in his book *The Innovator's Solution,* points out "when customers become aware of a job they need to get done in their lives, they look around for a product or service they can 'hire' to get the job done." Carpenters hire saws to cut wood, teenagers hire cell phones to communicate with friends, and doctors hire stethoscopes to listen to the heart and lungs. Christiansen goes on to say that knowing what job a product gets hired to do (and knowing what jobs are out there that aren't getting done very well) gives a clearer road map towards improvement from the customer's perspective.

Anthony Ulwick, in his book *What Customers Want,* takes the concept of hiring products to achieve some purpose one step further, redefining the concept of outcome. He states that an outcome is "a metric that customers use to measure how well they are getting a job done." The ability to structure jobs so that they meet a customer's desired outcome can be critical to the success of an organization.

Up to this point, we have talked about Process Mapping's ability to use key metrics to determine whether the process is accomplishing its overall objective. In particular, we have focused quite a bit on improving efficiencies in some obvious areas—looking at opportunities to decrease rework, to eliminate handoffs, or to shorten cycle times. This seems intuitively correct, since most customers would see value in any changes which resulted in faster turnaround times. If, however, we are striving for more than just process improvement—more than just tweaking our way to success—then we need to analyze processes in a way that creates true innovation. This is innovation that greatly increases the value to either internal or external customer. As we've stated, to achieve increased value, we need to look closely at the jobs people are trying to get done. And that really means looking more closely at the outcomes they desire.

In other words, it's time to take the basic concepts of Process Mapping we previously discussed and turn them around to provide more focus on the customer. It is time to start delving into some of those differences.

Customer Mapping versus Process Mapping

The job the customer is trying to get done is just like any other process. There are inputs, a transformation occurs, and an output is generated. (And, using our new definition, the output is the customer getting the job done to her satisfaction.) By mapping the customer's job processes, focusing on the actions the *customer* must take to accomplish the job, an organization has a visual representation of the customer's journey. It can then analyze these maps to determine what the company can do to enhance the value of the job the company performs for the customer. This visual map can help identify unnecessary actions the customer must take to accomplish the job, as well as redundancies, wasted time, and rework that directly affect the customer. These are often the same things we identify in Process Mapping. However, notice the key word we are consistently using—*customer*. Process Mapping focuses on the processes affecting the company; Customer Mapping focuses on those processes affecting the customer. Analysis of the outcomes of each Customer Process focuses on answering the question, "What would bring more value to the *customer*?"

So, it all comes back to a very central question—how can we determine what customers want? As we did during the Process Identification step of Process Mapping, we need to start rolling the camera and look at the process through the customer's eyes. This time, we will do so with a renewed focus on the customer's desired outcomes. As Larry Bettencourt and Anthony Ulwick point out in their *Harvard Business Review* article "The Customer-Centered Innovation Map," the focus needs to be on the jobs the customer is trying to get done, not on what the company is currently doing. These jobs can be broken down into actions, and the actions can be examined for opportunities to improve the desired outcomes for customers.

The Steps of Customer Mapping

The initial foray into Customer Mapping will seem very similar to the Process Mapping project. Some of the process identification steps are almost identical to those used in Customer Mapping. (That is the reason we used the concept of visualizing the process through the customer's eyes in our Process Mapping example.) And throughout the Customer Mapping project, many of the same techniques are also used. However, the different concepts and definitions we have identified for Customer Mapping will result in a slightly different approach to the project. The steps are as follows:

- Define the job the customer wants done.
- Identify the key customer tasks and the actions required to accomplish those tasks.
- Identify inputs and outputs for each task.
- Identify measures of success for each task.
- Rank the importance of the measures of success.
- Determine how successful the company is at meeting each measure.
- Build the Customer Map.

It is quickly apparent that the concepts of the Process Profile Worksheet lend themselves quite well to the Customer Mapping process. In Process Mapping we identify the objective of the process and a description of the process. The same is true in Customer Mapping; we start by defining the job the customer wants to get done (the objective) and describing outcomes that are valued by the customer. Process Mapping looks at events that start the process, events that end the process, and key events in between. In addition, Process Mapping looks at inputs, outputs, and key controls. Customer Mapping follows the same basic outline—with a focus specifically on the job the customer wants to get done, the tasks the customer must perform to accomplish the job, and the customer's key measures of success. All critical aspects of the job the customer wants to get done are identified, described, and mapped.

Defining the Job

As we have noted, during the Process Mapping project we identified the objective of the process, usually from the company's perspective. In Customer Mapping, we want to identify the objective from the customers' perspectives. Toward that end, we want to identify the job customers want to get done. The goal is to develop an accurate description of the true job the customers seek to accomplish, not the specific solutions that have been developed by the company. We also want to get away from defining this as the specific solutions customers think they want.

For example, if the job customers want to accomplish is "listening to music," we don't want to restrict this job by specifying the solution "listening to CDs." A broader definition expands the process beyond the accomplishment of providing a positive CD-listening experience. Likewise, an insurance company might make the mistake of defining the job the customers want to get done as "buying insurance." The broader definition of "obtaining protection" allows the company to see service solutions that the first definition might not have brought to light.

One of the best sources for defining the job is, obviously, the customer. However, you will find that customers fall into these same traps in trying to explain what job they want done. They will describe solutions and details rather than jobs. A solution or detail is "buying a smaller car." A job is "buying a fuel-efficient car," or even "buying a car that will fit in my garage." Solutions provide information on *how* the job is done instead of *what* needs to be done. The *what* does not generally change that much over time, but the *how* can change dramatically, through technology or innovation. Customer Mapping focuses first on what job the customer wants to get done, not on how they want to get the job done.

Further, the customer may tend to talk in general terms— "better, faster, more dependable." These are the kinds of phrases advertisers love. But the reviewer must dig deeper into what the customer thinks these terms mean to understand the job that is desired. Even a phrase like "fuel-efficient" may mean 50 miles per gallon to the environmentalist and 5 miles per gallon to the owner of an SUV. The amount of drill down in this area will depend on the needs of your individual project. (Your mileage may vary.)

The reviewer is just as susceptible to every one of these pitfalls as the customer. To ensure you are focusing on the actual job, take a look at your identified objectives. First, determine whether it looks at how, not what. Next, determine whether the objective is stated as a specification. If so, ask why that specification is important and how it gets a job done. Finally, look to see if the terms are too general—looking at benefits and needs that are too broad. Ask what is being accomplished by those needs. All these reviews will help ensure that you have gotten to the actual job being done for the customer.

One other approach to better understand the jobs that are being done is to classify them by the types of jobs customers are trying to accomplish—functional, personal, and social. In *What Customers Want*, Ulwick states, "Functional jobs define tasks people seek to accomplish, personal jobs explain the way people want to feel in a given circumstance, and social jobs clarify how people want to be perceived by others." In our example of purchasing that fuel-efficient vehicle, the customer may have the functional job of transporting people, the personal job of contributing to the greening of the earth, and the social job of being seen as proactive during times of high gas prices.

Defining Tasks

Once the job has been defined, it is time to look at the tasks that make up the job. This is very close to the process identification that we have already described for Process Mapping. However, in that instance our focus was on the moments of truth—the moments where the company had its chance to interact with the customer. In defining tasks for the Customer Map, the focus is on the moments of required action—the actual actions the customer must take. In other words, these are actions that must be taken by the customer to ensure the process continues.

Given the job definition, identify the first task the customer must do to initiate the job. Then determine the last thing the customer must do to make sure the job is finished. In between, you want to identify the key tasks the customer undertakes as the job progresses from beginning to end. Notice we are not focusing on the tasks that the organization undertakes, but instead on the tasks the customer must initiate. To truly identify the tasks, we are also using the same approach we did for the objective of the overall process—focusing on *what* must be accomplished, not on defining *how* the customer does the tasks. Capturing this information by using the verb–noun format can help facilitate this understanding.

Inputs/Outputs

Having identified the various tasks that make up the overall process (defining those tasks around actions the customer must take), we now want to determine what the customer is bringing to the table with each task, and what the expected outcome is. The inputs are most likely tangible products or information—very often, the requirement to provide that information to the company.

From that input, the customer is expecting some output. This expectation should correspond to the output (to the customer) that the company is expecting to produce. Keep in mind, there may be a number of other outputs within the company, but these are not necessarily the end of the task. In addition, there may be (as noted in Chapter 6) wastes, surprises, and invisible consequences. Never are these more evident as an impediment to customer satisfaction than when they get in the way of accomplishing the customers' tasks.

Very often, the outputs are the trigger leading to the next task. In other words, it is an output that provides the customer with the impetus to take the next action in the process. As an analysis consideration, remember that the output should be perceived by the customer as an important step to getting the overall job done.

Measures of Success

When we define the job the customer wants to get done, we begin to understand how the customer measures success. The desired outcomes are legitimate measures relating to how well a job is executed. Information about the customer's desired outcomes can be gathered in many ways: surveys, focus groups, one-on-one interviews, or it can even be inferred. The source is not as important as focusing on the right type of information—the desired outcome. How do customers differentiate between vendors or products they select? What would cause them to select one company over another? What are the characteristics of a "perfect" job? All these are measures of success that can be used for the process.

At this point, it is important to once again differentiate between *how* a job gets done and *what* job is getting done. This process should focus on getting accurate and precise descriptions of the outcomes and constraints for a particular job. In our example of a fuel-efficient car, we would talk about the measures of success that revolve around an increase in miles per gallon; an increase in utilization of electrical power; minimizing the use of gasoline; or minimizing the number of fill-ups required. (Note in the last instance, this may not be a function of fuel-efficiency but, rather, a function of tank size. If this is the measure of success you are finding from your customer, fuel-efficiency may not be the true job they want done. This is a chance to make sure you've properly identified that job.) The goal is determining how customers measure value. Simple terms like "minimize" and "increase" can provide a clear indication of the customer's desired outcome. Depending on how well you understand the customers' needs, you may even be able to become more specific. Is it to increase miles per gallon by ten percent? Is it to reduce gasoline consumption by 20 percent? And it may also relate to overcoming a constraint (also a legitimate measure of success for the customer). In our example, the customer may want to no longer rely on gasoline for power.

Ranking Measures

We have determined how the customer is defining the job, what inputs and outputs they expect, and what they might consider as measures of success. Working through the Customer Mapping project, you will generally find additional tasks that will lead to a larger number of success measures. What we do not know is how important each measure is to our customers. This is valuable information, because it helps reveal where the focus of our analysis should take place. Just as determination of the measures of success can be accomplished by using surveys, focus groups, or one-on-one interviews, these same tools can be used to rank these measures. As noted earlier, the reviewer's personal knowledge of the process can also be used to determine the rankings. Likewise, it may be appropriate to interview individuals within the organization who work directly with the customer to provide some insight on the value of each measure.

Results

Finally, after gathering all the information about the job the customer wants done and analyzing the tasks and actions in the customer's process, we want to determine where the organization meets or does not meet the customer's measures of success. Once again, this can come from the same sources used for the measures of success and rankings. This process will require examining the analysis conducted as well as details of the customer's interaction with the company to determine whether the measures were met. If an area is ranked high in importance and the measures of success are not met, then this area is ripe for process improvement. Drill-down Process Maps may be useful at this point to determine how the process can be restructured to better meet the customer's desired outcomes.

Very often, the construction of the Customer Map (described in the following section) will lead to additional analysis regarding how well the company is getting the customer's job done. Accordingly, these two steps may be completed in either order, allowing the information in the Customer Map to help determine these results.

Building the Map

At this point, a true Customer Map can be constructed, identifying every action the customer must take. The same fundamental concepts used with Process Mapping can be used in construction of the Customer Map. The difference is that the Customer Map focuses on the actions taken by the customer, not the company. Accordingly, rather than each column being a person or department taking some action, the columns represent the detailed steps the customer must take. Once developed, this information can be combined with the prior analysis to find the internal process (the company's process) where improvement can be pursued.

Also, during the construction of the map (in particular as cycle times are taken into account), new areas of concern may become apparent. For example, it may have been determined that a measure of success is to minimize the amount of time a customer has to wait. In the initial results it was determined that customers were satisfied with the results for the measure of success. However, the process map showed that the amount of time was much longer than anyone expected. Now, the result can be adjusted to reflect that it is not meeting the customers' needs, and a deeper review can be done of that area.

The Customer Profile Worksheet

Much like the Process Profile Worksheet introduced in Chapter 3 can be used to capture the relevant information about a process, a Customer Profile Worksheet can be used to accumulate key information from the customer's perspective. This worksheet (shown in

Exhibit 9.1 Customer Profile Worksheet

Job Description: _____

Trigger: _____
Functional Job: _____
Personal Job: _____
Social Job: _____

Task	Actions	Input	Output	Measure of Success	Ranking 1 = low 5 = high	Results

Start →

End

Exhibit 9.1) is designed to show the relevant information of each task while reinforcing the underlying process flow.

The top of the worksheet captures information about the aspects of the overall job the customers wants done—functional, personal, and social. It also includes the trigger that starts the overall process. The first column captures information regarding the tasks to be completed. This can be taken directly from the Customer Process Timeline Worksheet (which will be introduced in the next section). The tasks making up the process (from start to finish) are listed beginning in the first column and move sequentially to the last task. This approach allows for a better comparison of outputs to inputs and will match well with the final Customer Map. The remaining columns capture the Actions, Inputs, Outputs, Measures of Success, Customer Importance Ranking, and, finally, the Results. In this particular example, we have used a scale of one to five for the Ranking. Any scale will do, as long as you are consistent throughout the project.

A completed Customer Profile Worksheet is shown in Exhibit 9.2. You can see from this example how the information has been included and how the interrelationships come forward. We have also used a "stop light" approach for the results: *R* for red, *Y* for yellow, and *G* for green.

Let's see how this information was gathered and completed.

Customer Mapping Example

With these concepts in mind, let's apply them to a service example. WeTrainU is a company that offers continuing education to business professionals. They offer a wide variety of training programs, and some of their off-site sessions are held in five-star hotels at great vacation spots. They also offer virtual, Web-based, and onsite training. The company just implemented a new computer system that allows students to register for classes, obtain any continuing education credits, and provide instructor feedback online.

Defining the Job

Most business professionals need to expand their business knowledge and keep their knowledge current and relevant. Some professionals are required to take continuing education courses as part of a professional certification requirement. The functional job

Exhibit 9.2 Customer Profile Worksheet—Obtain Training

Job Description: Obtain Training

Trigger: Need professional continuing education credits, want to increase knowledge on certain topic
Functional Job: Obtain training
Personal Job: Get away from office, spend time in a nice place
Social Job: Be perceived as a "Professional," interact with peers

Task	Actions	Input	Output	Measure of Success	Ranking 1 = low 5 = high	Results
1. Determine Options	- Research options	- Vendor marketing materials	Potential vendors	1. Minimize time to locate potential training resources	3	G
2. Select Vendor	- Assess credibility - Review training offering - Determine cost	- Vendor marketing materials - Colleague recommendations - Budget	Preferred vendors	2. Minimize time required to review vendor options, training offerings, location, vendor credibility, and price	3	R
3. Select Training	- Examine training details - Prioritize options	- Vendor training descriptions	Preferred training	3. Minimize time required to review course options	2	R
				4. Increase usability of course information: valid descriptions, training method, time, location, cost	3	G
4. Register for Training	- Determine availability - Complete registration	- Vendor registration materials - Information	Verification of registration	5. Minimize time required to determine availability	3	G
				6. Minimize time required to register	3	Y
				7. Minimize cycle time between registration and confirmation	5	Y
5. Pay for Training	- Submit payment	- Vendor payment materials - Information	Verification of payment	8. Minimize time required to pay	3	R
				9. Increase security of payment	5	R
				10. Minimize cycle time between payment and confirmation	5	R
6. Coordinate Logistics	- Obtain details - Make arrangements - Obtain training materials	- Vendor attendance instructions - Travel vendors - Vendor provided materials	Book travel and hotel obtain materials	11. Minimize time required to make travel arrangements	2	G
				12. Increase availability of materials	2	G
7. Complete Training	- Attend training - Complete requirements	- Completion requirements	Confirmation of completion	13. Increase the quality of materials	4	G
				14. Increase the quality of instruction	4	G
				15. Minimize cycle time between training completion and confirmation	5	R

Start

End

a business professional wants to get done (ignoring the most basic one—obtaining CPEs) could be to obtain knowledge in a particular subject, for a variety of reasons. The personal job, however, may be seeking knowledge while going to a luxury location where they can enjoy amenities they might not get at home. The social job could be enhancing their reputation or being perceived as "professional." Any one individual may have a variety of jobs they want to accomplish. We will start by looking at the functional job that satisfies the desire to obtain knowledge through "hiring" the job of Obtain Training.

Defining the Tasks

We will start by looking at the events that start and end the process. Remember, this is through the customer's eyes. To accomplish *Obtain Training*, the process may start with Determine Options. The customer has to examine what options are available before she can make a decision on training. Once training has been received, the end of the process may be Complete Training. In between, key tasks may include: Select Vendor, Select Training, Register for Training, Pay for Training, and Coordinate Logistics.

To record this information, we will use a form similar to the Business Process Timeline Worksheet. The Customer Process Timeline Worksheet (see Exhibit 9.3) achieves the same purpose, but focuses on the tasks undertaken by the customer. Notice these tasks are generic for any customer and do not include particular solutions—an approach facilitated by the use of verb–noun construction. We will transfer this information to a second form shortly. But for now, this helps us determine whether we have identified the key tasks. Then we can drill down into the specific inputs and outputs of each task.

Exhibit 9.3   Customer Process Timeline Worksheet

Obtain Training						
Start						End
Determine Options	Select Vendor	Select Training	Register for Training	Pay for Training	Coordinate Logistics	Complete Training

Actions, Inputs, and Outputs

First, we will look at the actions that make up each task. From that, we will have a better understanding of the inputs that start each task. Note that we will try to identify an input for each action. Ultimately, we want to determine the potential inputs a customer must assemble to 1) accomplish each action within a task and 2) accomplish each task within the job of *Obtain Training*. Then, for each task, we will determine the output; effectively, the information that becomes the trigger to the next task.

1. *Determine Options.* There is one key action within this task—research options. Note that we might have just identified the action as determine options or the task as Research Options. However this helps indicate that the initial analysis of tasks is at a higher level than the step analysis, and research options versus determine options shows that deeper analysis by providing a better, more specific indication of the job this task is accomplishing. We will define this task as the customer identifying what is available in the market in order to determine what type of training they want to pursue. At this stage, the customer is still determining content, not method. She may conduct the research independently, or vendors may assist her by providing information through solicitation. This leads us to the inputs—vendor marketing materials. From the previous points, it is evident that these materials can come in many forms—mailers, Web sites, e-mails, and so on. The output from this task is a list of potential vendors. From our analysis standpoint, this represents our company making the first cut.

2. *Select Vendor.* There can be three key steps in this task: assess credibility, review offerings, and determine costs. After reviewing the potential options, the customer would generally narrow her choices down to a particular vendor. That choice is most likely driven by the subjects of these three tasks—credibility, breadth of offerings, and costs. And while the customer may not be specifically recognizing these as tasks, they are, more than likely, being accomplished. Note that by taking a closer look at the actions involved in the tasks, we are already identifying processes that can be streamlined to make

the customer's job that much easier. The related inputs for this task could be vendor marketing materials, colleague recommendations, and budget information. At this point, also recognize that the same input may be used for more than one task; meaning the input may have to do more than one job (in this case, attract the initial attention and help persuade the vendor selection). From this task, the output is the selection of the preferred vendor. From our perspective, we now have a true potential customer (as long as we don't mess up the next steps).

3. *Select Training.* Having identified the particular vendor that will be used, there are two actions within the next task: review details and prioritize options. This is the point where the customer determines which training option would do the best job. She might compare the details of each offering and prioritize the particular options based on how she feels each will meet her desired outcomes. The inputs for this action are the vendor training descriptions. It becomes quickly apparent that this is the point where an understanding of the personal and social jobs the customer is trying to accomplish will be important—the company will want to use that information to develop the descriptions. This will all lead to the next output—the selection of the preferred training.

4. *Register for Training.* There are two actions related to this task: determine availability and complete registration. It may appear just as logical to include determine availability in the Select Training task. However, in this particular process, the customer is required to determine whether the course is full after identifying the training she wants to take. Accordingly, it is included in the Register for Training task. (This is the kind of information that would be discovered as the Customer Mapping project progresses.) To accomplish this task, there are two types of input needed. The first is the vendor registration forms—manual or electronic. The second is the information the customer provides—name, address, and so on. The output from this task is deceptively simple: the verification of registration. However, this is the first real one-on-one customer contact that occurs and, as we will show, the customer will learn a lot from how well this one simple piece of correspondence is handled.

5. *Pay for Training.* Before describing the associated actions, note that the placement of this task is based on our understanding of the process. The customer may have specific needs relating to payment that require flexibility in the timing for this task—perhaps payment at the time of training, or shortly thereafter. By placing this task here, we have made the assumption this will be the primary approach customers use to accomplish it. With that in mind, there are two associated actions: determine amount due and submit payment. There are inputs to this task that are similar to those listed in the previous task—the vendor payment forms and the information provided by the customer. The output from this task is verification of payment. Note that it is very similar to the previous output, so similar that these outputs are often combined. While this could all be seen as one task, we have split this into two tasks to better facilitate our analysis.

6. *Coordinate Logistics.* Once everything has been put in place, there can be a number of logistical issues that need to be sorted out before the training can be completed. The underlying actions are obtain details, make arrangements, and obtain training materials. The customer needs the details about when and where to attend. If travel is necessary, she will also need details on accommodations. In addition, she would want to know when course materials will be received and whether there are any preliminary or special requirements. The inputs necessary to accomplish this task include the attendance instructions from the vendor, guidance for accommodations, and vendor training materials. The outputs from this task include travel confirmations and pre-training materials.

7. *Complete Training.* Finally, the job the customer has really wanted to accomplish is happening. There are two actions within this task: attend training and complete requirements. These two tasks help recognize that, often, just attendance is not sufficient to complete the training process. The inputs to this task are the vendor course and vendor instructions. Since this is the heart of the process, it contains some of the key outputs, including confirmation of completion and the most important output, obtaining knowledge.

Measure of Success

We can now match our overall understanding of the job the customer wants to accomplish with the specific information we have gathered around tasks, actions, inputs, and outputs. This approach allows us to recognize how we know when we have success. Ideally, as previously noted, this would involve discussions with the actual customers. However, while we have not conducted specific interviews, we can easily infer the following measures of success based on our general knowledge. Ultimately, we are basing this on the understanding that business professionals are busy people and would value any process that minimizes time they must spend on each action. Exhibit 9.4 shows each task with the measure of success. Note that we have focused on the desired outcomes, recognizing that we are evaluating what job is accomplished rather than how it is accomplished.

Exhibit 9.4   Measures of Success

Determine Options
 1. Minimize time required to locate potential training resources
Select Vendor
 2. Minimize time required to review options
Select Training
 3. Minimize time required to review course offerings
 4. Increase accuracy and completeness of course information
Register for Training
 5. Minimize time required to determine availability
 6. Minimize time required to register
 7. Minimize cycle time between registration and receipt of confirmation
Pay for Training
 8. Minimize time required to make payment
 9. Increase security of payment environment
 10. Minimize cycle time between payment and receipt
Coordinate Logistics
 11. Minimize time required to make travel arrangements
 12. Increase availability of materials
Complete Training
 13. Increase the quality of course materials
 14. Increase the quality of instructions
 15. Minimize cycle time between course completion and confirmation

Ranking Measures

The determination of ranking results is dependent on the needs of the customer—what part of the job is important to them. If, for example, a professional is attending training to meet professional certification requirements, the most important outcome may be timely receipt of the confirmation that the course was complete. If the most important outcome for a professional is knowledge, then the quality of instruction or quality of course materials may be most important. For purposes of this example (refer to Exhibit 9.2), we have made assumptions on the various rankings showing that the most important measures of success are "minimize cycle time between registration and confirmation," "increase security of payment," "minimize cycle time between payment and confirmation," and "minimize cycle time between completion of training and confirmation." We have determined that the least important measures of success are "minimize the time required to review course options," "minimize the time required to make travel arrangements," and "increase availability of materials."

This helps focus the review on those areas where the customer will receive the most benefit. For example, notice that both measures of success for *Coordinate Logistics* are low. While we don't want to ignore this area, it does indicate that there is less benefit from a change in that task than any other. Likewise note that the highest overall rankings are in the P*ay for* T*raining* and *Complete* T*raining* tasks.

Results

As previously noted, the analysis of results can occur at this point or be built on the information obtained during the construction of the Customer Map. To better understand this process and the success of the various tasks, we will discuss this results analysis after completion of the Customer Map.

WeTrainU Customer Mapping Example

One Customer's Experience

Before starting on the development of WeTrainU's Customer Map, let's examine their process by looking at one customer's experience. Sally has received an e-mail from WeTrainU regarding some course offerings. She was interested in a leadership course offered in Hawaii in April.

She started by clicking on the link to the Web site and found it full of information about WeTrainU. There was a lot of information, but she could not find the course selections. She tried the search function several times without any luck. After about 15 minutes of browsing the Web site, she finally found a section called "WeTrainU EP." (Later, she learned this was a pathway to WeTrainU Education Programs.) When she entered this area of the Web site, she learned she needed to register as a "new user" and create a new user id and password. That took another ten minutes. Since she was running late for a meeting, she had to log off the Web site.

When she returned later that day, she went to the Web site and tried to logon to WeTrainU EP, but she forgot her password. It took five more minutes to generate a new password. She finally started searching for the class she found in the e-mail. The classes were separated by Conferences, Seminars, Virtual Classes, and Web-Based Training. She searched through Conferences and could not find the class. She finally moved to the Seminars section and, after another ten minutes, was able to locate the class and review the description. She selected the class and completed the registration form. This required her to look up Industry Codes, ID numbers, and other information she did not have readily available. Accessing the additional information took about ten minutes. She was then told to print out the form and fax it to WeTrainU, along with information about her preferred method of payment.

She was concerned about faxing her payment information, so she called WeTrainU, was put on hold for five minutes, and finally was able to discuss her payment arrangements. The representative let her provide the payment information by phone. This took about five more minutes. Sally expected to receive an e-mail verification confirming her registration for the course, and also a receipt for her payment. When she had not received this in one week she called WeTrainU to ask about the status of the confirmation. They explained she should receive it in another week (which she did).

Although the trip to Hawaii was a major incentive, Sally attended the course primarily so she could get her CPE credits for her professional designation. Sally enjoyed the course and was satisfied with the materials and instruction. At the conclusion of the course she asked the instructor when she would receive her CPE certificate. The instructor informed her she would be sent an e-mail in about a week. This e-mail would request feedback on the course and, after she completed the survey, she would be sent her CPE credits. Sally stated she needed to have her certificate sooner, as she had to file her renewal within one week. It took two weeks for Sally to receive her certificate, so she had to file her renewal late and pay a penalty.

Building the Map

With these facts in hand, it is time to create the Customer Map, reflecting the customer's experience with the WeTrainU organization. We place the tasks across the top of the map and list the key actions the customer has undertaken to accomplish those tasks. Since many of the key outputs the customer desires are to minimize the time require to accomplish certain tasks, we want to highlight the cycle times for each task. If there were some other key requirements, we may want to highlight those as well. The completed Customer Map is shown in Exhibit 9.5.

There are a few additional things to note in the way the Customer Map was created. You will see that, once again, the verb–noun approach is used to maintain simplicity and to focus on what is being done. In addition, we have added comments to help isolate problem areas—the areas where Process Maps might be created to help streamline the overall process. Finally, we have included some analysis regarding probable causes. This will also help focus the Process Mapping part of the project on the underlying issues.

Analyzing the Map

After creating the map, we want to analyze the customer's experience to determine whether there are areas where the company did not meet the customer's measure of success. We can examine each of the measures of success and ask the question, "Did the outcome experienced by the customer meet the measurement criteria?" If it did not, we will determine whether the gap in expectation is a large or small one. These will represent the areas where improvements can be made in the process to better serve the customer.

After looking at the WeTrainU map, do you think the outcome of this process satisfied Sally's requirements? She did not have to spend much time locating the vendor—they solicited her with an e-mail. But her time was not minimized in locating an appropriate class, in registering for a class, in receiving confirmation for

Exhibit 9.5   WeTrainU Customer Map

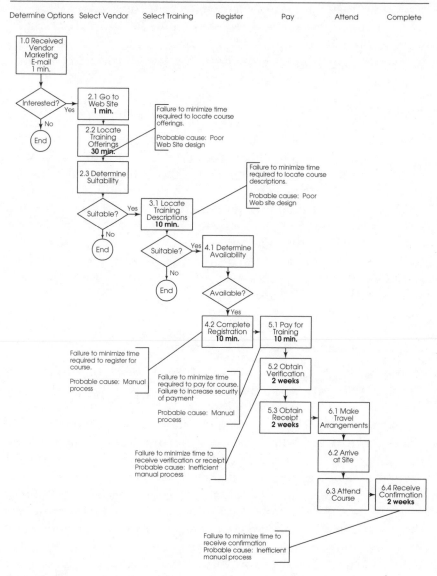

her registration, in the security of her payment, or in the receipt of her CPE certificate after attending the class. If Sally ranks these outcomes as highly important, then the lack of satisfaction related to these outcomes could make Sally select another vendor next time she needs to obtain training. But if Sally values other jobs as more important, then failure on these outcomes may not be as detrimental. Maybe the job Sally really values is more personal—she wants to go to Hawaii and have her company pay for the trip. She may be willing to forego other outcomes to satisfy her personal job requirement of going to Hawaii. But, even in that situation, the large number of dissatisfiers involved in the process may override her desire for a free trip to Hawaii.

Results

With this analysis of the overall operation, we can identify the areas needing improvement. Then a Process Map can be prepared, focusing on the processes supporting the highest ranked measures of success that were not met. In general, this would mean considering how we could minimize time the customer has to spend on a task, minimize the time the customer must spend "checking" on an outcome, or increase some other outcome the customer desires. With this background, compare the Customer Profile Worksheet in Exhibit 9.2 with the Customer Map developed for Exhibit 9.5. You can see that the information under *Results* is driven by the Customer Map.

Process Mapping the Customer Experience

Review of the Customer Map and Worksheet conclusions can provide WeTrainU with some insights on how they are doing in meeting their customer's requirements in both the overall job and the tasks required to accomplish the job. By analyzing the customer's experience, they can assess where they are meeting the customer's needs and where they could improve their process. If we look at Sally's experience, potential areas for further analysis by WeTrainU might be the *Select Vendor, Select Training, Pay for Training,* and *Complete Training* tasks. Within these, the measures of success that ranked highest and had the poorest performance include numbers nine (Increase security of payment), ten (Minimize cycle time between payment and confirmation), and fifteen (Minimize cycle time between training completion and confirmation.) To better understand how these might be improved, let's take a closer look at both the *Pay for Training* and the *Confirmation* processes for WeTrainU and see if we can identify areas for improvement.

The first area we have identified is one where Process Mapping probably will not help. The steps within the *Pay for Training* task that relate to the measure of success "increase security of payment" are manual, and do not allow payment over a secure server. There is no obvious way to enhance security without developing automated solutions that will provide the additional security required. The analysis of this task will probably only be of assistance to this measure of success if or when a secure automated solution is developed. With a completed Process Map of this task, the designers will have a better idea how to integrate the system and ensure customer satisfaction is not sacrificed.

However, an analysis of the *Pay for Training* task will be a great benefit to the next measure of success, "Minimize the cycle time between payment and confirmation." Exhibit 9.6 shows the completed Process Map for this area. By examining this process, we can see that the minimum cycle time for a customer to obtain a receipt for their payment is six days and the maximum is twelve days. This is probably not acceptable in today's world of real-time confirmation within minutes of payment. Again, a more sophisticated automated solution is required. In the absence of such a solution, priority should be given to decreasing the cycle times as much as possible. An objective of a one-day turnaround time by the Receivables Clerk for all payment receipts would improve results. The delays are primarily due to the Receivables Clerk working on other activities and on the hold for verification of electronic checks. If they remove the requirement that checks be held and process all payments on a priority basis, the cycle time could be greatly reduced.

An analysis of the *Confirmation* process within the *Complete Training* task can help focus on the measure of success "Minimize cycle time between training completion and confirmation." The Process Map for this area is shown in Exhibit 9.7. We can see that students will not normally get a confirmation within one week. The minimum time is most likely ten days, with a maximum time of fifteen days. This is due to mailing of rosters and delays in preparation of confirmations. If rosters were faxed instead of mailed, and confirmations were prepared and e-mailed within 24 to 48 hours after receipt, the cycle time could be reduced by 8 to 13 days. This would probably satisfy most customers. Alternatively, the instructors could sign and distribute the confirmations at the end of the course, providing verification to the vendor at a later date. Both of these would be easy fixes if a better automated solution is not available.

Exhibit 9.6 Pay for Training Process Map

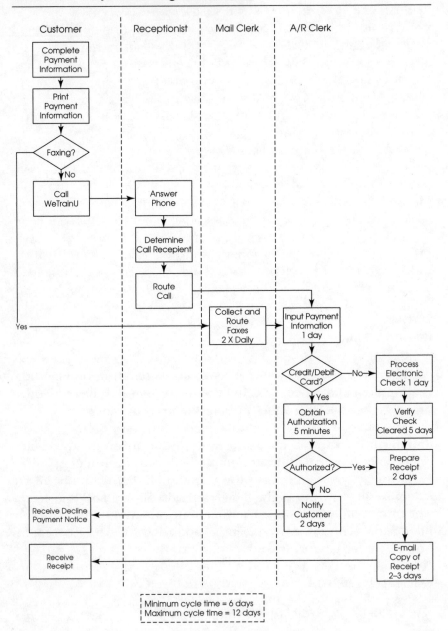

Exhibit 9.7   Confirmation Process Map

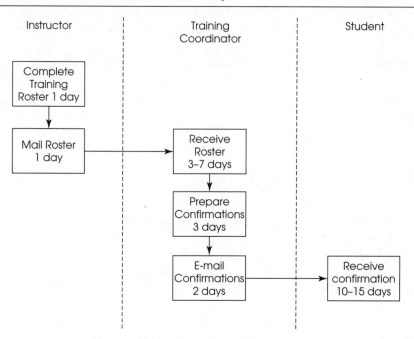

From this example, you can see how focusing on the job the customer wants to accomplish can lead to a better understanding of where process improvements should be focused. Just a note—the example we have used focused on a service industry example. That doesn't mean that this approach cannot be used in the development of products. In analyzing what job your product is doing for the customer, an analysis of the process the customer goes through in using that product will help you generate ideas for product improvement. The methods above work perfectly well for that. You can find additional information on how to complete these types of analyses in the book *What Customers Want* by Anthony Ulwick.

Spaghetti Maps

Visualizing the Detailed Process Flow

While they are not a function of Customer Mapping per se, this is a good time to introduce the concept of Spaghetti Maps—another valuable tool in analyzing process improvements.

Spaghetti Maps or Diagrams are a visual way to show the flow of material or information through a particular process. They are often used in manufacturing organizations to determine whether the floor plan in a manufacturing setting is configured in a way that optimizes efficiency. As an example, hospitals use these diagrams to identify ways to determine the optimal floor layout and minimize the distance traveled by patients or staff for key tasks. Just as Spaghetti Maps can be used to identify inefficiencies in physical work areas, they can also be used to identify inefficiencies in process work flows.

One way to think of Spaghetti Mapping is to imagine you are taking a ball of string and anchoring it to the floor at the start of the process. The string then travels with the work as it is passed from one person or department to the next. At each passing point or key action, the string is anchored in the floor again. Once the process is finished, we take a bird's-eye view of the string to see the complexity of the process. If there are very few lines and the paths are direct, we might conclude the process flow is reasonably efficient. If, however, the string resembles spaghetti, generally work can be done to improve the efficiency of the process.

Spaghetti Maps are usually first drawn to represent the "As Is" flow of the process. Analysis of the maps may often reveal areas where the process can be immediately streamlined. A new "To Be" map is then created to depict the improved process. One advantage of Spaghetti Maps is they are easy to prepare once you have identified the key tasks in a process. You are not distracted by numerous symbols or words; therefore, you can focus your attention on the process flow. When you are analyzing the maps, you will look for ways to combine tasks, eliminate tasks, have less people involved, and decrease cycle times—anything that will make the process flow more efficiently. Just like a Process Map, the Spaghetti Map helps you "see" processes and procedures in a different way.

Exhibit 9.8 is an example of a Spaghetti Map representing the expense process described in previous chapters. Many of the issues we identified in our Process Mapping project also become readily apparent with this approach.

"As Is" Spaghetti Map

Spaghetti maps can be completed very quickly using the same techniques used in Process Mapping. The first step in creation of an

Exhibit 9.8   Spaghetti Map—Expense Process—As Is

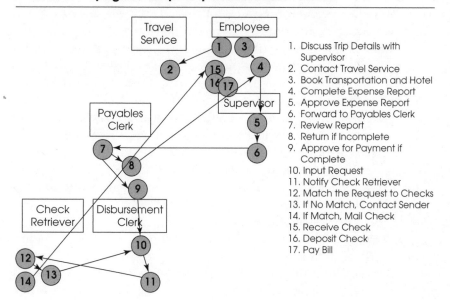

1. Discuss Trip Details with Supervisor
2. Contact Travel Service
3. Book Transportation and Hotel
4. Complete Expense Report
5. Approve Expense Report
6. Forward to Payables Clerk
7. Review Report
8. Return if Incomplete
9. Approve for Payment if Complete
10. Input Request
11. Notify Check Retriever
12. Match the Request to Checks
13. If No Match, Contact Sender
14. If Match, Mail Check
15. Receive Check
16. Deposit Check
17. Pay Bill

"As Is" map is to identify the key actions in the process and who is performing those actions. They should then be listed in numerical order. On the page where the map is being created, list the actions, in order, on the right side of the paper. Then, think of placing a pin on a map showing where the first action of the process begins, then another pin where the next process begins. Start at the upper right hand column with your first action. Label the box with the person or location. Place a circle with the action number in the box. If the process moves to another person or location, then the circle will also move. Move the circle down for related entities and across to the left if the process is moving locations, and down again as appropriate. You can do this with columns or free form if it is not too complex. Once your "pins" are in place, start stringing the string to see the pattern (draw the lines). Finally, just as with any review process, verify your "As Is" view is accurate.

"To Be" Spaghetti Map

Developing a "To Be" map starts by analyzing the "As Is" map for "spaghetti" tangles, which indicate that inefficiencies exist in the process. Also analyze for delays in the outcome due to the length of the process. Move the "pins" around to try and create a more streamlined, efficient process. Look for places where actions can be eliminated, made shorter, or reworked to make a smoother, more direct flow. Involve clients where you can to provide suggestions on how to improve the process. You may use sticky-notes to depict your pins; then you can move them around and see your "To Be" map as it progresses.

With that understanding, we will construct a Spaghetti Map of WeTrainU's *Confirmation* process. (See Exhibit 9.9.) At first blush, since this does not seem particularly convoluted, it doesn't appear that significant change is needed. However, it does look like one, long spaghetti noodle. And we can observe that the student is at the end of this laborious process.

If we look at how we might streamline the process, we can identify ways to shorten the length of time it takes for the student to receive her confirmation. One possibility is shown in Exhibit 9.10. We can see that the process is much shorter and the student is at the beginning of the process. All the back office work can be done without the student having to be involved, and we could provide them same-day service in this new process—no delay.

Exhibit 9.9   Spaghetti Map—Confirmation—As Is

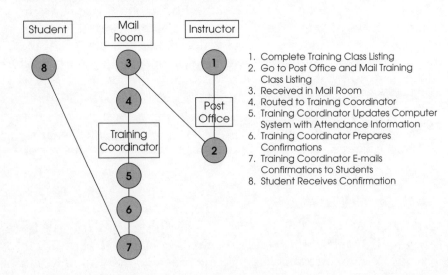

Exhibit 9.10   Spaghetti Map—Confirmation—To Be

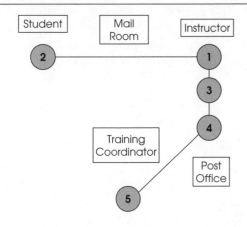

1. Sign/Adjust Confirmation
2. Receive Confirmation
3. Update Training Listing
4. E-mail to Training Coordinator
5. Update Computer System with Attendance Information

Recap

Customers are hiring your products or services to perform a job. Don't focus on what job the company is doing. Instead, focus on the job the customers are trying to get done and on how they are measuring the success of the job. In other words, focus on what actions the customers must take to get the job done and what they value as outputs.

Customer Mapping is very similar to Process Mapping. Both are attempting to gain information about where the process is working well and where improvements can be made. The steps for Customer Mapping are:

- *Define the job.* Identify the job the customer wants done.
- *Define the tasks.* Determine what the customer must do to initiate the job and end the job, and identify the key actions between the start and the end of the process.
- *Define inputs/outputs.* For each task, identify the customer inputs and expected outputs.
- *Identify measures of success.* Determine the outcome the customer desires from each task.
- *Rank the measures.* Identify the measures of success that customers value more than others.

- *Examine results.* Use the results of the Customer Mapping project to ask questions about the process. Compare the various tools to identify opportunities.
- *Create Process Maps for failing measures.* Create Process Maps for those tasks and actions for which customer importance is high but results are low.

Spaghetti Mapping is another tool to use in analyzing processes. By identifying steps in the process and "pinning" them to the appropriate office, department, or individual, this approach can provide a bird's-eye view of the process. Spaghetti Maps can be built "As Is" (the current situation) as well as "To Be" (how it will look after suggested changes). The latter allows you to quickly test your assumptions about the changes to see whether an optimal solution can be developed.

Key Analysis Points

What Job Is the Process Hired to Do?

To understand what the customer is looking for in a process, you need to understand that the customer is hiring that product or service to get a job done for them. The better that service or product does at getting the job done, the more likely the customer is to go for that service or product in the future. And making that service or product more efficient—making it so it does a better job—increases the likelihood that the customer will "hire" it again.

What, Not How

Making sure you have truly defined the job the process is getting done for the customer can be tricky. Often, definitions of customer satisfaction are couched in hazy terms (better, faster, dependable), or they describe satisfaction around solutions, rather than the actual job. In general, the definition should be around *what* is getting done, not *how* it is getting done. This approach leads to a definition of the job that better identifies what it is that will provide customer satisfaction.

Measures of Success

Determining the appropriate measures of success is contingent upon first identifying the proper job. Once that job is identified, the measure of success is based on how well that job is done. Again, it can be very easy to fall into the trap of using "fluffy" words to help describe these measures. Instead, strive for simple measures such as "minimize," "increase," or even overcoming a constraint.

Customer Maps Lead to Process Maps

The Customer Mapping process is about determining the steps that the customer must take to ensure the process moves forward. Within that map, an analysis can show which steps in the customer's process are least likely to meet the customer's needs. Once identified, the underlying processes, tasks, and actions can then be analyzed using traditional Process Mapping approaches, which will lead to better efficiencies and innovation.

Unscramble the Spaghetti and Shrink the Noodles

Spaghetti maps can visually show how the work moves between offices, departments, and individuals. Once completed, look for those situations where lines constantly cross. These represent opportunities to streamline the process. Likewise, look for longer strands that, while not crossing, indicate too large a separation between the start of the process and the customer. These represent opportunities to cut down the amount of time spent getting to the customer—improving service by bringing the customer to the conclusion of the process more quickly.

CHAPTER

10

RACI Matrices

If we could find out who's in charge, we could kill him.

—George Carlin

Process versus Authority

Process Maps do an excellent job of identifying the actual tasks that are being accomplished and the individuals (or positions) who do that work. However, in some situations it may become apparent that there is a problem that goes beyond the processes themselves. It may have first become apparent as you tried to determine the owner of a process. It may be that no one really took ownership, or that more than one person was thought of as ultimately responsible. And even though a Process Map may have information about the hierarchies involved (for example, the documentation of approval levels), there may be evidence in the maps that other departments have more active roles than first thought, or employees may actually be on their own with no management oversight. Ultimately it often comes down to the most important question: Who's really in charge here?

In any of these situations, there is a need to delve further into the roles and responsibilities of the individuals involved in the process. A RACI Matrix is an excellent tool that helps isolate responsibility issues within a process or department. Just as Process Mapping is a visual representation of a process flow, the RACI Matrix is a visual representation of each individual's role within that process—identifying those who are Responsible, Accountable, Consulted, and Informed (RACI). When these tools are used together, the Process Map can help identify areas where accountability is held too tightly, and the RACI Matrix may bring to light invisible consequences of accountability. The RACI Matrix can also serve to eliminate misunderstandings about each person's role, reduce duplication of effort, and help build consensus within the team.

How Do I Know There's a Problem?

The first indication that issues regarding responsibilities may exist can arise during the identification of process owners. As shown in the Process Owner Charts, there can be one-to-one, one-to-many, or many-to-one ownership relationships. As you talk to those owners, you may find they have conflicting interpretations regarding ownership. Two people may share ownership but each thinks he or she is the only owner; two may share ownership but there are gaps in ownership of the entire process; a person who has ownership of more than one process may not recognize his or her role in all processes; or (the worst situation) no one may take any ownership of a process. In particular, if the department or company has a matrix organization, there is a heightened chance of misunderstanding responsibilities.

You may also recognize the need for a RACI Matrix during the mapping phase. This can manifest itself in a number of ways. First, it may be as simple as individuals indicating that no one is taking responsibility. Second, the Process Map may reveal that decisions are being made at too low a level, there is no clear understanding of where the decision is made, or there are delays in the decision making that indicate no one person wants to accept responsibility. Third, the map may show numerous approvals across many layers, an indication that too many people have taken responsibility. Finally, the Process Map may show that individuals outside the influence of the process owner are providing input or making decisions. Any one of these, in and of themselves, is not necessarily an indicator that a RACI Matrix should be constructed. However, based on the overall tone and information received from interviewees, the reviewer should seriously consider whether the use of a RACI Matrix is warranted.

And, just in general, keep alert during discussions with all levels of employees to see if there are misunderstandings, confusions, or even disagreements about authority and responsibility. Leading the department through creation of a RACI Matrix can assist in better determining the required roles and responsibilities.

What Is a RACI Matrix?

Responsibility charting (the process that results in the RACI Matrix) is an approach used to identify where ambiguities may exist related to accountability and responsibility. When used in a collaborative approach, differences are brought into the open and resolved with the entire team. Building on the active participation of management and others in the development of process maps, the RACI Matrix clarifies the responsibilities each person plays in relation to the identified processes.

The final RACI Matrix is a grid showing the activities or tasks down the left-hand side and the functional roles across the top. Exhibit 10.1 shows a blank RACI Matrix. The functional roles are positions accomplishing an action or task. The activities are the key steps in the process.

In identifying the activities, you can use information already created for the Process Maps. Many of the guidelines used for Process Mapping are applicable to the RACI Matrix approach, so

Exhibit 10.1 The RACI Matrix

Process Name	Roles of Participants				
Activities or Decisions	Type or degree of participation				

if you are involved in creating a RACI Matrix prior to completion of the Process Map, you will find the work familiar. In particular, the verb–noun approach is still valid, although you may find situations where additional explanations are necessary to meet the needs of the matrix. However, never abandon the rule that descriptions should be short and concise.

Within the grid is the heart of the analysis process. For each activity, determine the role and degree of responsibility for each individual. There are four identified levels of participation—Responsible, Accountable, Consult, and Inform. (There is also a fifth option: The individual is not involved at all.) The definition of each of these four components is important to understanding how this all comes together.

Responsible (R) represents the doer, the individual who actually works on the activity. Using the *Expense Payment* process example, the person responsible is the check requester. This is the doer: the one who is actually requesting the check. Depending on the complexity of the action or task, there may be more than one individual identified as being Responsible.

Accountable (A) is the position with the actual yes or no authority over the activity; the person about whom it is said "The buck stops here." There should be only one Accountable for each activity. If there are more than one, you are seeing the results of divided accountabilities and, ultimately, confusion over ownership. In the check request process, the individual actually accountable for the initial request is the same as the doer—the check requester. First, note that it is possible for one individual to be Accountable and Responsible. Second, while there is an approval process, that approver is not accountable for the activity of requesting the check. Yes, they may be accountable for expenses or for approval—but the actual accountability for the activity is with the requester. (If you think about it, this does make sense. If something is wrong with the request, if something is wrong with the support, if there is an indication of fraud, the requester is the one who will take the blame, because he or she has the accountability.)

Consult (C) is an individual who is to be consulted before the process can move forward. It is important to remember that this individual is involved prior to completion of a decision or action. This means there must be two-way communication regarding the activity. More than one person may be consulted. In the check request process, the reviews by the first- and second-level reviewers represent two Consults for one activity.

Inform (I), the final identification in the RACI Matrix, is any individual who needs to know an activity is occurring, but is not required to be part of the process. They can be informed while the activity is occurring or even afterwards. As such, this is very much a one-way communication. This example demonstrates how the RACI Matrix can enhance the content of a Process Map. In the Process Map created for the check request process, there is no explicit indication of anyone who might be considered to be an Inform. However, the manager of the department may need to be informed if there are particular budget concerns. Likewise, an administrative assistant might need to be informed to continue development of a spreadsheet analysis of expenses.

This is an excellent time to reiterate that the Process Map should not be transferred to the RACI Matrix verbatim. As noted regarding Consult, approvals may represent the role of the individual rather than an additional activity in the RACI Matrix. The map previously developed for the check request process shows the requester completing the request and the supervisor approving the request. For the RACI Matrix (because it is focused on responsibilities rather than on a complete map), this can be combined into the activity request check. The requester is then a Responsible and an Accountable, and the supervisor would be a Consult.

Analyzing the RACI Matrix

Issues identified within some RACI Matrices are apparent after only a cursory look. However, a detailed analysis is best performed looking at information within each position (vertical analysis) and within each activity (horizontal analysis).

Vertical Analysis

The vertical analysis takes a structured look at the roles and responsibilities of a single individual or position. This represents an assessment of whether that person has the proper amount and proper level of involvement. First, look at how many Responsible and Accountable activities are under that individual. If there are a large number of Responsible activities, determine whether that person really needs to be involved in that many activities. Look for opportunities to break the activities into smaller, more manageable functions that can be delegated. If there are a large number of Accountable activities, make sure that a proper segregation of duties exists. Also, determine whether the requirement that all activities go through this one individual might be creating a bottleneck. Finally, if there are no Responsible or Accountable activities, question whether the functional role is actually necessary. This may represent a situation where processes have changed to a point where the resources could be reused.

Next, look at the white spaces. If there are a lot of empty spaces under the position, this may be another indicator that the functional role is no longer necessary. If, on the other hand, there are no empty spaces, question whether the individual needs to be involved in so many activities. If the person is acting as a "gate-keeper," it could be that management by exception will speed up the process. Also look for opportunities where a Consult role can be changed to Inform, and an Inform role can be eliminated.

The final review point is to determine whether the degree of participation fits the qualifications of the role. For example, if a manager is involved at a very detailed level, it might not be the best use of the manager's resources. On the other hand, if clerical or low-level positions are providing high-level approvals, it may indicate the need for stronger management involvement.

Horizontal Analysis

The horizontal analysis takes a structured look at the activities being performed. It is intended to determine whether the proper responsibilities have been established for each activity. Again, start by reviewing the Responsible and Accountable roles. If there is no one Responsible, no one is getting the job done. If there is no one Accountable, no one is ensuring the job is done correctly. In effect, if there is either no one Responsible or no one Accountable, then no one is taking ownership of the activity. If there are too many individuals Responsible, then quite simply, there are too many people involved in the activity. It may also be an indication that people are more concerned with "throwing it over the wall" than actually completing the activity.

Also, check whether there is more than one person Accountable. One of the basic rules of constructing a RACI Matrix is that there should only be one Accountable person. If there is more than one, then the individuals Responsible may not know where to go for final decisions. In effect, shared responsibility is no responsibility. Finally, determine whether there are too few people Responsible. If only one person is responsible for the activity (that is, only one person is doing all the work) this may represent a bottleneck in the process. At the furthest extreme, it may even represent that an activity is not necessary.

Next, evaluate the Consults and Informs. If there are too many of either, it may be an indication of an activity that is being over-controlled. Any Consult role represents a delay in the process and an investment of resources. Therefore, determine whether there are good reasons for having a large number of people involved. Similarly, with the Inform role, determine whether there are valid reasons for such involvement. In effect, look for opportunities to streamline the activity and free up individuals' time by eliminating Consult and Inform roles.

Finally, look to see if every box is empty or every box is filled in. Obviously, if every box is empty, then the activity is not necessary – no one is currently performing that activity and it has not been missed. If every box is filled, there is an excellent chance that too many people are involved in the activity. In particular, you will usually find that too many people are acting in Consult and Inform roles and, as already indicated, opportunities to reduce their involvement should be identified.

Expense Payment Process Example

To better understand how a RACI Matrix is constructed, we will use the *Expense Payment* process. This example will begin by determining the activities to be included and then assigning the appropriate degree of participation to the various roles.

Getting to the Right Level

When working with an existing Process Map, it is important to remember that you do not want to use the most detailed maps. As indicated earlier, in determining Responsibilities, you want to bring it to a higher level than the action level. As an example, you will note that detailed Process Maps have a step for completion of a task as well as entries for each approval. This is all combined in the RACI Matrix with one activity, which includes any necessary Consult or Inform roles.

For example, in the action-level map for the *complete request* process, the steps are as follows: prepare check request, prepare return check request (if needed), submit request, fax support, and notify supervisor. This then is followed by the *approve request* action level: review request, return for corrections (if necessary), approve request, and forward to appropriate level.

Exhibit 10.2 shows what the resulting RACI Matrix might look like. (We'll discuss how the roles are assigned in more detail later.) It is evident that there is more detail than is necessary. There are already nine steps in the process, meaning that this will result in an unwieldy listing for the entire process. (Just like Process Maps, RACI Matrices are intended to be easily grasped representations of the process.) In addition, there is little differentiation in each step regarding Responsible and Accountable roles. The first five have the requestor as Responsible and Accountable, and the remaining four have the supervisor as Responsible and Accountable. And there are likely to be no Consults or Informs. The focus on the trees means there is no assessment of the forest.

It is also ineffective to prepare the matrix at a level that is too high. This can be shown by translating the unit-level map to a RACI Matrix. This results in only three steps: prepare request, prepare check, and deliver check. While the resulting RACI Matrix (shown in Exhibit 10.3) shows more information regarding responsibilities than the prior example, it is at too high a level for any real discussion. It is tough to determine the key steps to be reviewed.

So, the level of review has to be at an appropriate level. Exhibit 10.4 shows a RACI Matrix at a more appropriate level for the check request

Exhibit 10.2   Action-Level RACI Matrix

Complete Check Request	Check Requester	Supervisor
Prepare Check Request	R/A	
Prepare Return Check Request (if needed)	R/A	
Submit Request	R/A	
Fax Support	R/A	
Notify Supervisor	R/A	
Review Request		R/A
Return for Corrections (if necessary)		R/A
Approve Request		R/A
Forward as Appropriate		R/A

Exhibit 10.3 Unit-Level RACI Matrix

Complete Check Request	Check Requester	Document Center	Supervisor	Second-level Approver	Disbursements (Local)	Check Issuer	Check Retriever	Disbursements Supervisor
Prepare Request	R/A	R	C	C	R			
Prepare Check					R/A	R	R	
Deliver Check								R/A

Exhibit 10.4 Check Request RACI Matrix

Complete Check Request	Check Requester	Supervisor	Second-level Approver	Disbursements (Local)	Check Issuer	Check Retriever	Disbursements Supervisor
Complete Request	R/A	C	C				
Verify Request				R/A			
Issue Check					R		A
Retrieve Check				R/A		R	A
Deliver Check							

example. Note that there are not many more activities than in the previous example. Yet, there is enough extra detail to provide better insight into the final product.

Let's see how this RACI Matrix was completed. The first step, complete request, is performed by the requester. It is evident that the requester is both responsible and accountable. Depending on the size of the request, at least two people (the supervisor and second-level approver) must be consulted before the process can continue. The next step is verify request (a step done by the local disbursements department). This could have been handled one of two ways. One approach is to include this in the complete check activity by indicating the role as Consult. In this case, the better approach is to emphasize that a separate unit is involved in the process. In this case the individual is Accountable and Responsible. If there was a particular need to emphasize the role of management in this situation, an additional column would be added for the supervisor. The disbursements clerk would be Responsible and the supervisor would be Accountable.

The next steps in the RACI Matrix are issue check and retrieve check. First, notice that there is no indication how the check request got from one place to the next. RACI Matrices are not intended to cover every step of the process—that is the role of the Process Map. Instead, the matrix focuses on broad tasks and responsibilities. It is assumed that the user of a RACI Matrix will understand the transitions between actions. Second, notice that although the two processes are within the same department (and could be considered part of one step), two distinct activities have been established. This is intended to recognize an important segregation of duties. Accordingly, each person is noted as Responsible for his or her own activity.

For this example, we have also made an assumption that the supervisor of the department has the ultimate accountability for these processes and included a column for that individual. When determining accountability in an activity, there are two things that can be considered. First is the active role a person takes in ensuring the correct work is done. You may assign accountability based on how you see work being completed. The second thing to be considered is the person that others perceive to have the authority. In that case, you may base your assignment of accountability on what you are told by employees. In most situations, the perception should match the reality, but be aware that a problem may exist when the two do not mesh.

The final step in the RACI Matrix is deliver check. Once again, we have not included the transfer of the check from the Home Office to the local center, as this is to be inferred. Responsibility and Accountability are once again directly assigned to the clerk charged with the job.

And so we have completed a relatively simple RACI Matrix. Analysis of this matrix shows a decent spread of accountability. Analyzing vertically, we see a proportionate amount of Responsible and Accountable activities indicating proper allocation—no one person with too many Accountable activities, and no overabundance of empty space. Analyzing horizontally, we again see a proportionate number of people assigned to Responsible and Accountable roles, appropriate empty space, and an appropriate number of Consults and Informs. All this only re-emphasizes the fact that the problems with the *Expense Payment* process lie in the process itself, not in the way responsibilities are handled.

RACI Matrix to Process Map

Process Maps and RACI Matrices can be used in conjunction with each other to identify problems that might not have been apparent from the use of just one of the tools. Construction of a Process Map after completion of a RACI Matrix may help isolate issues with convoluted processes.

We were once asked by a client to help analyze the process used to deliver analysis reports to internal departments. The process started with first contact with the client and included the analysis and reporting of the final results. The client worked as an internal consultant to various levels within the department, so she also worked with the internal departments in executing improvements that were designed based on the results within those reports. The reports were also rolled up on a quarterly basis to the company's executive management.

The client had two primary concerns. Because of the visibility of the product, she wanted to ensure the final report (the contents and the actual writing) were of the highest quality. At the same time, she was having trouble completing the reports within the proscribed time frames. The final straw on this camel's back was that the department of approximately 100 people was set up in a matrix structure, and there were questions about ultimate responsibility.

Exhibit 10.5   Analysis Report RACI Matrix

Analysis Report Process		Senior Analyst	Regional Manager	Functional Manager	Senior Manager	AVP	VP
Project Planning	Resource Allocation	R1	R/A	–	C	C	C
	Department Notification	R1	A	R2	–	C	C
	Data Gathering	R1	A	–	–	C	C
	Update Department	R1	A	R2	–	C	C
Fieldwork	Data Analysis	R1	A	C	C	–	–
	Summary of Results	R1	A	C	C	C	–
	Final Meeting with Department	R1	A	C	–	–	–
Reporting	Final Report	R1	A	R2	C	C	–
	Quarterly Roll-up to Executives	R1	A	–	C	C	–
Results Updates	Results Management	R1	A	–	–	–	–
	Monitoring	A/R	–	–	–		
	Closing	R1	A	–	C		

R1: person responsible for creating the document
R2: signature on the document and e-mail from that individual

In our initial discussions we found that their first priority was the issue of quality. In addition, it was obvious that the matrix structure was causing issues. We initially worked with the client to develop a RACI Matrix. Exhibit 10.5 is an approximation of the final matrix.

To better understand the overall process, the final RACI Matrix was first broken down into the units and then subdivided into the activities on which the RACI Matrix would be developed. The functional roles across the top were set up to mirror the department's corporate hierarchy. This also emphasized the issues with the matrix structure, as the senior analysts reported to the regional managers, the regional managers reported to the senior managers, and the senior managers and functional managers reported to the assistant vice president (AVP).

The matrix showed that our client's interactions with other departments were an important part of the overall process. Four of the activities identified related to keeping the department informed of our client's progress. It was also quickly apparent that a large number of people were involved throughout this process. In an attempt to help ensure quality, a number of touch points had been established.

Vertical Analysis

One of the first things to jump out in the vertical analysis was that the regional manager was listed as accountable for every step in the process. Our client felt it was important to place that accountability at the level where the actual work was being completed. However, that brought to light one of the potential flaws in this (and any matrix) approach. The functional managers, who had no authority over or accountability to those individuals on the regional side, had some responsibility for completion of the work. This represented an area of serious potential conflict.

There were also no empty spaces under the senior manager, regional manager, or senior analyst roles; and there is only one empty space for the functional manager. Most of the work was actually being done by the senior analyst, and a lack of empty spaces made sense at that level. But this analysis was our first indication that too many people were involved in the overall process.

Finally, the matrix indicated that the AVP and vice president (VP) were involved in a consulting role for every project that was executed. Again, this raised the question as to whether every project (as many as 100 to 200 annually) required that degree of participation.

Horizontal Analysis

The first thing that becomes evident in the horizontal analysis is the way Responsible individuals were noted in this matrix. As previously discussed, there is not a problem with more than one person being noted as Responsible. However, the client wanted additional information spelled out in the final product. Accordingly, we used R1 to indicate the person responsible for completing the document and R2 to indicate the person responsible for delivering the document. Note that, once again, the accountability lies with the person in charge of the individual preparing the document, but not the one delivering it. In addition, the person responsible for delivering the document (and, in this case, the person responsible for the relationships on a functional basis) had no authority over completion of the document.

It is also apparent that some activities have too many people involved (e.g., every box is filled in). Five of the activities show every level is involved in one way or another. While this may sometimes be an indicator that there has not been enough drill down in determining the RACI Matrix activities, in this instance it was a red flag that too many people were involved.

Related to the prior observation, there are a large number of Consults and Informs. An obvious concern came up that too many people were being consulted and informed as the process moved forward. In addition, there was an unusual idiosyncrasy whereby the functional manager was generally informed on each step but for two exceptions—the Summary of Results and the final meeting with the department. This, along with the number of R2s in the matrix, emphasized the responsibility issues that were inherent in the client's organizational structure.

The Process Map

Even a cursory review of this RACI Matrix shows there are issues with involvement and responsibility. To better understand the problems and the process, we developed a Process Map based on our discussions with the client. The final map is shown in Exhibit 10.6.

We made three adjustments to this final map to better serve the purpose of our project. The first was to show the activities as listed

Exhibit 10.6   Analysis Report Process Map

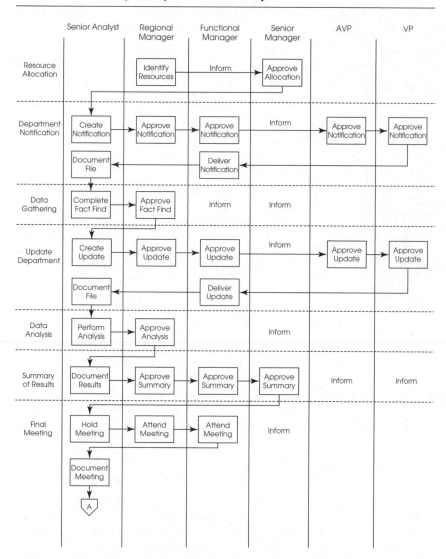

on the RACI Matrix. This allowed the client to better understand how the Process Map related to that matrix. Second was to indicate those individuals that were to be kept informed. This was done to emphasize the number of people involved in each step of the process. Third was to remove a number of the decisions that were inherent to the actual process and just indicate that approval was required. For example, creation of the department notification should have four separate decision points, one for each time a manager is asked to approve the document, with a corresponding referral back every time additional work was required. While this would have driven home the issue of too many decision points, it was not really necessary given the overall state of the process. (And this is a good point to re-emphasize something we have said a number of times. Process Maps are just a tool. What we have outlined in previous chapters is not the gospel, but an approach to better understand processes. Just as we did here, mold that tool to the needs of your project.)

What becomes strikingly apparent from just a cursory review is that this process does not flow well downhill. The large number of handoffs as well as the number of steps that go horizontally across the map revealed a process that focused too closely on collaboration and not enough on efficiency of the operation. Even something as simple as department notification required the involvement of six people, some twice. In addition, six of the processes required involvement of at least four people. And, even when they were not officially involved, there were 18 separate points where individuals were to be kept informed. The efficiency issues in this operation were never as evident as when this Process Map was presented.

However, in this instance, the client made an interesting choice. While our initial involvement was intended to help with both quality and timeliness, she felt that the quality issue was paramount. Therefore, they were loathe to change the overall process. To address the efficiency as well as the issues with the matrix structure, a solution based on touchpoint meetings was developed. Rather than each box in the process representing a handoff, it was determined that everyone involved attend one meeting. Rather than four steps, this became one. It had the benefit of streamlining the process while maintaining the quality control. In addition, there was the added benefit of all participants having buy-in to the final product. Finally, by bringing together all the players at one time to discuss issues, everyone gained a better understanding of each person's needs, reducing the amount of time required for rewrite because everyone better understood how the overall final product could relate to individual needs.

Process Map to RACI Matrix

Just as some issues relating to a RACI Matrix can be better viewed by using a Process Map, issues related to a process that are not apparent with a Process Map can be brought to light better with the RACI Matrix.

We developed a Process Map while working with a client on his approach to internal investigations. (See Exhibit 10.7.) The problems within the department were already well understood. In particular, there were delays in the handling of these investigations and questions about their completeness. It was recognized that the zone managers (the ones to whom the investigators reported) did not fully understand how investigations should be conducted, and the existing investigation process was built around a manual systems that caused delays. A process was developed in which the zone managers were kept informed, but the subject matter expert (the investigation manager) had a larger role in the final product. The resulting Process Map represented how the process would look rather than how it currently existed.

In general, the process seemed very straightforward. The investigator was allowed to do the necessary work with clerical support. As the process moved along, the investigations manager provided input and necessary approvals until final disposition of the case. The only interaction required from the zone manager was related to the planning process and the final report. This was done to accommodate issues related to the way the zone managers oversaw their operations. In general, it was felt that this new process would do a good job of satisfying the quality and timeliness needs of the department.

However, there was a nagging feeling that something was not right about this approach. In particular, it seemed the solutions ignored problems that had not surfaced under the current situation. Based on this proposed Process Map, we developed a RACI Matrix to better understand the responsibilities (see Exhibit 10.8).

The resulting RACI Matrix made the underlying issue easily apparent—the individual noted as Accountable for more than half of the activities had no authority over the people Responsible for the work. In almost every step of the process, the investigator and investigations manager were working closely on reaching the final conclusions of the investigation. However, the zone managers might need to use the investigator resources in other areas. With authority over the investigators and no accountability for the investigations, they were free to reallocate those resources as they saw fit. Because their success measures were not in alignment with those of the investigations manager, their use of investigator resources was

Exhibit 10.7   Investigations Process Map

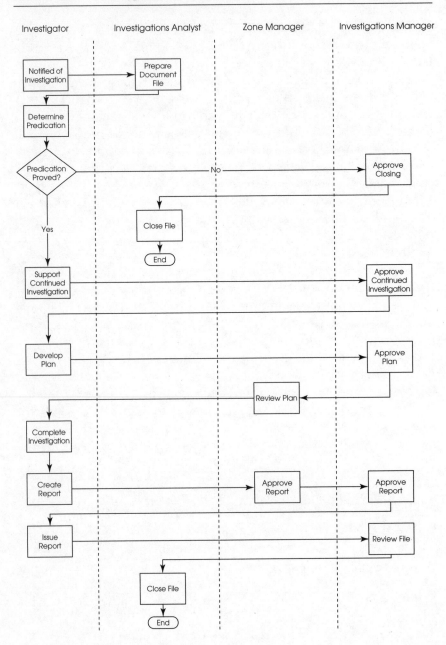

Exhibit 10.8 Investigations RACI Matrix

Investigations	Investigator	Investigations Analyst	Zone Manager	Investigations Manager
Notification	R/A			
Document Initial Investigation	A	R		
Determine Predication	R			A/C
Develop Plan	R		C	A/C
Complete Investigation	R		I	I
Report Results	R		C	A/C
Close Investigation	R	R		A/C

not always in the best interest of the investigations manager. While it might have been inferred from the Process Map, it became much more evident in the RACI Matrix.

At this point, the client had to choose between two options. The first was to reassign the investigators to work directly for the investigations manager. The second was to build accountability for the zone managers into the investigations process. They chose the latter, including successful investigations as part of their bonus structure and including collaboration with the investigations manager as part of that success.

Recap

While Process Mapping does an excellent job of identifying how work gets done, issues may become apparent regarding who has the ultimate responsibility for tasks, actions, and the overall process. The RACI Matrix is a perfect tool to help identify those issues.

A RACI Matrix is a graphical representation showing the activities within a process and the primary individuals involved in that process. For each activity, a determination is made regarding who is Responsible (the ones doing the work), Accountable (the person with the ultimate yes or no authority), Consulted (individuals involved prior to the action continuing), and Informed (those who need to know what is occurring without stopping the process).

The Process Map and RACI Matrix can be used in conjunction to provide a better overview of the entire operation. Process Maps built from RACI Matrices can show whether the process follows a logical flow. RACI Matrices developed from Process Maps can identify accountability issues that may not be apparent in the Process Map.

Key Analysis Points

The Process Profile Worksheet May Be a First Indicator

The first indication that a RACI Matrix may be invaluable in a Process Mapping project may occur in completion of the Process Profile Worksheet. Since the RACI Matrix is ultimately about who is in charge, a Process Profile Worksheet that shows either no one or everyone taking charge is an indicator of an accountability issue. Likewise, discussions with all employees may show similar issues.

Matrix Organization Have Accountability Issues

Another strong indicator that a RACI Matrix may need to be created is when working with a matrixed organizational structure. While companies have found that matrix structures solve various problems, they also open up new issues with responsibility and accountability. In particular, employees often have confusion regarding who to report to and where the final decision making lies.

Review for Accountability and Responsibility

In reviewing RACI Matrices, the first review should focus on the Accountability and Responsibility assignments. No activity should have more than one person Accountable. And, while more than one person can be noted as Responsible, be aware that too many people designated as Responsible may mean no one is actually taking ownership of completion of the activity. Likewise, look for those situations where too many people are involved with the Consult and Inform roles. These may be indicators of bottlenecks or over-control of an activity.

Too Many/Not Enough Blanks

Also review the RACI Matrix to see if there are too many or too few blank boxes. Too many blank boxes may indicate that an activity may not be necessary or one of the functional roles need not be involved. Too many boxes completed can be an indicator that one person may be overloaded, there may be bottlenecks, or too many people are involved.

Mold the Tools

Process Mapping and RACI Matrices are tools used to help analyze processes. As such, they can be adapted to fit the needs of each project. While a number of guidelines have been set up for developing these tools, they are only guidelines. Mold the tools to fit your needs.

11

Enterprise Risk Management and Process Mapping

Acknowledge the reality of risk. Denial is a common tactic that substitutes deliberate ignorance for thoughtful planning.
—Charles Tremper

Efficiency versus Effectiveness

Up to this point, we have focused on using the Process Mapping approach to help streamline the process—the efficiency. But Process Mapping is also an excellent opportunity to ensure the right work is being done—the effectiveness. As we have discussed, a process is in place to achieve some objective. Therefore, when we talk about the efficiency of the process, we are talking about achieving that objective in as expeditious a manner as possible. When we talk about the effectiveness of a process, we are talking about how well the process achieves that objective. Related to all this is the risk to that objective. Accordingly, the effectiveness of the process relates to how well those risks are mitigated.

One of the most important pieces of work to come out in the last few years related to risk is *Enterprise Risk Management—Integrated*

Framework. Many companies have adopted this framework to establish and evaluate their risk management processes, and it has become central to many companies' assurance activities. Because of its importance, many companies are looking for ways to ensure the integrated framework is working properly or to find ways for it to work more efficiently. Process Mapping can be an important tool in providing assurance that the framework is working as intended or for enhancing the assessments that are being completed as a part of any risk management approach.

Enterprise Risk Management: A Primer

To understand how the Process Mapping approach can be used to help a department or company better address risk issues, it is necessary to understand the basics of enterprise risk management. Even for those individuals who may already be familiar with the concepts, a refresher will help crystallize how these concepts relate to Process Mapping.

In 1992, the Committee of Sponsoring Organizations of the Treadway Commission (COSO—a question that will never come up on *Jeopardy*) produced its first publication, an integrated framework for controls and the control environment. This provided a framework for the overall establishment and evaluation of controls related to the achievement of companies' objectives. However, as additional scandals rocked the business world, the public began to realize that the control framework was only a part of a bigger picture; there needed to be a broader look at the full landscape.

Accordingly, in 2004 COSO introduced *Enterprise Risk Management—Integrated Framework* (commonly referred to as ERM). This framework was developed to provide a way for companies to better understand how to address and respond to various risks. For this model, risk was defined around the risk to the achievement of the company's objectives. And one of the most important aspects it brought to the discussion was the inclusion of strategic risk—the risk that high-level goals might not be aligned with or support the entity's mission.

The model for the framework is a cube which shows the interrelationships of the objectives, the entity and its units, and the eight components of the ERM framework. A version of this framework is shown in Exhibit 11.1.

Exhibit 11.1   ERM Framework

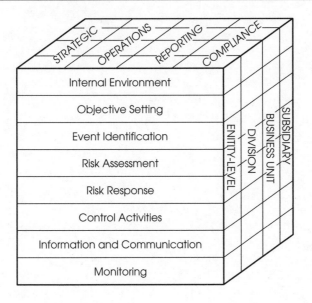

Objectives

The top of the cube shows the four categories of entity objectives—
Strategic, Operations, Reporting, and Compliance. Operations objectives relate to the effectiveness and efficiency of operations; Reporting
objectives support the reliability of the entity's internal and external
reporting of financial and nonfinancial information; Compliance
objectives are those addressing how the company conforms to applicable laws and regulations; and, as noted previously, Strategic objectives
represent high-level goals aligned with and supporting the company's
mission or vision. While there is no specific hierarchy, it is apparent
that the Operations, Reporting, and Compliance objectives derive
from the Strategic objectives.

The topics we have discussed in Process Mapping relate perfectly to this aspect of ERM. In particular, since Operations risks are
based on effectiveness and efficiency, it is easy to see that any Process
Mapping project will have that efficiency and effectiveness at the
heart of the project. However, Reporting risk and Compliance risk
can also be a part of a Process Mapping project. Process Mapping is
about understanding how processes and changes in those processes
affect operations, and that includes effects on appropriate reporting

and compliance. Finally, we have also talked about understanding the objectives of a process and how they relate to the overall strategy of the entity. This ties nicely to the concepts of Strategic objectives that exist in the ERM framework.

Business Level

The right-hand side of the cube shows the various levels within the business at which ERM can be applied—entity, division, business unit, subsidiary, and so on. The intent is to show the relevance of ERM to all levels within a company. In addition, this serves as a reminder that the ERM framework should be evaluated at all levels. On one hand, a company may drill down too far; they may not recognize that using a silo approach to their self-analysis has caused them to miss risks at the entity level. On the other hand, a company may miss an opportunity to improve local conditions if only a broad assessment is performed at the entity level.

Again, this matches the possible approaches of a Process Mapping project. Analysis can occur at any level within the company. We have described analyses at the division, business unit, and subsidiary level. But an entity-wide analysis could be performed in much the same manner.

Components

The heart of the ERM framework is the eight components that actually comprise the ERM process. These start with the high-level concepts within risk management and work down to the tactical applications. The first layer is Internal Environment. This represents the tone of the organization; how it influences employees' attitudes and approach regarding risk management. This includes everything from risk appetite and risk management philosophy to the integrity, ethical value, and competence of the people working for the company. It is the basis for all other components of the framework.

The next four sections work closely together to establish the relationship between objectives and managing the risk of achieving those objectives. The first step is to actually set the objectives the entity will try to accomplish (Objective Setting). Once the objectives are established, the next step is to identify all those events that, if they occur, can affect the entity's objectives (Event Identification). As defined, these can have positive as well as negative impacts. Once the events are identified, the entity considers the extent to which these potential events can impact achievement of objectives (Risk Assessment). Next is to determine what steps the entity will take related to each identified risk (Risk Response). This response can be anything from avoidance (exiting the activity) to reducing or mitigating the risk (establishing controls) to acceptance of the risk (taking no action). These responses are designed to reduce the risks to the point where they are within the entity's risk tolerance.

The final three components focus on the details related to the risk response. The first of these three components is the establishment of Control Activities—the policies and procedures developed to help ensure management's risk responses are carried out. Pertinent information must also be captured and effectively communicated (Information & Communication) to enable people to carry out their responsibilities related to risk management. Finally, Monitoring is the assessment over time of the presence and functioning of the ERM components to ensure the risk management process is working effectively.

In each of these components there is a role for Process Mapping. Much of our earlier work has a direct relation to such concepts as Control Activities, Information & Communication, and Monitoring. But every component is itself a process that can be addressed through Process Mapping analysis. Various processes within the company help support each of the ERM components, and those subsidiary processes can likewise be analyzed through Process Mapping.

And Now for Process Mapping

Any risk management process is a candidate for Process Mapping, because, whether articulated or not, risk management approaches represent processes. ERM can serve as a blueprint for best practices in the risk management field—a benchmark against which any risk process can be measured. Therefore, to understand how a Process Mapping approach can be used with ERM, it is first necessary to have a better understanding of the ERM process.

Exhibit 11.2 shows the relationship among the various attributes of ERM at the entity level. The Internal Environment (including the influencing factors within that environment) works together with Risk Management Philosophy and Risk Appetite to drive Objective Setting. Considering all four types of objectives, events are identified. If opportunities arise, this information will feed back into new objectives. The identified risks are then quantified through the

Exhibit 11.2   ERM Information and Communication Flow—Entity Level

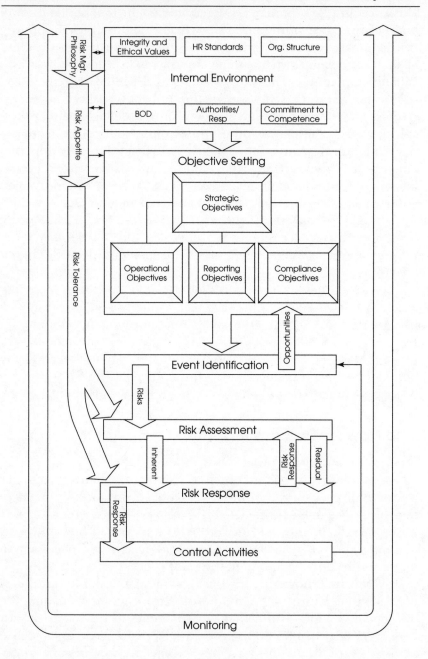

Risk Assessment process. With additional consideration of the Risk Tolerance and Risk Appetite, a Risk Assessment is completed. The inherent risk values are then used to determine the Risk Response. Based on this response, another Risk Assessment may be undertaken to determine whether the residual risk is now within the Risk Tolerance. Control Activities are established over the Risk Responses. These Control Activities can then feed back to Event Identification to strengthen the Risk Responses. Finally, Monitoring activities are established to ensure the entire process stays on track.

While this flow of information is true at any level within the entity, it is important to keep in mind how the entity-level flow affects the business unit level flow. Exhibit 11.3 enhances this understanding by showing the relationship of the entity-level flow

Exhibit 11.3　ERM Information and Communication Flow—Business Unit Level

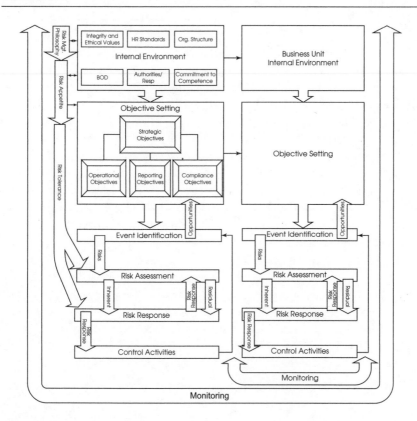

to the business unit–level flow. Note that the overall processes are the same. However, it is the entity's Internal Environment, Risk Management Philosophy, and Risk Appetite that helps make up the business unit's Internal Environment. Likewise, the entity's Objective Setting process helps drive the Objective Setting of the business unit. These relationships continue to be true as you drill deeper into the company (e.g., divisions, subsidiaries, even individual departments).

With this understanding of the overall process, we can start applying the basic concepts of Process Mapping to an analysis of the ERM approach in an entity or business unit. The ERM framework provides the units within the overall process—the process identification. From this, it is a matter of going through the various aspects of information gathering to better understand the process. Exhibit 11.4 shows a potential Process Profile Worksheet that could be developed from this assessment.

You can see how the information in this worksheet is driven by the ERM framework. For example, we have identified the process owner as the CEO. ERM is defined as a process effected by the board of directors, management, and other personnel. From this definition, we identify the ultimate owner of the process as the CEO. As another example, the description of the process is derived from the definition of ERM and focuses on the actual work that is done— identifying events and managing risks.

It is an interesting dilemma determining triggers, inputs, and outputs for the ERM process. In actuality, ERM is a continual process and, as such, the trigger event that starts the process is the establishment of the entity in the first place. While we might just use the first component as the starting point, we have the same issues with internal environment. (We will specifically address that component later.) Therefore, we have used the setting of strategy as the beginning of this process, with the risk responses and monitoring system representing the end. The events throughout the process relate to the components of ERM. (Even if the entity under review has a structured approach to ERM that is different than the COSO model, this still makes a good framework for evaluating the entity's approach.) The units within the process are represented by the ERM components just as the events were. And, ownership of those individual units will vary greatly depending on the entity.

Exhibit 11.4   Process Profile Worksheet—ERM

Process Name—Number	Process Owner
Enterprise Risk Management	CEO

Description	
A process designed to identify potential events that may affect the entity and manage risks to be within its risk appetite.	

Triggers	
Event beginning: Established strategy Event ending process: Risk management approach Additional events: The components of ERM	

Input—Items and Sources	
The entity's strategic direction	

Output—Items and Customers	
Risk Responses Monitoring System	

Process Units	Process Unit Owners
Components of ERM	Various

Business Objective(s)	Business Risks
Provide reasonable assurance regarding the achievement of objectives	Poor internal environment Objectives not established Important events not identified Etc.

Key Controls	Measure of Success
Ethics hot line Annual re-evaluation of objectives Annual risk profile completed	Achievement of objectives

The business objective comes from the last part of the definition of ERM. The business risks and key controls shown are just examples. In this situation, we have identified one for each of the components. Finally, there may be several measures of success that can be considered. However, we have only listed the ultimate measure—successful achievement of the objectives.

As mentioned previously, the use of ERM will provide a good framework for discussions with executive management. Unless executive management has a very good knowledge of the concepts of ERM, the discussions will not necessarily revolve around the specific components. However, the reviewer's understanding of the information needed for the Process Profile Worksheet, as well as the ERM components, will provide a solid basis for wide-ranging discussions about executive management's approach to enterprise-wide risk management.

There are really three approaches to evaluating ERM using Process Mapping. The first relates to the previous discussion and will result in a map of the overall ERM process. This will be completed at a very high level—perhaps at the task level, just below the components. This will give a sense of what is occurring, but does not lend itself to in-depth analysis.

A greater value comes from the second approach that can be used—drilling deeper into the individual components, seeing them as individual processes that work together to accomplish the objectives of ERM. This allows in-depth analysis of each component and can be tailored to focus on specific components. Related to this, Process Maps can be created for combined components that work in conjunction. For example, in our prior discussion we described the components Objective Setting, Event Identification, Risk Assessment, and Risk Response as working closely together to establish the relationship between objectives and risks. Accordingly, the four can be evaluated as an entire process to better ensure they work in harmony.

The third approach is to use current Process Mapping projects to also provide feedback on the overall ERM approach. In this situation, all information related to the ERM process is rolled up to the process owner on a periodic basis. Even if there is no such agreement, a situation may occur in which significant issues related to ERM are identified during an individual project. These should be brought to the attention of the ERM process owner through available communication channels. (It may be that such findings become the impetus for executive management to take on a more comprehensive review of the ERM process.) If you are unable to directly approach the ERM process owner, these results can still be incorporated in the final report, pointing out to management that this is an issue requiring action for reasons related to risk management.

In the following sections, we will explore each component of ERM more closely. We will first show how a Process Mapping project over that component might be approached. Then we will provide information on how any Process Mapping project can provide input into that component of ERM.

The Internal Environment

Mapping the Internal Environment

The Internal Environment provides the context for the other components of the ERM framework. Completing the Process Map of the Internal Environment is one of the more challenging projects in an ERM mapping project. It does not define itself as a process as well as other components. Instead, it is defined as "the tone of the organization, influencing the risk consciousness of its people." The key to understanding how to evaluate this component, then, is understanding what it is comprised of—risk appetite, board oversight, integrity, ethical values, competence, and so on.

Accordingly, the better approach is to analyze each of these defined parts of the Internal Environment through Process Mapping. The results of these analyses then provide an assessment of the Internal Environment. As an example, we might do a separate analysis of integrity and ethical values. (Even though they are separate components of Internal Environment, they are intertwined sufficiently to allow us to evaluate them together.) Exhibit 11.5 is the Process Profile Worksheet that might result from our initial analysis of the process.

We have identified the CEO as the owner. It is possible that the company has an Ethics Officer and that individual might be the owner of this process. However, for something as important as ethics and integrity, putting this under the CEO may still be the best approach. As with our analysis of the ERM process, the description provided for this exhibit is based on the definitions and information provided by the ERM model.

The identification of an actual process called *Integrity and Ethical Value* is again a challenge (just as it was with ERM and Internal Environment). Because this is a core piece of the Internal Environment, we have used the established strategy as the event beginning (just as we did with the ERM process). The input uses this same approach. The ending is defined as employees applying the behavior. This recognizes that the success of this process is not just about delivery and acceptance, but of actual application. Likewise, the output includes a set of standards and people

Exhibit 11.5 Process Profile Worksheet—Integrity and Ethical Value

Process Name—Number	Process Owner
Integrity and Ethical Value	CEO

Description	
Convey the message that integrity and ethical values cannot be compromised and management must continually demonstrate a commitment to high ethical standards	

Triggers	
Event beginning:	Established strategy
Event ending process:	Employees apply the message
Additional events:	Develop standards
	Deliver message
	Obtain feedback
	Update approach

Input—Items and Sources
The entity's strategic direction

Output—Items and Customers
Standards of behavior
Observed behavior

Process Units	Process Unit Owners
Development and update of standards	Various
Ongoing delivery of message	
Obtain feedback	

Business Objective(s)	Business Risks
Demonstrate the highest level of integrity and ethical values throughout the organization	Executive management does not provide model
	Message is not delivered and/or received

Key Controls	Measure of Success
Ethics hot line	Use of upward communication
Open door policy	Feedback results
	Customer and vendor feedback
	Consistent application of disciplinary measures

properly applying them. Events between the start and finish are establishment of, communication on, application of, and feedback regarding the standards. The process units mirror this approach and the owners of those units would be identified throughout the Process Mapping project.

The objective is based on information in the ERM framework and shows a serious commitment to integrity and ethics. The two business risks relate to management not "walking the talk" and problems in message delivery. Accordingly, the key controls have to do with the openness of communication and the ability to provide feedback when there are problems. It should be noted that the ERM model lists a number of controls that should exist, including "Entity's standards of behavior reflect integrity and ethical value," "Penalties are applied to employees who violate the code," and "Mechanisms encourage employee reporting of suspected violations." The list provided in the model is an excellent tool and should be considered when evaluating the integrity and ethical values portion of the project. But the Process Profile Worksheet is intended to record just the key controls and should relate to the primary risks you have previously identified. Finally, there are a number of measures of success that also relate to the objectives, risks, and key controls that were previously noted.

This same approach can then be used for each of the factors that make up the internal environment—the risk management philosophy, the entity's risk appetite, oversight by the board of directors, the competence of the entity's people, and the way management assigns authority and responsibility and organizes and develops its people. And, just as we did earlier, some of these can be combined to provide a more holistic picture of that internal environment.

Feedback on the Internal Environment

Many aspects of Internal Environment are touched on by Process Mapping projects. In particular, this type of information is obtained during the Process Identification and Information Gathering stages of any Process Mapping project. In particular, discussions with upper management will provide insight regarding the true tone at the top. Most of this information will not be the result of questions directly related to the Internal Environment. Rather, you will learn this from the way they speak of others, the way they speak of the company, and the general tone of the discussion. As an example, listen for executive management who speaks of its employees with a sense of trust. And, likewise, listen for those touches of mistrust that can intrude.

As you work your way down from executive management, you will have the chance to compare their perceptions with those of everyone else. As you gather information for documents such as the Process Profile Worksheet, you will gain information on the

Internal Environment. When discussing the risks to objectives, include broader questions about the existence of a specific or implied risk management philosophy. A discussion of key controls can also be the springboard for questions about the risk appetite. (For example, numerous key controls may be an indicator of low risk tolerance.) You can ask specific questions related to leadership, competency, communication, and accountability; even if you are not specifically asking about the Internal Environment, you will begin to get a feel for it.

During the construction of the maps, use the same radar to determine whether employees are receiving the same message management is trying to convey, and whether the employees believe it. Listen for messages from employees that imply a mistrust of management or other employees. Don't feed that mistrust if it is identified, but try to get to the root of what is being said. We have had numerous situations where employees indicated concerns about management or fellow employees. It is a natural course of work that people may be disgruntled, and we take any individual complaint with a grain of salt. However, if more than one person has an issue, or there are specific indications of a concern, then we will carefully pursue them to see if there is an issue with the environment. In one situation, we asked an employee if there was anything else she would have liked us to ask. She immediately replied she wished we had asked if there were any questionable activities going on in the office. When we followed up, she provided information relating to the integrity of one of the supervisors—information that led to follow-up by management. While at first blush this might imply an environment problem (and at a very limited level this was true), we also saw this as evidence that the overall environment was in decent shape. Not only had the person felt secure enough to bring us specific information, but the department took immediate action when advised of the issue.

Finally, even in the map itself, look for information relating to the internal environment. Numerous approvals or low authority levels could be indicators of a low risk tolerance or even a high degree of mistrust. As another example, construction of a higher-level process map might reveal that processes are performed in a vacuum—one department not working with associated departments—which could be an indication of an organizational issue related to the overall environment.

Objective Setting

Mapping Objective Setting

While Internal Environment provides the context for ERM, Objective Setting is the precondition for all that follows. Objectives represent an articulation of (usually) measurable goals by which the company will achieve its mission; they are the skeleton upon which the entity's Internal Environment and vision rest. Therefore, the setting of objectives is the first true process in the ERM framework.

Evaluating the process of Objective Setting is a much easier task, as it is usually an annual event, executive management usually understands it as an integral part of planning, and everyone understands (or thinks they understand) the concept of setting objectives. The challenge is that people do not always see the connection between objectives and vision. In most operations, the objective-setting process has become a mind-numbing annual event during which prior results are run through a process, tweaked, and sent out to be achieved. People involved in the act of setting objectives (or those who are recipients of the results) have lost sight of how the mission should drive the establishment of objectives.

Exhibit 11.6 is a sample Process Profile Worksheet for the Objective Setting process.

The owner of this process will vary depending on the company. It may also be owned by a committee of executives. If you run across that scenario, be sure you list the committee chair as the owner, not the committee. As we have emphasized previously, success for any process is dependent upon having one person responsible. And success of the Process Mapping project is also dependent upon having one person ultimately be responsible for the results.

The description is simple, describing the role of the entity's mission in building the objectives, the various types of objectives to be developed, and the purpose of the objectives related to the mission.

In the example we have here, we are using the annual objective-setting process as the start of the event. This process will also vary widely depending on the operation. For a start-up, the trigger is the company coming into existence. For some operations, the update of objectives is a quarterly process, and for others it might be every two or three years. In some cases, it may be more ad hoc, based on someone's perception that it is time to take another look

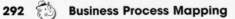

Exhibit 11.6: Process Profile Worksheet—Objective Setting

Process Name—Number	Process Owner
Objective Setting	Various

Description	
Use the entity's mission to develop strategic and related objectives intended to achieve that mission	

Triggers	
Event beginning:	Annual reassessment of objectives
Event ending process:	Full set of strategic and related objectives
Additional events:	Develop strategic objectives
	Distribute strategic objectives
	Develop operational, compliance, and reporting objectives

Input—Items and Sources
Entity's Mission Statement
Prior objectives
Historical data

Output—Items and Customers
Updated Objectives

Process Units	Process Unit Owners
Develop strategic objectives	Various
Develop related objectives	
Distribute objectives	

Business Objective(s)	Business Risks
Develop and distribute objectives that are aligned with risk appetite and drive risk tolerance levels for activities	Related objectives are not aligned with strategic Objectives are not completed in time to support successful achievement of mission

Key Controls	Measure of Success
Objectives committee reviews completed objectives for alignment Project Manager oversees timely completion of objectives	All objectives completed per schedule Feedback from employees regarding understanding of objectives Achievement of mission

at the objectives. Another event that might trigger the setting of new objectives would be a change in the mission of the company. Such changes should not occur frequently (if they do, it may be an indicator of another problem), but when they do, it is important to remember that this should cause a re-evaluation of the objectives.

We have identified three related inputs. The first is the mission statement, which drives all objective setting. The next is the prior objectives. These can be used to benchmark past successes and failures to better understand this year's objectives. The final input is general historical data. This might include industry trends and prior financial results. One other input that we have not identified in the Process Profile Worksheet deserves mention. This comes from Exhibits 11.2 and 11.3, which show the ERM information and communication flow. You will see information flowing back up from the event identification component. One other input that may be used to drive new objectives is the identification of positive events— that is, opportunities that may not have been properly addressed in the initial determination of the objectives.

The final event of the process is distribution of the completed objectives. This matches the output identified later. The additional events show a separation between strategic objectives and compliance, reporting, and operational objectives. This separation emphasizes the role of strategic objectives in helping establish the related objectives. We have also included the distribution of the strategic objectives prior to establishment of the related objectives to show that the strategic objectives have to be available before the related ones can be completed. The process units reflect this approach.

The objective of this process derives from the information in the ERM model—in particular, the focus on using the objectives to align risk appetites and drive risk tolerance. The related risks then include the objectives not being aligned and problems with timeliness. This second risk is intended to focus on the issue of objectives coming out after the year has started. Particularly with aggressive objectives, if the content is unknown, the entity spends the remainder of the year playing catch-up and runs the risk of not meeting those objectives.

We have set up two different controls in this particular example. The first is a committee that oversees the objective process. In particular, this would help ensure alignment. The second control is the use of a project manager—someone to make sure that the trains run on time. The first measure of success relates to timeliness. The next one has to do with how well the objectives are understood by employees. While this particular risk was not identified, nor was there a key control, it reveals that employee understanding of objectives is an integral part of those objectives being successful. In an actual Process Mapping situation, this would represent an opportunity to go back and ensure the measures, risks, and key controls are correct. The final measure of success is the ultimate one, and while it is true that a mission is seldom met each year (mission statements are about long-term strategies), it is still a good practice to measure how well the company is progressing in that regard.

Feedback on Objective Setting

During any Process Mapping project, making an assessment of the objective-setting component would seem easy, as this is one of the primary questions asked during the Information Gathering stage. However, an in-depth review will include deeper questions than just asking people what they think the objectives are. When talking to management, it is important to not only ask what the objective of the process is, but to also ask what the overall objectives (strategic, operational, etc.) of the department and company are. From this, there should be a discussion of how the objective of the process supports the objectives of the department and how the objectives of the department support the objectives of the entity.

This can be an even more important discussion if multiple departments are involved in the process. The first step is to determine whether the departments are even in agreement regarding the objective of the overall process. The next step is to see if the objectives of each department are in conflict. This is the type of problem that is often encountered when reviewing sales operations. Almost any sales department can articulate an objective regarding increased sales. They can also articulate how this supports the growth initiative of their company. However, to achieve these numbers, they may try to sell below the price suggested by corporate management or make promises about customer service that cannot be met. The growth, then, is at the expense of objectives related to profitability, customer service, or even ethics.

We experienced a similar situation in the review of a *Marketing Quality Assurance* process. The company had set the objective of increasing profitable growth—that is, an increase in unit sales coupled with profitable sale of those units. The numbers associated with this growth were aggressive, but well within the company's risk tolerance levels. The department in charge of the sales force had a related objective of increasing growth. Their success was measured in an increase of unit sales. The department actually doing the quality assurance analysis had the objective of reducing errors in the sales process. Initially, because they both supported parts of the overall objective, it was not apparent that there might be a conflict. However, further inspection revealed that the department in charge of the sales force also controlled the corrective actions resulting from the quality assurance findings. Although they agreed that sales quality was important, they did not want to strictly enforce the quality assurance review results, because this would adversely affect sales. Error ratios were not improving. The final assessment was that the department in charge of sales had to build more accountability into its objectives related to profitability vis-à-vis the error ratios.

As the Process Mapping project moves into the various interviewing stages (even at the mapping stage), it is a good idea to see if individuals can articulate the objectives of the company and the department. First, it is an indicator of how well people understand the way their work supports the overall objectives. Second, it can be an indicator that the "true" objectives (those that people perceive as being real) may not match or may even contradict the actual objectives. Third, it can tell the interviewer a lot about the environment. For example, when people do not know the overall objectives (and are effectively being asked to work in a vacuum), there is a heightened chance that the closed environment is not conducive to the trust and honesty that is exhibited by successful companies.

Event Identification

Mapping Event Identification

Identification of events is the first step towards determining how an entity will respond to risk. If all pertinent events are not identified, the company may not be taking appropriate action to reduce the resulting risk. Further, as event identification includes positive events, the company may be missing out on opportunities to better achieve its objectives. In particular, reviews over this area focus on how well risks are linked to objectives, how feedback mechanisms ensure the company is warned of impending events, and whether important risks have been overlooked. Exhibit 11.7 shows a potential Process Profile Worksheet for Event Identification.

As with the previous Process Profile Worksheet, the owner of the overall operation will be dependent upon the makeup of the entity. This is a situation where it will be very easy for an entity to farm out pieces of the overall project. The important point in this situation, once again, is to have one person overseeing the overall operation, which will ensure a standardized approach and the inclusion of all objectives and all potential events.

Exhibit 11.7 Process Profile Worksheet—Event Identification

Process Name—Number	Process Owner
Event Identification	Various
Description	
Identify events that can have a negative or positive affect on the entity's ability to successfully implement strategy and achieve objectives.	
Triggers	
Event beginning: Objectives are developed Event ending process: Identify potential risks and opportunities Additional events: Analyze objectives Analyze potential events	
Input—Items and Sources	
Entity's objectives Industry events General current events	
Output—Items and Customers	
Risks and opportunities related to the objectives	

Process Units	Process Unit Owners
Analyze objectives Analyze potential events	Various

Business Objective(s)	Business Risks
Identify the significant risks and opportunities that might have an impact on the entity's achievement of its objectives	Unable to establish a full collection of potential events All objectives not considered

Key Controls	Measure of Success
Checklist of sources and approaches to event identification maintained Project manager oversees event identification process	Achievement of objectives No surprises

The objective comes from information in the ERM model. The important factors are that this includes negative and positive events, and it focuses on the entity's ability to achieve objectives.

This process starts once objectives are set. The first input is the objectives. The other inputs relate to sources of information that will help in the determination of events that might occur. Industry events represent the set of events that typically happen within an industry. Each industry should have its own resources for such information, and this can be invaluable for ensuring that a comprehensive list is established. The second is general current events. These represent political, financial, and other trends occurring that could give rise to an event impacting the objectives.

At the end of the process, sufficient analysis should have been conducted to transform these events into potential risks or opportunities. If they are neither, then they need not be considered. The additional events within this operation are relatively simple—analyze the objectives, analyze the events. The process units are similarly titled.

The objective of the process also shows the transformation from events to risks and opportunities. Two risks have been identified—both related to not evaluating the full palette of information. The first is the risk of not having all events, and the second is not having all objectives. To help mitigate those risks, one of the key controls is the establishment of a project manager charged with overseeing the entire process. The second control ensures that the fullest possible list of sources has been used. The first measure of success matches one we have seen in previous Process Profile Worksheets—achievement of the objectives. The second relates very closely to the concept of identifying events. "No surprises" does not mean that an event does not occur. Rather, it means that any event that does occur was foreseen.

Feedback on Event Identification

Once again, the Information Gathering stage of the Process Mapping project lends itself to supporting analysis of this component. The issue of risks to achievement of the process's objectives is included in the discussions that lead to completion of the Process Profile Worksheet. In developing the risks to the process, ensure that the identified risk is not only pertinent to the objective of the process, but also to the objectives of the department. These discussions may lead to the realization that the identified risk is not as large as first thought. If it is found that the risk does not have much impact on the company, then one of two things may be true—either the wrong risk has been identified, or the process may not as important as first thought. In fact, this may be an indicator that a process may not be needed.

Likewise, the measures of success are also a part of discussions related to development of the Process Profile Worksheet. However, this discussion should go beyond a fundamental discussion of measures of success to include an understanding of the actions taken when these measures go outside tolerances—something that might be called "measures of failure." Similarly, go beyond the discussion on how success is measured and include how increased risk is measured. The department may have never thought in these terms, but start them out by discussing what the objectives are and how they monitor to determine whether the objectives will not be met. From this, determine what actions might be taken if it seems that objectives may not be met. Also, determine whether employees monitor these situations as a warning before a problem occurs.

In the Interview and Map Generation stage, the reviewer should be aware of processes that can support the Event Identification process. In particular, reviews of compliance and quality assurance areas lend themselves to this concept. These departments focus on risk and opportunity issues more than most others. However, they are often not viewed as event identifiers. While Chief Compliance Officers and their ilk generally take the broad view of compliance and how it affects the overall entity, individual compliance departments (ones that work within specific business units or departments) often can be too mired in the detail. They focus on ensuring the correctness of individual transactions without seeing the broader risk issues.

In addition, few people working in a compliance environment (no matter what level) think of the issues they work with as opportunities. However, compliance changes can just as easily represent an opportunity for a company as a risk. Likewise, quality assurance departments often are deep in the details of transactions, and even if they are looking for broad root causes related to quality issues, they do not see them in the broader picture. The information they collect in their reviews is an excellent source of risk and opportunities that can lead to better Event Identification. In supporting the Event Identification component, anyone involved in a Process Mapping project should look for the chance to work with individuals in these types of departments.

In general, if companies do a good job in the area of Event Identification, it relates to identifying risks. However, most companies really have no good mechanism for identifying missed opportunities. This is where the Process Mapping project can also provide great insight. We have previously mentioned that many of our best ideas for process improvement have come from the individuals we are interviewing. Likewise, employees who are doing the actual work may have different insights regarding events that can impact their jobs. Asking the correct questions is key. Even asking executives questions like "What risks are there to getting your job done and what opportunities do you see?" can elicit wide-eyed "dumb-foundedness." However, questions such as "What do you think would have the most impact on getting this job done?" or "What could happen to make this job better?" can lead to identification of events that have not been considered at the process level, the department level, or even the entity level.

Risk Assessment

Mapping Risk Assessment

The risk assessment portion of ERM focuses on the extent to which potential events can impact achievement of objectives, looking at these from the aspect of likelihood and impact. Risk assessment includes examining the negative impacts of events across the entity, and includes an assessment of both inherent and residual risks. You may have noticed that our discussion about opportunities is no longer included. As noted in the objective-setting discussion, "opportunities" become an opportunity to adjust objectives. From this point forward, the focus is on the things that can go wrong.

As we move further along the components of ERM, it becomes apparent that the centralized approach is harder to maintain. Some companies will approach risk assessment through the use of a Chief Risk Officer acting as a coordinator, but others will leave this to individual departments. As you analyze the components, be aware that this trend can result in less coordination and poorer results.

Exhibit 11.8 is a sample Process Profile Worksheet for Risk Assessment.

As previously mentioned, the owner of these processes becomes less apparent as we move through the components. If there is a Chief Risk Officer, then that individual is a good candidate for the owner of the Risk Assessment process. In our example, there is a Chief Risk Officer (see controls), but that individual is not the owner. In this scenario, the risk officer is acting as an oversight control and therefore has not been given the ultimate authority over the process. This is a good third-party review, but it still leaves the question of ultimate ownership up in the air.

Exhibit 11.8   Process Profile Work Sheet—Risk Assessment

Process Name—Number	Process Owner
Risk Assessment	Various

Description	
Consider the extent to which potential events might have an impact on achievement of objectives.	

Triggers	
Event beginning:	Identified risks and opportunities
Event ending process:	Ranking of identified risks
Additional events:	Evaluate impact of events
	Evaluate likelihood of events

Input—Items and Sources
Identified risks

Output—Items and Customers
Risks ranked by priority

Process Units	Process Unit Owners
Evaluate impact Evaluate likelihood Prioritize risks and opportunities	Various

Business Objective(s)	Business Risks
Prioritize identified risks in order to determine the entity's appropriate action for each	Different approaches to risk assessment throughout company Improper evaluation of events

Key Controls	Measure of Success
Chief Risk Officer to oversee operations Standardized risk assessment approach	Timely completion of risk assessments As events occur, results match models

The description uses information in the ERM model and hits the primary points of potential events and their effect on objectives. This process is triggered by receiving the identified risks and opportunities, which are also reflected in the input. The event ends with the ranking of these risks and priorities, as reflected in the output. Additional events are the evaluation of the impact and the likelihood of an event. This reinforces an important concept in risk assessment (and one of the suggested approaches from the ERM model)—evaluation based on impact and likelihood. This is also reflected in the Process Units.

The objective speaks to the prioritization and how it will be used to determine the entity's action regarding those risks and opportunities. This helps establish the importance of this step in the ERM process. Two primary risks are identified. The first relates to inconsistency within the company, and the second relates to poor quality. The first key control (the Chief Risk Officer) addresses both risks, while the second control (standardized approach) addresses the inconsistency issue. The measures of success in this scenario include timeliness. It seems obvious that the sooner the risk assessment is completed, the less likely it is that the company will suffer adverse effects from the underlying event. The second measure is much like the "no surprises" notation from the Event Identification worksheet. In this case, not only does the entity not want to be surprised by an event, it wants to be prepared for the impact and likelihood of that event.

Feedback on Risk Assessment

When discussing a process with the client, there are two phases to the discussion of risk. The first has already been addressed when we discussed Event Identification—that is, identifying the risks that can affect the objectives. The second relates to Risk Assessment and the focus of the discussion should be on the true impact of those events. It should also include a discussion of inherent versus residual risk. While discussing the risks to the objectives, make sure the initial discussion is on inherent risk—the worst that could happen if no actions were taken. This will provide insight on the importance of controls built into the process. Then discuss the residual risks to determine the client's interpretation of the effectiveness of controls.

In these discussions, determine the client's assessment of the importance of each risk. As noted, this is usually done by combining the likelihood with the impact. If likelihood and impact are high, then there is a significant need for controls. If both are low, then few controls may be needed. Based on this assessment, you can determine whether the client has overcompensated with a convoluted process that is unnecessary for the risks involved, or may need more key controls in an unprotected process.

And the ultimate question to be asked whenever discussing risk with a client? "What keeps you up at night?" When using a term like risk, people often fall into patterns—providing the answers that seem right. However, when put in more human terms (what keeps you up), people will do more soul searching, trying to find the real problems. This discussion can lead to a better assessment of the risks, which leads to better opportunities for process improvement.

Risk Response

Mapping Risk Response

Risk response is often thought of as the control structure that is put in place to mitigate risks. However, this is only part of the picture and can lead to a myopic review of the process. The full picture of risk response includes avoidance, reduction, sharing, and acceptance. Using the likelihood and impact, management makes a decision on how best to respond. Exhibit 11.9 is a sample Process Profile Worksheet for the Risk Response process.

This description shows a change in focus—there is a greater emphasis on risk tolerance and risk appetite. While risk appetite was considered as a part of the risk assessment, it takes on greater importance at this point. As noted, Risk Response is all about getting the residual risks (those left over after mitigating factors have been put in place) to a level that the entity can tolerate. So the description speaks to developing responses that achieve this.

The start of this is triggered by the completion of the risk assessment. This is also reflected in the input. The ending process is development of the various responses. The output is these responses. It could also be possible to include the various types of responses in the output—for example, lists of activities to avoid, of areas where additional insurance is needed, and of activities that will be continued with no additional change. The additional events are testing out the various responses, performing cost/benefit analyses, and applying the results to the risk appetite. The Process Units match these events.

The objective focuses on effectively getting risks within the risk tolerance. The risks to achieving this objective come from poor communication and poor analysis—as in, poor communication results in a misunderstanding of what the entity will accept and poor analysis results in too much or too little residual risk. To address the communication issue, a corporate risk statement has been developed. Obviously, the effectiveness of this document has to do with how well it has been circulated, how robust it is, and whether it is actually applied. To address the risk of incorrect residual risk calculations, a standardized approach has been developed. The measures of

Exhibit 11.9 Process Profile Worksheet—Risk Response

Process Name—Number	Process Owner
Risk Response	Various
Description	
Using the entity's risk appetite and risk tolerance, determine the appropriate entity's response to the identified risks.	
Triggers	

Event beginning: Complete risk assessment
Event ending process: Identify appropriate risk response
Additional events: Apply various responses to risks
                                  Evaluate costs and benefits
                                  Weigh risk against risk appetite	

Input—Items and Sources	
Completed risk assessment	
Output—Items and Customers	
Responses to significant risks	

Process Units	Process Unit Owners
Evaluate risk Evaluate alternatives Ensure residual risk is within risk appetite	Various

Business Objective(s)	Business Risks
Develop effective risk responses that place residual risk within the entity's risk appetite	Misunderstanding of the entity's risk appetite Incorrect determination of residual risk

Key Controls	Measure of Success
Corporate risk statement Standardized residual risk approach	No events occur that result in losses greater than risk appetite Amount of residual costs from actual events is within expectations

success in this case look at both sides of the issue. The first is much like ones we have seen in previous examples—another way to state "no surprises." The second, however, addresses more than just having things under control—it also takes into consideration having too much control. The term "within expectations" means we don't want it to be over, but we also don't want it to be under.

Feedback on Risk Response

This provides the next section for discussion with management—determining the ways they will respond to the risks. And this will be the final evaluation that shows whether response to risk is a true process or just a reaction to events. In general, if they cannot explain how each process is a response to a risk, then they do not understand the ERM process.

As noted before, this discussion is just as important to have during the actual map generation as in the initial management meetings. Our previous discussions of process mapping have focused on discussions related to "What do you do next?" However, this can easily be followed up with "Why do you do that?" In that respect, the reviewer gets a better picture of the actual actions, and learns the degree to which employees understand how their work supports the overall objectives and responses to risk. It is also worth asking employees what they think is the worst thing that can happen. They may have additional insights into the entire risk process—insights that management cannot see at their high level.

Control Activities

Mapping Risk Response

Control activities are the policies and procedures established to help ensure that risk responses are properly working. This is not the same as every control activity in the entity. Rather, it is the set of controls over the risk responses. For example, if the risk response was avoidance, a control would be put in place to ensure that activity is not occurring. If the risk response was sharing, then the control might be a periodic review of insurance levels. Any control activity can both ensure the risk response is being carried out and be a risk response itself. Accordingly, it can be difficult to identify the control activities related to risk responses. However, this is where an entity using a rigorous ERM process will be able to better show these connections. Exhibit 11.10 is a possible Process Profile Worksheet for Control Activities.

The description of this process focuses on the proper implementation of control activities as they apply to ensuring risk responses are carried out correctly. The trigger that starts this process (as well as the input) is the risk responses themselves. The ending event is the development of the overall approach to these control activities. This is based on the premise that establishment of a set of control activities is only part of the solution and may lead to a helter-skelter approach to this assurance. Accordingly, once the basic activities are developed, there should be an overall approach that will provide assurance regarding the entire framework, not just

Exhibit 11.10   Process Profile Worksheet—Control Activities

Process Name—Number	Process Owner
Control Activities	Various

Description	
Identify and implement the activities necessary to ensure risk responses are carried out properly	

Triggers	
Event beginning:	Complete risk response
Event ending process:	Develop entity-wide control activity approach
Additional events:	Evaluate risk responses
	Determine appropriate controls for each response

Input—Items and Sources
Risk responses

Output—Items and Customers
Integrated control activity strategy

Process Units	Process Unit Owners
Evaluate responses Determine individual controls Develop entity-wide approach	Various

Business Objective(s)	Business Risks
Ensure the entity's risk responses are implemented as designed	Controls designed but not implemented Controls not appropriate for risk response

Key Controls	Measure of Success
Controls designed by controls experts Quality assurance review of key controls	All control activities taking place No surprises

a set of individual controls. The additional events relate to understanding the responses and developing appropriate controls.

With all this in mind, the objective of the process focuses on assurance for the overall implementation. The risks that have been identified are controls that are designed but not implemented, and inappropriately designed controls. The first key control in this scenario focuses on using experts to help design the controls in the first place. After that, there is a quality control review intended to show that controls are working as expected. The first measure is simply that every control is actually being done. The second one is starting to sound redundant—"no surprises."

Feedback on Control Activities

It should already be apparent that these control activities are an integral part of what is being documented in the Process Mapping project. Discussions at all levels of a Process Mapping project should coincide with the needs of this portion of ERM. If the Process Mapping project is specifically intended to include issues related to ERM, an important aspect is the proper identification of controls that are also acting as control activities for ERM. This may not be readily apparent in an individual Process Mapping project, and may mean going back through some of the steps of the project to better understand the risk responses. However, the controls related to ERM may well be some of the more important, and properly isolating and evaluating them can provide additional value to the Process Mapping project.

Information and Communication

Information and Communication is probably the one component of ERM that has the least applicability to a pure process analysis approach. In the Integrated Control Framework developed by COSO (a precursor to ERM), Information and Communication was shown linking the various components together. And that represents a better understanding of its role within ERM—providing value across the entire spectrum of components. Accordingly, rather than talk about Process Mapping the Information and Communication component, we will focus on how Process Mapping projects can provide information about Information and Communication, particularly when that project is being completed on one of the other components.

The ERM model indicates that pertinent information is to be identified, captured, and communicated in a way that allows people to do their jobs effectively. Communication should flow up the organization as well as down, and those messages should clearly convey the intent of the deliverer. It also includes clear communication with outside parties. With that in mind, you can see how there is a lot of value in the proper evaluation of this component.

The evaluation of Information and Communication starts with the first meetings. As discussed in the Internal Environment section, this meeting should ensure that all personnel understand the Internal Environment and are taking steps to communicate it properly. Information and Communication then permeates all discussions. At all levels, the reviewer should be asking what information is needed and whether effective communication is taking place. As one example, the Process Mapping project will have identified measures of success. For those measures, the reviewer should determine whether the information necessary to measure success goes where it needs to go, and whether the message of success (or failure) was properly communicated.

In the map generation, look for those situations where information is generated, where it is communicated, and where it is received. Then ensure that there are no gaps among them. These gaps represent opportunities to improve the communication of information.

Monitoring

Mapping Monitoring

The final aspect of ERM is monitoring. There may be a perfect process in place, one that has properly identified and reacted to risks related to achievement of objectives. It may be that the necessary control activities have been built in response to those risks and information flows everywhere it should. However, if there is no check on that process to ensure it continues to work as designed, there is no assurance that risks have been properly addressed. In particular, the ERM model indicates that there should be ongoing monitoring as well as separate evaluations. It is quickly evident that monitoring is really just the final piece of control activities—albeit a piece that looks over the entire operation. Accordingly, the Process Profile Worksheet for Monitoring (Exhibit 11.11) has a broader scope and feel.

The description section of the worksheet speaks to the overall ERM process and shows the broader approach of this process. The trigger to this process is the implementation of the ERM process, and the input reflects this. The final event is an overall assessment of ERM, and the additional events relate to getting information on how well the ERM process works and providing the necessary feedback. This is also reflected in the outputs and process units.

The objective of this process once again speaks to the broad scope of its operation—nothing less than the effective implementation of ERM. Two risks that might be identified are poor communications

Exhibit 11.11 Process Profile Worksheet—Monitoring

Process Name—Number	Process Owner
Monitoring	Various

Description
Assess the presence and functioning of ERM components over time

Triggers
Event beginning: Implementation of ERM
Event ending process: Assessment of the state of the ERM process
Additional events: Evaluate individual activities within the ERM process
Provide feedback as needed

Input—Items and Sources
The ERM strategy

Output—Items and Customers
Assessment of ERM

Process Units	Process Unit Owners
Evaluate activities Provide feedback Provide overall assessment	Various

Business Objective(s)	Business Risks
Ensure the effective implementation of the ERM process	Communication goes only one direction Inaccurate data

Key Controls	Measure of Success
Specific procedures regarding communication requirements Quality control reviews	Adjustments to the ERM process No surprises

(the issue of information coming down from above, but not being fed back up to executive management) and bad data. This last is important because effective monitoring of control activities is heavily contingent upon accurate management report data. (It is interesting to note that the two areas identified are exactly the pieces of the prior component—Information and Communication. As noted in that section, these two items tie all ERM activities together.) The key controls identified speak to having a protocol that ensures upward and downward communication, and quality control reviews to ensure good data is reported. Finally, the first measure of success speaks to the point that no system is perfect. If Monitoring is working correctly, there should be changes to the system. And the final measure of success is, again, "no surprises."

Looking at the various aspects of Monitoring, it is easy to see that a Process Mapping project over ERM might well be the ultimate monitoring step for ERM.

Feedback on Monitoring

In the Process Mapping project, ongoing Monitoring should be built into each process being reviewed. When combined with an ERM assessment, the map should indicate how information is shuttled up the organization to ensure the continuous reviews are effective. Likewise, all evaluations that impact a process should be included in the map. Very often, the groups responsible for evaluations (often the quality control groups) are not a part of the actual operations. While they are a part of the department, they are often not seen as part of the process. However, there are two important reasons to include them in the overall assessment of a process. First is the impact they may have on delaying the process. If they have an intrusive effect, they may not be a transparent process and may affect customer satisfaction. Second is their ability to provide broad oversight to improvements. It is one thing to elevate concerns to management; it is another to use those concerns to help drive improvements. In particular, ask whether the separate evaluation actually uses results to improve the process (much like the Process Mapping project).

Recap

As an integral part of its approach, Process Mapping has a focus on objectives and ensuring the process helps achieve those objectives. This means that it can be a very valuable tool in evaluating risk assessment processes. At the same time, Enterprise Risk Management (ERM) has come forward as one of the most important frameworks to be used in developing risk strategies. Accordingly, there is a natural marriage between Process Mapping and ERM.

The core to the ERM process is the eight components—Internal Environment, Objective Setting, Event Identification, Risk Assessment, Risk Response, Control Activities, Information and Communication, and Monitoring. Each one of these is also, effectively, a process. Therefore, there are three approaches whereby Process Mapping can assist ERM activities within a company.

The first approach is to conduct a Process Mapping review of the entity's overall ERM approach. This does not lend itself to a deep dive into how the process is working, but it can provide a general feel for the effectiveness of the ERM process.

The second approach is to look at each of the components as individual processes and complete a Process Mapping evaluation on selected components. Determining which ones to include will depend on the needs of the entity, but this approach will provide more detail and a better assessment of the entire ERM approach.

The final approach is to ensure that any Process Mapping project includes consideration of the components of ERM. This will not result in an assessment of ERM, but it may lead to a better under-standing (although somewhat apocryphal) of the effectiveness of ERM. In particular, results from these projects could help support the need for additional specific work in ERM.

CHAPTER 12

Where Do We Go from Here?

Somewhere, something incredible is waiting to be known.

—Carl Sagan

Additional Applications

The Process Mapping approach is more than just a method for making extensive flowcharts. It is a holistic approach to analyzing a business, an entity, or a function. As such, many of the techniques described can be used in whole or in part in other disciplines. When we issued the first edition of this book, we included a separate section in this chapter indicating Process Mapping could be used in the risk assessment process. Now, Enterprise Risk Management has become a topic unto itself. Likewise, Sarbanes-Oxley was just a glimmer in the regulators' eyes then. But the principles outlined for Process Mapping can be applied to the walk-throughs and the recording of key controls.

In this chapter, we will discuss how Process Mapping can be a valuable tool in control self-assessment, re-engineering, and training. However, with a constantly changing world, the uses for Process Mapping will likewise constantly change. If you keep your eyes open and look for the opportunities, Process Mapping may be the tool you need for the next big thing.

Control Self-Assessment

Control self-assessment is a tool that, among other things, was devised to bring all necessary parties together to determine the obstacles and strengths affecting achievement of key business objectives. It has been defined as "a formal, documented process in which management and/or work teams directly involved in a business function judge the effectiveness of the processes in place and decide if the chances of reaching some or all business objectives are reasonably assured." Much of this is the result of the Committee of Sponsoring Organizations of the Treadway Commission (COSO) report issued in 1992, which was previously mentioned in Chapter 11. Our focus in that chapter was on the subsequently issued report on Enterprise Risk Management. However, the report on Internal Control—Integrated Framework issued in 1992 is just as valid. Ultimately, the earlier report (along with similar reports issued by similar commissions in England and Canada) helped redefine the meaning of control structures.

According to the COSO report, "internal control is defined as a process, effected by an entity's people, designed to accomplish specific objectives." The remainder of the report represents a focus that is changing from traditional "hard" controls (e.g., policies, procedures, approvals, and two-party controls) to less traditional "soft" controls (e.g., trust, leadership, openness, and high ethical standards). Accordingly, new approaches had to be found to analyze these controls. Control self-assessment has been one of the most popular of these tools.

While every control self-assessment practitioner uses his or own methods, there are some steps that are basic to all. Generally, teams are brought together from similar functions to discuss the control framework. A facilitator introduces the purpose of the project and helps ensure that the discussions stay on track. The focus of the discussions from this point on usually includes identifying the business objectives, the risks, and the controls and determining whether the control framework is sufficient to ensure achievement of the objectives. One of the primary benefits of this method is that the members of the department are determining the answers themselves. Because it is their evaluation, they have buy-in to the project.

This description helps point out how Process Mapping can be used to facilitate or enhance the control self-assessment project.

The most obvious point is that many of the introductory steps in completing the Process Mapping project are similar to those used in control self-assessment. The forms and skills learned from Process Mapping can be easily translated into the control self-assessment situation. The reviewer can facilitate this by using the Process Profile Worksheet to capture the objectives, risks, controls, and monitoring systems. Looking at inputs and outputs, as well as process beginning and ending points, can help control self-assessment participants assess the information and communication aspects of the process. This is a perfect opportunity to show process owners how controls can help them accomplish business objectives. It can also help establish ownership of both the controls and the measures of success. The systematic completion of profile worksheets for all critical business processes can be the starting point for determining whether the processes in place provide management with reasonable assurance that business objectives will be reached.

A second, less obvious use of Process Mapping is in those situations in which process owners or upper management are leery of the control self-assessment approach. Many people have trouble believing that team members can be counted on to successfully participate in these types of projects, and some team members are afraid to become true participants because of disconnects between management and employees. As mentioned previously, the Process Mapping approach lays the groundwork for control self-assessment. This approach allows people to begin thinking in terms of business objectives, associated risks, and the other trappings of process assessment. In addition, as the project continues and the maps are developed, it gets everyone used to a collaborative process in which everyone's ideas are respected. In this way, Process Mapping can be used to obtain an initial analysis while laying the groundwork for future control self-assessment projects.

Re-Engineering

Re-engineering projects became a mainstay for many companies and consultants beginning in the late 1980s. They are still an important tool in redesigning processes. Most re-engineering efforts focus on streamlining processes and eliminating non-value-added activities. They tend to focus on radical changes, rather than on incremental changes.

As we have seen in the previous chapters, Process Mapping provides a visual representation of the process that can highlight inefficiencies, such as multiple handoffs, areas where rework is required, or areas where delays are occurring. Whether you are starting with an existing process and trying to determine where appropriate changes can be made or starting with a blank piece of paper and re-engineering the whole process, you still need a map to see where you have been and where you are going. The complete story still must be captured so everyone can see it from the same perspective.

If the purpose of the re-engineering project is to change an existing model, Process Mapping can be used to get that initial snapshot. If the process is being blown up and the company is starting over, Process Mapping can be used to graphically show the new system.

Re-engineering often begins with a change agent and an idea. Not unlike Walt Disney's attempt to convey the story of *Pinocchio* to his animators, the change agent must convey his or her idea to others so they can conceptualize the new theme. Everyone must understand the overriding theme so that changes made to the business remain consistent with the theme. The best way to verify that the theme is remaining consistent is to visually capture the re-engineering effort in a Process Map. It is much easier to make changes on paper, before people are involved, than to fix problems due to a lack of foresight.

The primary pitfall for most re-engineering projects is losing focus on how the process fits in with the corporation as a whole. This is often the result of a lack of attention to the details. It may be a failure to recognize how one event affects another. It may be a failure to recognize moments of truth. It may be a focus on minimum cycle times instead of maximum cycle times. It may be a failure to consider all the risks. Or it may be a failure to consider the soft issues—how people interact in the process. However, using the holistic approach to Process Mapping, including creating complete process definitions, identifying business objectives, identifying risks, and identifying measures of success, can help ensure that critical details are not missed. Mapping the actual process and analyzing those maps can help create the road map to a successful re-engineering project.

Training

The saying "a picture is worth a thousand words" is very true, especially when it comes to training people on how to perform a specific job. A company may have very detailed procedure manuals with explicit instructions on how to complete the job, but it may find that people just do not read the manuals. Most of us, with the exception of a few auditors, never take the time to read the actual procedure manuals. We may look up things from time to time, but we never review all of the areas that relate to our job. We are trained on how to perform specific tasks, but we often do not know why we are performing them or how they impact the entire operation.

Process Mapping is an excellent tool for developing training materials. Overview maps can be created to give the employee a sense of how his or her work fits in with the whole. Detailed maps can also be created at the task level to visually show individuals where the work comes from, what they need to do with it when they get it, and where it goes when they complete the task. The drill-down technique can also be used to link the detailed procedure manual to the actual tasks.

For example, the map may show a task (1.1) as *verify customer data*. A drill-down map of this task could be created that may have actions such as log onto computer, input customer name, review address information, and so on. However, if all of these steps are in a particular procedure manual, it may be just as easy to reference task 1.1 to a drill-down narrative that is the procedure manual, with the various steps involved in the process. At some point, drawing more boxes does not make sense, and you can just refer to a narrative that includes the appropriate details for the task.

The development of the maps is also an excellent training tool on a number of other levels. First, the employees involved are beginning to learn how their work interrelates with everyone else's work. At the same time, they may begin understanding what the overall objectives are and how their job helps.

Second, management's involvement may help the managers better learn the operations they supervise. In some instances, just going over the maps helps instruct them on correct procedures. During a recent review, a new supervisor was put in place after we started reviewing a particular area. Rather than reviewing the maps to make sure we understood the process, we reviewed them with him to help teach him what the processes were.

Third, a member of management may become part of the team and learn how processes work directly from the employees. You must be careful with this approach—the involvement of management may mean people feel less secure in talking. However, their involvement will mean they learn a lot about day-to-day operations. In one instance, we brought in a manager from another part of the country. In this way the employees felt secure while management was trained.

At the very least, when you leave a mapping project, the detailed maps are valuable as documentation of the process. They can be used as a future training tool or a reference for procedures. Ultimately, it is a graphic representation of what everyone is doing.

That's Not All, Folks!

After Walt Disney talked with his animators, they gathered information, mapped the movie with storyboards, and eventually provided the world with another animated gem. Then they went home, flush with success, never to produce again.

Well, we know that is not true. There was a lot more work to do—more projects, more storyboards, and more international successes. And they did not wait until *Pinocchio* was completed to begin work on other films. Animated movies take years to go from idea to movie house. There is no way a company can wait until one project is finished before beginning the next. While *Pinocchio* was in production, additional classics were already being started—*Bambi, Dumbo, Fantasia*. And as each of those was begun, another idea was in the background waiting to take its turn. While it is never easy, the process was streamlined by the skills the animators learned from each project. Principle among these was storyboarding.

You have been reading about a similar tool—a tool that is the cornerstone of a valuable assessment technique. Its versatility has been shown in many different ways. We have tried to pass on the successes and failures so that you can gain an appreciation of the power of this tool. And we have tried to provide you with the basic information necessary to take this tool and make it your own.

There is nothing fancy in what has been discussed, and there is nothing sacrosanct either. Take these tools and suggestions and bend them to your needs. Take the ideas and build newer and better projects. Learn from your successes and failures. But most of all, take the first step and become involved in a Process Mapping project. After that first success, you will not want to look back. It is really up to you. Just like Walt Disney, you have to sell your ideas.

Then you have to count on success—selling the next idea before the last one is finished. Eventually, your string of successes will be your Oscar that opens additional doors.

Ultimately, Process Mapping is just one more analytical technique meant to make businesses run better. But, ultimately, *Pinocchio* was just one more story meant to make people feel better. The final success is up to you.

And they all lived happily ever after.

Index